Storytelling in Psychotherapy with Children

Storytelling in Psychotherapy with Children

RICHARD A. GARDNER, M.D.

Clinical Professor of Child Psychiatry
Columbia University, College of Physicians and Surgeons

JASON ARONSON INC.
Northvale, New Jersey
London

First softcover edition 1993

Copyright © 1993 by Richard A. Gardner

10 9 8 7 6 5 4 3 2 1

Library of Congress Cataloging-in-Publication Data

Gardner, Richard A.
    Storytelling in psychotherapy with children / by Richard A.
Gardner.
        p. cm.
    Includes bibliographical references and index.
    ISBN 1-56821-032-9 (pbk.)
    1. Storytelling—Therapeutic use.   2. Child psychotherapy.
I. Title.
    [DNLM: 1. Psychotherapy—in infancy & childhood.
2. Psychotherapy—methods. 3. Communication.   WS 350.2   G228s   1993]
RJ505.S75G367   1993
618.92′8916—dc20
DNLM/DLC
for Library of Congress   93-14898

Manufactured in the United States of America. Jason Aronson Inc. offers books and cassettes. For information and catalog write to Jason Aronson Inc., 230 Livingston Street, Northvale, New Jersey 07647.

To Patricia Ann

> You and this book
> both represent
> a culmination and
> a commencement

Other Books by Richard A. Gardner

The Boys and Girls Book About Divorce
Therapeutic Communication with Children:
  The Mutual Storytelling Technique
Dr. Gardner's Stories About the Real World, Volume I
Dr. Gardner's Stories About the Real World, Volume II
Dr. Gardner's Fairy Tales for Today's Children
Understanding Children: A Parents Guide to Child Rearing
MBD: The Family Book About Minimal Brain Dysfunction
Psychotherapeutic Approaches to the Resistant Child
Psychotherapy with Children of Divorce
Dr. Gardner's Modern Fairy Tales
The Parents Book About Divorce
The Boys and Girls Book About One-Parent Families
The Objective Diagnosis of Minimal Brain Dysfunction
Dorothy and the Lizard of Oz
Dr. Gardner's Fables for Our Times
The Boys and Girls Book About Stepfamilies
Family Evaluation in Child Custody Litigation
Separation Anxiety Disorder: Psychodynamics and Psychotherapy
Child Custody Litigation: A Guide for Parents
  and Mental Health Professionals
The Psychotherapeutic Techniques of Richard A. Gardner
Hyperactivity, The So-Called Attention-Deficit Disorder,
  and The Group of MBD Syndromes
The Parental Alienation Syndrome and the Differentiation
  Between Fabricated and Genuine Child Sex Abuse
Psychotherapy with Adolescents
Family Evaluation in Child Custody Mediation, Arbitration,
  and Litigation
The Girls and Boys Book About Good and Bad Behavior
Sex Abuse Hysteria: Salem Witch Trials Revisited
The Parents Book About Divorce - Second Edition
The Psychotherapeutic Techniques of Richard A. Garnder - Revised
The Parental Alienation Syndrome: A Guide
  for Mental Health and Legal Professionals
Self-Esteem Problems of Children: Psychodynamics
  and Psychotherapy
Conduct Disorders of Children: Psychodynamics and Psychotherapy
True and False Accusations of Child Sex Abuse

Contents

ACKNOWLEDGMENTS   xi

INTRODUCTION   xiii

1 THE MUTUAL STORYTELLING TECHNIQUE   1

HISTORICAL BACKGROUND   1
THE BASIC TECHNIQUE   5
SPECIFIC TECHNIQUE FOR ELICITING
   SELF-CREATED STORIES   7
FUNDAMENTALS OF STORY ANALYSIS   10
CLINICAL EXAMPLES   12
   The Case of Martin
      (The Bear and the Bees)   12
   The Case of Mark
      (The Farmer and the Stone)   14
   The Case of Evan
      (The Killed Guide and the Grilled-Cheese Sandwiches)   26
   The Case of Todd
      (The Club of Mean Tigers)   27
   The Case of David
      (The Family with Sixteen Children)   34
   The Case of Harry
      (Valentine Day's Candy from a Loving Mother)   41

The Case of Frank
  (The Nutcracker and the Three Peanuts)   48
    Freud's Theory of the Oedipus Complex   48
    Freud's Theory of the Resolution of the Oedipus Complex   49
    The Author's View of the Oedipus Complex   49
    The Author's Approach to the Alleviation
      of Oedipal Problems   51
    The Case of Frank   53
CONCLUDING COMMENTS   61

2 DRAMATIZED STORYTELLING   62

INTRODUCTION   62
CLINICAL EXAMPLES   65
  The Case of Adam
    ("Can a Dead Frog Be Brought Back to Life?")   65
  The Case of Frank
    ("Gonga Wants Too Much")   67
  The Case of George
    ("This Damn Magic Wand Is No Good")   96

3 MUTUAL STORYTELLING DERIVATIVE GAMES   116

INTRODUCTION   116
THE BOARD OF OBJECTS GAME   120
  Clinical Example: The Case of Norman
    (The Cowboy Whose Gun Was Missing)   124
THE THREE GRAB-BAG GAMES   129
  The Bag of Toys Game   129
    Clinical Example: The Case of Bernard
    (Let Sleeping Dogs Lie, But Give Him a Bone)   130
    Clinical Example: The Case of Tom
    (The Bed That Dumped Its Occupants)   136
  The Bag of Things Game   140
    Clinical Example: The Case of Betty
    ("Get Off My Back")   141
    Clinical Example: The Case of Ronald
    (The Robot Baby Who Receives Unconditional
      Positive Regard)   145
  The Bag of Words Games   147
    Clinical Example: The Case of Marc
    (The Man Who Picked the Big Coconuts Off the Palm Tree)   150
SCRABBLE FOR JUNIORS   155
  Clinical Examples   158
    The Case of Cary (The Frog and the Seal)   158
    The Case of Timothy (The Seal and the Cat)   162

THE FEEL AND TELL GAME   167
   Clinical Example   169
      The Case of Mary (The Kangaroo in the Mother's Pouch)   169
THE ALPHABET SOUP GAME   174
   Clinical Example   176
      The Case of Larry (The Boy Who Felt His Mother's Breasts)   176
THE PICK-A-FACE GAME   186
   Clinical Example   188
      The Case of Gloria (Make Believe There's No Trouble,
         and You Won't Be Bothered by Things)   188
THE MAKE-A-PICTURE STORY CARDS   192
   Diagnostic Utilization   192
   Therapeutic Utilization   195
      Clinical Example: The Case of Ruth (The Army of Babysitters)   195
CONCLUDING COMMENTS   204

4 THE STORYTELLING CARD GAME   206

EQUIPMENT   207
BASIC FORMAT OF PLAY   208
TECHNIQUES OF PLAY   209
   The Creation of the Child's Picture   209
   The Creation of the Child's Story   210
   Eliciting the Lesson or Moral of the Child's Story   212
   The Therapist's Response to the Child's Story   212
   The Therapist's Responding Story   212
   The Therapist's Initiated Story   214
   The Child's Response to the Therapist's Story   215
   Ending the Game   215
INDICATIONS AND CONTRAINDICATIONS   215
   Age Range   216
MODIFICATIONS   216
GENERAL DISCUSSION   218
CLINICAL EXAMPLE   219
FINAL COMMENTS   228

5 BIBLIOTHERAPY   230

INTRODUCTION   230
THE EXPOSITORY BOOK   232
   MBD: The Family Book About Minimal Brain Dysfunction   233
   The Boys and Girls Book About Divorce   234
   The Boys and Girls Book About One-Parent Families   238
   The Boys and Girls Book About Stepfamilies   240
   The Parents Book About Divorce   240
   Understanding Children—A Parents Guide to Child Rearing   241
REALITY-ORIENTED STORIES   243

FABLES   246
FAIRY TALES   250
  Introduction   250
  Reasons Why Fairy Tales are Extremely Attractive
    to Children (of All Ages)   251
  What Should We Do with Fairy Tales?   255
  Fairy Tales for Today's Children   256
  Modern Fairy Tales   257
  Dorothy and the Lizard of Oz   260
CONCLUDING COMMENTS   265

REFERENCES   267

INDEX   273

Acknowledgments

I deeply appreciate the dedication of my secretaries Linda Gould, Carol Gibbon, Donna La Tourette, and Susan Monti to the typing of this manuscript in its various forms. I am grateful to Barbara Christenberry for her diligence in editing the manuscript. She provided useful suggestions and, at the same time, exhibited respect for my wishes regarding style and format. I am grateful to Colette Conboy for her valuable input into the production of the first edition of this book, from edited manuscript to final volume. I appreciate the efforts of Robert Tebbenhoff of Lind Graphics for his important contributions to the revised edition.

My greatest debt, however, is to those children and families who have taught me so much over the years about the development and alleviation of psychopathology. What I have learned from their sorrows and grief will, I hope, contribute to the prevention and alleviation of such unfortunate experiences by others.

Introduction

Eliciting stories is a time-honored practice in child psychotherapy. From the stories children tell, the therapist is able to gain invaluable insights into the child's inner conflicts, frustrations, and defenses.

A child's stories are generally less difficult to analyze than the dreams, free associations, and other therapeutic verbalizations of the adult patient. Via the vehicle of storytelling, the child's fundamental difficulties are exhibited clearly to the therapist, with less of the obscurity, distortion, and misrepresentation that are characteristic of the adult's presentations. The essential problem for the child's therapist, however, has been how to use these insights therapeutically.

The techniques described in the literature on child psychotherapy and psychoanalysis are, for the most part, attempts to solve this problem. Some are based on the assumption, borrowed from the adult psychoanalytic model, that bringing unconcious processes into conscious awareness can itself be therapeutic. My own experience has been that few children are interested in gaining conscious awareness of their unconscious processes, let alone utilizing such insights therapeutically.

Children do, however, enjoy both telling stories and listening to them. Because storytelling is one of the child's favorite modes of communication, I wondered whether communicating back in the same mode might not be useful in child therapy. The efficacy of the storytelling approach for the impartation and transmission of values and insights is proved by the ancient and universal appeal of fable, myth, and legend.

It was from these observations and considerations that I developed the *Mutual Storytelling Technique,* a proposed solution to the question of how to utilize therapeutically the child patient's self-created stories. In this method the child first tells a story; the therapist surmises its psychodynamic meaning and then tells one that includes the same characters in a similar setting, but he/she introduces healthier adaptations and resolutions of the conflicts that have been exhibited in the child's story. Speaking in the child's own language, the therapist has a better chance of being heard. One could almost say that here the therapist's interpretations bypass the child's conscious and are received directly by the unconscious. The child is not burdened with psychoanalytic interpretations, which are often alien to him. Direct, anxiety-provoking confrontations, so reminiscent of the child's experience with parents and teachers, are avoided. Last, the introduction of humor and drama enhances the child's interest, pleasure, and receptivity. As a therapeutic tool, the method is useful for children who will tell stories, but who have little interest in analyzing them. It is not a therapy per se, but rather one technique in the therapist's armamentarium.

The first chapter of this book details the implementation of the technique with illustrative clinical examples that should be of assistance to therapists who wish to utilize the method. The next chapter elaborates upon the dramatization of stories both by the patient and therapist—an elaboration that generally adds to the therapeutic efficacy of the technique.

There are some children, however, who are particularly resistant to telling stories. It was for these that I developed the mutual storytelling derivative games. These games, most of which are based on standard board-game play, utilize token reinforcement, prizes, and the exitement of a mildly competitive game as vehicles for enhancing the child's motivation to provide self-created stories. I have found *The Storytelling Card Game* to be the most effective of these derivative games. Accordingly, I have devoted a full chapter to the game's utilization. *The Storytelling Card Game's* value as a diagnostic instrument is also described. Whereas the *Children's Apperception Test* (CAT) and the *Thematic Apperception Test* (TAT) are useful instruments for eliciting projective material, they have an intrinsic contaminant in that the pictures are structured and have a certain pull in specific directions. When *The Storytelling Card Game* is used as a diagnostic instrument, the child creates his/her own pictures and so circumvents this drawback to these traditional instruments.

Legends, myths, fables, parables, and allegories have traditionally been useful ways for educating children and imparting to them the behavioral patterns that are considered to be desirable in a particular society. Psychotherapy is, in part, an educational process—especially for children. In this chapter I focus on my own bibliotherapeutic contributions, that is, the stories and books I have devised and found useful for children and their parents, especially as they relate to the psychotherapeutic process.

Taken as a whole, this book provides a full statement of my therapeutic use of storytelling ranging from the free fantasies provided by the child when utilizing the mutual storytelling technique to the bibliotherapeutic stories provided by the therapist.

ONE

The Mutual
Storytelling Technique

Originality is a return to the origin.

Antonio Gaudi

HISTORICAL BACKGROUND

The use of children's stories as a source of psychodynamic information is well known to child psychotherapists. To the best of my
knowledge, this was first described in the literature (in German) by
Hug-Hellmuth in 1913. (The first English Translation appeared in
1921.) A fundamental problem for the child therapist has been that
of how to take the information that one can derive from such stories and bring about psychotherapeutic change. Children's stories
are generally easier to analyze than the dreams, free associations,
and other verbal productions of adults. Often, the child's fundamental problems are exhibited clearly to the therapist, without the
obscurity, distortion, and misrepresentation characteristic of the
adult's fantasies and dreams.

A wide variety of psychotherapeutic techniques have been devised to use therapeutically the insights that the therapist can gain

1

from children's stories. Some are based on the assumption, borrowed from the adult classical psychoanalytic model, that bringing into conscious awareness that which has been unconscious can in itself be therapeutic. The literature is replete with articles in which symptomatic alleviation and even cure quickly follows the patient's gaining insight into the underlying psychodynamic patterns. My own experience has been that very few children are interested in gaining conscious awareness of their unconscious processes in the hope that they can use such insight to alleviate their symptoms and improve their life situation. I believe that one of the reasons for this is that the average child of average intelligence is not cognitively capable of taking an analytic stance and engaging in a meaningful psychoanalytic inquiry until about the age of ten. This corresponds to Piaget's level of formal operations, the age at which the child can consciously differentiate between a symbol and the entity which it symbolizes.

Of course, brighter children are capable of doing this at early ages. But even those children are generally not interested in assuming the analytic stance and delving into the unconscious roots of their problems—unless there are significant environmentally stimulating factors. The child who grows up in a home in which both parents are introspective and analytic is more likely to think along these lines as well. Accordingly, it is only on rare occasions that I do direct analytic work with children under the age of 10 or 11. And when this occurs, it is usually a patient who, 1) is extremely bright, and 2) comes from a home in which the parents have been or are in psychoanalytic treatment themselves, and who in addition, are deeply committed to introspective approaches to dealing with life's problems. But even in adult therapy, professions of commitment to analysis notwithstanding, most of my patients are not deeply committed to psychoanalytic inquiry. And they are generally even more resistant to analyzing their resistances to such inquiry. Hence, I attempt to employ a psychoanalytic approach to the therapeutic utilization of children's stories very infrequently.

In the 1920s Anna Freud and Melanie Klein—both influenced deeply by Hug-Hellmuth's observation—attempted to work analytically with children, and the analysis of their stories was essential to their therapeutic approaches. Although they differed significantly regarding the interpretations they gave to children's stories, they agreed that the gaining of insight into the story's underlying psychodynamic meaning was crucial to meaningful therapeutic change. Beginning in the 1930s Conn (1939, 1941a, 1941b, 1948, 1954) and Solomon (1938, 1940, 1951, 1955) described the same frustrations this examiner experienced with regard to getting children to analyze meaningfully their self-created stories. They were quite happy to analyze those children who were receptive to such inquiries. But for those who were not, they were equally satisfied discussing the child's story at the symbolic level. They believed that therapeutic changes could be brought about by communicating with the child at the symbolic level. For example, if a child told a story about a dog biting a cat and was unreceptive to analyzing it, they found that discussions about why the dog bit the cat and what better ways there were to handle the situation could get across important messages without producing the anxiety of analytic inquiry.

During my residency training in the late 1950s I first began to suffer the frustration of children's unreceptivity to analysis. I was much more comfortable with the work of Conn and Solomon. It was from these experiences that I derived in the early 1960s the technique that I subsequently called *the mutual storytelling technique*. Basically, it is another way of utilizing therapeutically children's self-created stories. It stems from the observation that children enjoy not only telling stories but listening to them as well. The efficacy of the storytelling approach for imparting and transmitting important values is ancient. In fact, the transmission of such values was and still is crucial to the survival of a civilized society. Every culture has its own heritage of such stories that have been instrumental in transmitting down the generations these important messages.

It is reasonable to speculate that in the early days of civilized society attempts were made to impart directly important messages necessary for people to learn if they were to cooperate meaningfully in the social group. It was probably learned quite early that such direct confrontations, especially in the presence of others, might not be the most effective way to teach individuals in the hope that they would incorporate these messages into their psychic structures. It is reasonable to speculate that a subsequent development involved the recognition that storytelling might be a useful vehicle for incorporating such messages in a disguised and therefore less threatening way. After all, storytelling is an ancient tradition and, up to the twentieth century, it was probably one of the most popular forms of evening entertainment.

It was in such storytelling sessions that people would relate the events of the day and, considering the fact that external sources of entertainment were limited and infrequent, a certain amount of elaboration of events was probably welcomed. Furthermore, it is reasonable to speculate that a certain amount of "expansion of the truth" was not seriously criticized because of the extra entertainment value that such elaboration provided. It is reasonable to assume further that the popularity of this form of entertainment made it an attractive vehicle for the incorporation of messages that were important to impart to individuals for immediate purposes as well as for perpetuation down the generations. It was probably appreciated that one could circumvent listeners' defensiveness regarding being told about their wrongdoings by describing the transgressions of *others* and the lessons *they* learned from their departures from acceptable patterns of behavior. The basic principle was: "Of course, none of us here would ever do such terrible things, and most of us probably wouldn't even think of such terrible things. However, it's interesting to hear about others who did these things and what they learned from them." Adding violence and sex (traditionally attractive modalities in any story) enhanced their attractiveness to listeners. Ultimately, these stories became the primary vehicle for transmitting down the generations important messages necessary for the survival of the group. In fact, I would go further and state that societies that did *not* have such a heritage did not survive because they did not have this important vehicle for transmitting their values to subsequent generations.

Much more recently, with the development of the written language, these stories achieved a new permanence. Our Bible is one example of such a document. The Old Testament is basically a collection of those stories that were prevalent from the period around 750 BC to 250 BC. Most consider these stories to be combinations of fact and fantasy. Each individual, of course, must make a decision regarding how much of these two elements are present. There are some who claim that everything in the Bible is completely true and others who go to the other extreme and claim that it is complete fantasy. Although people may differ regarding what they consider the fact/fantasy ratio to be, most will agree that these stories have had a profound influence on mankind and have contributed significantly to moral development and the perpetuation and survival of civilized society.

The mutual storytelling technique is in this tradition. It attempts to rectify one of the fundamental problems of storytelling as a vehicle for transmitting important messages, namely, that any story, no matter how well tailored to the needs of a particular audience, is likely to be relevant to only a small fraction of those who listen to it. After all, an audience generally consists of men and women of varying ages from childhood through old age. It is unreasonable to expect any particular story to "turn on" more than a small fraction of such a heterogeneous group. The mutual storytelling technique attempts to circumvent this drawback by using a story that is designed to be specifically relevant to a particular person at that particular time. The stories are tailor-made to the individual and therefore, they are more likely to be attended to with receptivity and incorporated into the listener's psychic structure.

THE BASIC TECHNIQUE

In this method the therapist elicits a self-created story from the child. The therapist then surmises its psychodynamic meaning and then tells a responding story of his or her own. The therapist's story utilizes the same characters in a similar setting, but introduces healthier resolutions and adaptations of the conflicts present in the child's story. Because the therapist is speaking in the child's own language—the language of allegory—he or she has a better chance of "being heard" than if the messages were transmitted directly. The direct, confrontational mode of transmission is generally much more anxiety provoking than the symbolic. One could almost say that with this method the therapist's messages bypass the conscious and are received directly by the unconscious. The child is not burdened with psychoanalytic interpretations that are generally alien and incomprehensible to him. With this technique, one avoids direct, anxiety-provoking confrontations so reminiscent of the child's experiences with parents and teachers.

The technique is useful for children who will tell stories, but who have little interest in analyzing them (the vast majority, in my experience). It is not a therapy per se, but one technique in the therapist's armamentarium. Empirically, I have found the method to be most useful for children between the ages of five and eleven. I generally do not treat children under the age of four (I find it more efficient to counsel their parents). In addition, children under the age of five are not generally capable of formulating organized stories. In the four- to five-year age bracket, one can elicit a series of story fragments from which one might surmise an underlying psychodynamic theme which can serve as a source of information for the therapist's responding story. The upper age level at which the technique is useful is approximately eleven. At that time, children generally become appreciative of the fact that they are revealing themselves. They may rationalize noninvolvement with the technique with such justifications as, "This is baby stuff," and "I don't feel like telling stories." Lastly, the technique is contraindicated for children who are psychotic and/or who fantasize excessively. One wants more reality-oriented therapeutic approaches such as *The Talking, Feeling, and Doing Game* or else one may entrench their pathology.

Dolls, drawings, and other toys are the modalities around which stories are traditionally elicited in child psychotherapy. Unfortunately, when these facilitating stimuli are used, the child's story may be channeled in highly specific directions. They have specific forms that serve as stimuli that are contaminating to the self-created story. Although the pressure of the unconscious to create a story that serves a specific psychological purpose for the child is greater than the power of the facilitating external stimulus to contaminate the story, there is still some contamination when one uses these common vehicles for story elicitation. The tape recorder does not have these disadvantages; with it, the visual field remains free from distracting and contaminating stimuli. The tape recorder almost asks to be spoken into. Eliciting a story with it is like obtaining a dream on demand. Although there are differences between dreams and self-created stories, the story that is elicited by a tape recorder is far closer to the dream than that which is elicited by play material.

In earlier years I used an audio tape recorder. In more recent years I have used a video tape recorder. For the therapist who has this instrument available, it can enhance significantly the child's motivation to play the game. Although hearing one's story on the audio tape recorder can serve to facilitate the child's involvement in the game, watching oneself on television afterwards is a much greater motivating force. But the examiner should not conclude that these instruments are crucial. They are merely devices. Long before they were invented children enjoyed relating self-created stories, and the therapist should be able to elicit them from most children without these contrivances. They should be viewed as additional motivating facilitators and, of course, they have the additional benefit of the playback which provides reiteration of the therapeutic messages. In earlier years many children would bring their own tape recorder and simultaneously tape the stories with me, and then listen to them at home for further therapeutic exposure. Recently, I added a second video cassette recorder to my office closed-circuit television system. A child can now bring his or her own video cassette (to be found with increasing frequency in homes these days), tape the story sequences along with me, and then watch him- or herself at home.

SPECIFIC TECHNIQUE FOR ELICITING
SELF-CREATED STORIES

I begin by telling the child that we are now going to play a game in which he or she will be guest of honor on a make-believe television program. In earlier years I would ask the child if he or she would like to be the guest of honor on the program; in more recent years I seduce him or her into the game without the formal invitation. Of course, if the child strongly resists, I will not pressure or coerce. We then sit across the room from the mounted camera, and the video cassette recorder, lights, and camera are turned on. I then begin:

> *Therapist:* Good morning, boys and girls. I would like to welcome you once again to "Dr. Gardner's Make-Up-a-Story Television Program." We invite boys and girls to this program to see how good they are at making up stories. The story must be completely made up from your own imagination. It's against the rules to tell stories about anything that really happened to you or anyone you know. It's against the rules to tell a story about things you've read about, or heard about, or seen in the movies or on television. Of course, the more adventure or excitement the story has, the more fun it will be to watch on television later.
>
> Like all stories, your story should have a beginning, a middle, and an end. And after you've made up your story, you'll tell us the lesson or the moral of your story. We all know that every good story has a lesson or a moral. Then, after you've told your story, Dr. Gardner will make up a story also. He'll try to tell one that's interesting and unusual, and then we'll talk about the lesson or the moral of his story.
>
> And now, without further delay, let me introduce to you a boy(girl)

who is with us for the first time. Tell us your name young man(woman).

I then ask the child a series of questions that can be answered by single words or brief phrases. I will ask his or her age, grade, address, name of school, and teacher. These "easy" questions reduce the child's anxiety about the more unstructured themes involved in "making up a story." I then continue:

Therapist: Now that we've heard a few things about you, we're all interested in hearing the story you've made up for us today.

Most children at this point begin with their story, although some may ask for "time out to think." Of course this request is granted. There are some children, however, for whom this pause is not enough, but will still want to try. In such instances the child is told:

Therapist: Some children, especially when it's their first time on this program, have a little trouble thinking of a story. However, I know a way to help such children think of a story. Most people don't realize that there are *millions* of stories in everyone's head. Did you know that there are millions of stories in your head? (Child usually responds negatively.) Yes, right here between the top of your head and your chin (I touch the top of the child's head with one finger, and the bottom of his or her chin with another finger), right between your ears (I then touch the child's two ears), inside your brain which is in the center of your head are millions of stories. And I know a way how to get out one of them.
The way to do this is that we'll tell the story together. And this way, you won't have to do all the work yourself. The way it works is that I start the story and, when I point my finger at you, you say exactly what comes into your mind at the time that I point to you. You'll see then that your part of the story will start coming into your brain. Then after you've told the part of the story that comes into your mind, I'll tell another part, and then I'll point to you. Then we'll go back and forth until the story is over. Okay, here we go. (The reader will note that I again did not ask the child if he or she wished to proceed, rather I just "rolled on.")
Okay, here we go (I now speak *very slowly*). Once upon a time . . . a long, long time ago . . . in a distant land . . . far, far away . . . far beyond the mountains . . . far beyond the deserts . . . far beyond the oceans . . . there lived a. . . .

I then quickly point my finger at the child (jolting the child out of the semi-hypnotic state that I have tried to induce by this "introduction" which basically says nothing). It is a rare child who does not offer some associative word at that point. For example, if the word is "cat," I will then say, "And *that* cat. . . . " and once again point firmly to the child, indicating that it is his or her turn to tell more of the story. I follow the next statement provided by the child with, "And then. . . . " or "The next thing that happened was. . . . " Or, I will repeat the last few words of the patient's last sentence, with such intonations that continuation by him or her is implied. Every statement the child makes is followed by some connective term supplied by me and indicates to the child that he or she should supply the next statement. At no point do I introduce any specific material into the story. The introduction of such specific phrases or words would defeat the purpose of catalyzing the child's production of his or her *own* created material and of sustaining, as needed, its continuity.

This approach is successful in eliciting stories from the vast majority of children. However, if it is unsuccessful, it is best to drop the activity in a completely casual and nonreproachful manner, such as: "Well, today doesn't seem to be your good day for storytelling. Perhaps we'll try again some other time."

While the child is telling his or her story, I jot down notes. These help me analyze the story and serve as a basis of my own. When the child completes the story, I then elicit its lesson or moral. In addition, I may ask questions about specific items in the story. My purpose here is to obtain additional details which are often helpful in understanding the story. Typical questions might be: "Is the dog in your story a boy or a girl, a man or a woman?" "Why did the horse do that?" or, "Why was the cat so angry at the squirrel?" If the child hesitates to provide a lesson or a moral, or states that there is none, I will usually reply: "What, a story without a lesson? Every good story has some lesson or moral! Every good story has something we can learn from it."

Usually, after completing my story, I will ask the child to try to figure out the moral or the lesson of my story. This helps me ascertain whether my message has been truly understood by the child. If the child is unsuccessful in coming forth with an appropriate lesson or moral to my story, I will provide it. Following the completion of my story, I generally engage the child in a discussion of its meaning to the degree that he or she is capable of gaining insight and/or referring the story's message to him- or herself. Many children, however, have little interest in such insights, and I do not press for them. I feel no pressure to do so because I believe that the important therapeutic task is to get across a principle, and that if this principle is incorporated into the psychic structure (even unconsciously), then therapeutic change can be brought about.

FUNDAMENTALS
OF STORY ANALYSIS

Obviously, the therapist is in no position to create a story of his or her own unless there is some understanding of the basic meaning of the child's story. The greater the familiarity with the child, the greater the likelihood the therapist will be in the position to do this. Also, the more analytic training and experience a therapist has, the more likely he or she will be able to ascertain correctly the meaning of the child's story. I first try to ascertain which figure(s) in the child's story represent the child him- or herself and which symbolize significant individuals in the child's milieu. Two or more figures may represent various aspects of the *same* person's personality. There may, for example, be a "good dog" and a "bad dog" in the same story, which are best understood as conflicting forces within the same child. A horde of figures, all similar, may symbolize powerful elements in a single person. A hostile father, for example, may be symbolized by a stampede of bulls. Malevolent figures can represent the child's own repressed anger projected outward, or they may be a symbolic statement of the hostility of a significant figure. Sometimes both of these mechanisms operate simultaneously. A threatening tiger in one boy's story represented his hostile father, and the father was made more frightening by the child's own hostility, repressed and projected onto the tiger. This is one of the reasons why many children view their parents as being more malevolent than they actually are.

Besides clarifying the particular symbolic significance of each figure, it is also important for the therapist to get a general overall "feel" for the atmosphere of the story. Is the ambiance pleasant, neutral, or horrifying? Stories that take place in frozen wastelands or on isolated space stations suggest something very different from those that occur in the child's own home. The child's emotional reactions when telling the story are of great significance in understanding its meaning. An 11-year-old boy who tells me, in an emotionless tone, about the death fall of a mountain climber reveals not only his anger but also the repression of his feelings. The atypical must be separated from the stereotyped, age-appropriate elements in the story. The former may be very revealing, whereas the latter rarely are. Battles between cowboys and Indians rarely give meaningful data, but when the chief sacrifices his son to Indian gods in a prayer for victory over the white man, something has been learned about the boy's relationship with his father.

The story may lend itself to a number of different psychodynamic interpretations. It is part of the creativity of the unconscious, even in the child, that these can be fused together in the same symbols. The themes may exist simultaneously or in tandem. In selecting the theme that will be most pertinent for the child at that particular time, I am greatly assisted by the child's own lesson or moral. It will generally tell me which of the various themes is most important for the storyteller him- or herself. At times, however, the child may not be able to formulate a relevant moral or lesson. This is especially the case for younger children and/or older ones with cognitive or intellectual impairment. In such cases the therapist is deprived of a valuable source of information.

I then ask myself: "What is the main pathological manifestation in this story?" or, "What is the primary inappropriate or maladaptive resolution of the conflicts presented?" Having identified this, I then ask myself: "What would be a more mature or a healthier mode of adaptation than the one utilized by the child?" I then create a story of my own. My story generally involves the same characters, setting, and initial situation as the child's story. However, very quickly my story evolves in a different direction. The pathological modes are not utilized although they may be considered by various figures in the story. Invariably, a more appropriate or salutary resolution of the most important conflict(s) is achieved.

In my story I attempt to provide the child with more *alternatives*. The communication that the child not be enslaved by his or her psychopathological behavior patterns is crucial. Therapy, if it is to be successful, must open new avenues not previously considered by the patient. It must help the patient become aware of the multiplicity of options that are available to replace the narrow, self-defeating ones that have been selected. After I have completed my story, I attempt to get the patient to try to figure out its lesson(s) or moral(s). It is preferable that the child do this, but if the child cannot, then I present it for them. (It is nowhere written that a story must have only one lesson or moral.) My lesson(s) attempts to emphasize further the healthier adaptations I have included in my story. If, while telling my story, the child exhibits deep interest or reveals marked anxiety, then I know that my story is "hitting home." I know then that I am on the right track, and that I have ascertained correctly the meaning of the story and have devised a responding story that is relevant. The anxiety may manifest itself by jitteriness or increased activity level. If the child is bored, it may mean that I am off point. However, it may also be a manifestation of anxiety, and the therapist may not know which explanation is most relevant.

Following the completion of my story and its moral, I usually try to engage the child in a discussion of our stories. For the rare child who is interested in gaining insight, we will try to analyze our stories. For the majority there may be a discussion along other lines, and these are usually at the symbolic level. In earlier years, when I used the audio tape recorder, children were sometimes interested in listening to the tape. In more recent years, since I have been utilizing the video cassette recorder, the interest in watching the program has been much greater. Playing the program makes possible a second exposure to the messages I wish to impart. And, as mentioned, I have recently purchased a second video cassette recorder—which enables the child to bring his or her own tape and replay it at home. This not only provides the opportunity for re-iteration of the therapeutic messages, but also serves to entrench the therapist-patient relationship.

CLINICAL EXAMPLES

The Case of Martin
[The Bear and the Bees]

Martin, a seven-year-old boy, was referred because of generalized apathy, lack of involvement with peers, and disinterest in school in spite of high intelligence. His mother was an extremely angry woman who stated during the first session: "Doctor, my father died when I was two and I have no memory of him. I grew up with my mother and two older sisters. I don't know anything about men and boys. To me they're like strangers from another planet. I can't relate to them. My daughter I can relate to. We're on the same wavelength. I can understand her. Although I know nothing about men, I do know one thing about them and that is that I *hate them all.*" Very early I found the mother to be a bitter, self-indulgent woman who used biting sarcasm as a primary mode of relating to men. She told me about a series of male therapists she had seen herself and who had seen her son, and she had only critical things to say about each of them. I could not help thinking while she was talking that my name might soon be added to the list and be mentioned with an equal degree of denigration to the next therapist. (This prophesy soon proved to be true.) The patient's father was obsessively involved in his work, was away for weeks at a time on business trips, and when home had practically no interest in his son. He had a passive-dependent relationship with his wife and served as a scapegoat for her.

In his first session, Martin told this story:

> Once upon a time there was a bear. He was trying to get some honey from a beehive. He got it from the beehive. He went home with it. The bear ate the honey.

I considered the beehive in the story to represent Martin's mother. She is the source of honey, that is, love; but this love is covered with stinging, poison-injecting, potentially painful contaminants. Seeking affection from her inevitably exposes one to her venom. In the story the bear easily acquires honey from the beehive without any interference at all by the bees. This is an atypical element in the story that is our best clue to its meaning. Typically, bees do not sit silently by while bears put their paws in their beehives and gobble up their honey. Rather, they usually sting the bear in the obvious hope that it might retreat. The absence of this reaction on the part of the bees in Martin's story is a statement of his wish that his mother's hostility not manifest itself when he attempts to obtain love and affection from her. In short, the story reveals his wish to gain her love without being traumatized by her malevolence.

The story epitomizes well, in a few words, the mother's basic personality pattern and her relationship with the patient. It is an excellent example of how a child's first story may reveal core problems. Because the mother's psychopathology was deep-seated and because she had absolutely no interest in entering into treatment herself, I considered her prognosis for change to be extremely poor.

However, even if she exhibited motivation for treatment, under the best of circumstances it would have taken many years to bring about reasonable changes. By that time Martin might be an adolescent or even an adult. I considered it antitherapeutic to tell a responding story that would provide Martin with any hope for a dramatic change in his mother's personality, either in the present or the future. Accordingly, I told Martin this story:

> Once upon a time there was a bear. This bear loved honey very much. There was a beehive nearby, but he knew that the bees were not always willing to let him have some. Sometimes they were friendly, and then they would give him a little bit. Other times they were not, and he knew then that it was wise to stay away from them or else he would get stung. When the bees were unfriendly, he would go to another part of the forest where there were maple trees which dripped sweet maple syrup. When the bees were friendly, he would go to them for honey.

In my story I attempted to accomplish two things. First, I tried to help Martin accept his mother as she really was at that time— someone who could, on occasion, provide him with some affection but who, at other times, could be punitive and denigrating of him. In my story I advise him to resign himself to the situation and to take her affection when it becomes available, but not to seek it otherwise. Second, I attempted to provide Martin with alternative sources of gratification by suggesting that there are others in the world who can compensate him somewhat for his mother's deficiency. This is an important therapeutic point. It is unrealistic to expect patients to resign themselves to giving up an important source of gratification if one does not, at the same time, offer some kind of compensatory satisfactions. Martin might not be able to have the bees' honey at times, but he certainly could have sweet maple syrup as a reasonable substitute.

The Case of Mark
[The Farmer and the Stone]

Mark, a nine-and-a-half-year-old boy, was referred for treatment because of disruptive and hyperactive behavior in the classroom. At home he was difficult to manage and frequently uncooperative. Particular problems existed with regard to Mark's doing his homework. He frequently refused to do it, and his parents' warnings and threats regarding the consequences of his not doing homework proved futile. He generally subscribed to the life philosophy: "I'll worry today about today and I'll worry tomorrow about tomorrow." Another dictum by which Mark lived was: "I'll cross that bridge when I come to it." His parents' concerns and warnings about the future repercussions of his inattentiveness to his school work were continually of no avail.

Investigation into the background of Mark's difficulties, did not reveal factors that I were certain were playing a role in his difficulties. The one factor that I considered possibly operative was the fact that his father had made significant contributions in his field, and Mark probably had the feeling that he could never reach his father's level of competence and renown. He didn't want to confront the fact that he might not achieve his father's levels of competence. This reaction, however, is inappropriate because if it were indeed justified, then all the children of distinguished contributors would end up academic failures. There are still many things to be done in this world and many ways of achieving a sense of competence. Furthermore, one need not be a super-achiever or well known to lead a gratifying life.

During his second month of treatment Mark told a story which lends itself well to being divided into three parts. Accordingly, I will present each of the parts separately and describe what I considered to be its meaning.

> *Patient:* Well, once there was this farmer and he liked to plant all kinds of crops, and he raised chickens and cows and horses. He liked to work out in the garden. He liked to feed the chickens and get their eggs.
>
> One day he took an egg out of underneath a chicken and the chicken bit him. And he didn't know what to do because the chicken never bit him before. So he sold the chicken to a man and this man got mad and he sold the chicken to another man. And this person that he sold the chicken to got mad and said he didn't want it. So he gave it back to him and that man gave it back to the farmer. And then that chicken died so he was kind of glad.

Generally, the protagonist of a story represents the patient. In this case, the patient depicts himself as a farmer. The other "protagonist" of the first part of the story is the chicken. The chicken lends itself well to representing a female in that it is the layer of eggs—the origin of life and a source of food. In this case, I considered the chicken to represent Mark's mother. This speculation is further supported by the fact that the chicken bites the farmer. I considered the biting to symbolize the mother's harping on Mark to do his homework. Mark would like to get rid of the chicken, that is, "get his mother off his back." But Mark, like all other human beings, is ambivalent in his relationship with his mother. A part of him would like to get rid of her, and yet another part of him recognizes that to do so would be a devastating trauma. The chicken, then, goes back and forth between Mark and two prospective purchasers. Selling the chicken involves some comfort with duplicity on Mark's part in that the farmer does not inform the buyer of the chicken's alienating defect (biting) which caused him to sell it. The buyer, presumably after being bitten himself, similarly exposes the bird to a third person. The latter, equally dissatisfied, returns the chicken to the second who, in turn, gives the unwanted creature back to the original owner.

Having learned that one cannot so easily rid oneself of people who irritate us, the farmer utilizes a more expedient solution: the chicken conveniently dies. This solution, often resorted to in inferior novels, provides a quick solution to a complex problem and is generally not particularly adaptive in reality because those who hound, persecute, and otherwise make our lives miserable generally do not die so conveniently. In fact, they often appear to live longer than those who treat us benevolently.

In addition, we are not told why the chicken suddenly decides to bite the farmer. All the farmer had done was to take an egg (equals love). The farmer is portrayed as innocent without having done anything to provoke this hostile act on the chicken's part. There is no consideration of the possibility that the farmer may have contributed to the chicken's behavior by some provocation or negligence, as is so often the case in reality. This segment of the story is also a statement of Mark's desire to solve the problem with the biting chicken (equals mother) by hostile acting out rather than civilized discussion. And now to return to the second part of Mark's story.

So he went along with his farming and when he was planting his crops—you know corn—in his cornfields, he found like a little, whatever you want to call it, stone. And he kept it because it was kind of pretty. So when he was keeping it, he kept it in his dresser, you know.

And every time when he went out to work in his crops he had the stone with him. He would put it in his pocket and every year he held that in his pocket the crops would come up just the way he wanted them to, and when he didn't have it with him something went wrong. So he always had the stone with him. And then he thought that it was a magic stone.

Here, the farmer finds a magic stone which brings him good fortune as long as he keeps it in his pocket. He need only keep the stone in his pocket and his crops will flourish; failure to do so causes them to "grow wrong." I considered this part of the story to be a manifestation of Mark's life philosophy that he need not exert any effort; things will somehow work out. He need not show any forethought or planning; somehow all will go well. He need not put in any effort to accomplish things in life, especially learning in school. He utilizes the magic stone to counteract the insecurity engendered in him by parental threats and suggests that at some level he is fearful that things will not work out. The magic stone provides him with the power to bring about a favorable outcome without any effort on his part. Again, this is a maladaptive response to his school difficulties. And now to the third and last part of Mark's story. I include here the post-story discussion which is also important if the examiner is to be certain about the meaning of a child's story:

And then one day when he was riding along in his wagon pulled by a horse, it went across the bridge and the wheel came off, you know. And the bridge started to crack. So he grabbed the stone and put it in his pocket and then just got up and walked across to the other side. And then he took the horse to the other side with him and the bridge fell out, you know. As soon as he took it [the stone] out of his pocket the bridge fell into the river. So he had to go and tell the people about it so they could put up a sign so nobody else could run into it. They put up a sign that said, "Bridge Out." And the townspeople paid to put up a new bridge.

And when the man found out that he lost the stone he was very unhappy and like he didn't tell anybody ever that he had the stone. So one time he was walking along in the same spot that he found the crop, he found the stone again. And he always had good luck forever on.

Therapist: Tell me something. Is it true that it was because the man had taken the stone out of his pocket that the bridge fell down?

Patient: Yes.

Therapist: And that if he had kept the stone in his pocket the bridge would not have fallen down.

Patient: Right.

Therapist: What about the wheel of his wagon? Would that have broken had he kept—

Patient (interrupting): Well, the wheel broke and the weight of it pushed and cracked the bridge.

Therapist: I see, but it was because he didn't have the stone that the bridge fell down?

Patient: Right.

Therapist: And what's the lesson of that story?

Patient: If you've got something you believe in, you should try to hold on to it, like you know, not try to lose it. If you really believe in it don't you know, fool around with it.

Therapist: Okay.

Here, the farmer is riding a wagon. The wagon lends itself well to symbolizing an individual's feelings about his or her ability to move along life's course. It is analogous to the automobile in this regard. A man, for example, has a repetitious dream in which his automobile is just sitting there with all four tires deflated. The dream is a statement of his sense of impotency with regard to his capacity to move along life's course. A neurologically impaired girl has a dream that she is driving her father's car and each time she puts her foot on the brake, the car doesn't stop. The dream reveals her feeling that she cannot "put the brakes on" her thoughts, feelings and actions. In Mark's fantasy the wheel of the wagon "came off." This is a statement of Mark's sense of instability. It probably reflects his awareness, at some level, that his failure to work in school is compromising his capacity to move along life's course. Furthermore, it may relate to his parents' warnings that if he does not "shape up" his future will be a bleak one.

But it is not only the wheel that comes off, the bridge itself "started to crack." This is a statement of an even more profound sense of insecurity in Mark. The supporting structure under the wagon is also weak. The wagon on the bridge symbolizes Mark's view of his capacity to move along life's course. After all, the bridge connects one point to another and facilitates such progress. If the bridge breaks, one is stopped (at least temporarily) from moving along life's path. In short, the breaking of the wagon's wheel and the falling of the bridge depict Mark's belief that his world is falling away under him. His difficulties at school and at home were interfering with his gaining a sense of competence in coping with life. In both the academic and behavioral realms he was not acquiring the talents and skills which are necessary if one is to feel confident about coping with reality. In compensation for his feelings of inadequacy in these areas, he provides himself with a magic stone which protects him from the dangerous results of his incompetence. Furthermore, the magic stone fantasy is consistent with his life philosophy that somehow things will work out.

In the post-story discussion, I questioned Mark in order to be certain that I understood completely the facts of his story. If the therapist is not completely clear about the incidents in the story, he or she is ill-equipped to analyze it. And, of course, any stories that the therapist creates that derive from an incorrect rendition of the child's story are likely to be completely off point and of little or no therapeutic value. Just as Mark's story lent itself well to being divided into three segments, I divided my responding story into three segments, each of which corresponded to one of the patient's. This was the first of the three segments of my responding story:

Therapist: Now I'll tell my story. The title of my story is "The Chicken and the Stone."

Once upon a time there was a farmer and this farmer had a chicken and this chicken would lay eggs. And one day he went over to the chicken to get an egg, and the chicken bit him. He got very angry and he thought, "I know what I'll do. I'll get rid of this chicken. I'll sell this chicken to someone else." He also thought, "Maybe it will die. Then I won't have any problems with it."

So another man came along and he said, "Would you like to buy a chicken?"

And the man said, "Well, tell me about this chicken. Is he a good chicken? Is he kind? Does he bite?"

The farmer said, "Well, he may bite."

"Look," the man said, "I don't want a biting chicken."

And the farmer didn't know what to do because there he was stuck with this chicken. He said, "Gee, I wish this chicken were dead."

The second man said, "Look, here you have a chicken that's biting. You want to get rid of him. You want him to die. Is that the only way you know how to solve a problem with a biting chicken? You know, you can't solve life's problems by killing off or selling off the people who are bothering you. You've got to work it out with them. You can't get rid of people so easily and you can't even get rid of biting chickens so easily. So I suggest that you try to figure out some way of solving this problem with the chicken."

Well, he talked to the chicken. (In my story this chicken talks.) And he found out that there were things which he was doing which were bothering that chicken and that's why the chicken bit him. And when they were able to settle that problem and he stopped doing the things which bothered the chicken, the chicken stopped biting him and then the chicken continued to lay many more eggs and he then no longer wished to get rid of the chicken to sell him and he no longer wished that the chicken were dead.

Whereas the first buyer in Mark's story gullibly buys the chicken without asking questions, in my story he inquires about the chicken's habits—especially whether he bites. I attempted thereby to communicate that buyers in reality may not easily be taken in by the seller's duplicity. I hoped to let Mark know that one doesn't easily get away with lying and in this way lessen his tendency to lie in order to achieve his ends. The farmer then tells the truth and hopefully serves as a model of honesty for the patient. Thwarted in his attempts to get rid of the malevolent chicken, the farmer expresses the wish that it die. Again, reality considerations reign and the chicken remains very much alive. At this point the buyer becomes more directly the transmitter of my healthier communications and adaptations. He advises direct inquiry into the difficulties in the farmer-chicken relationship in the service of resolving them in ways more civilized (discussion rather than hostile acting out) than those already attempted by the farmer.

Accordingly, the farmer invites the chicken to express his grievances ("In my story this chicken talks.") rather than act them out with biting. The chicken does so and the problems are resolved. Because the patient's story did not specify the nature of the chicken's source(s) of irritation, I made only general reference to them. Had I wished to get more specific I would have first asked Mark why the chicken bit the farmer. The information so gained could have served to provide me with specifics for my story. But I already had so much information to work with by the time Mark finished his complete story that I decided not to add any more material. Overloading can reduce the child's receptivity to the therapist's stories. My main message then was that if someone is hostile toward you, rather than trying to get rid of him or her by separation or death, try to work out the problem through civilized inquiry and nonviolent action.

Whereas in Mark's story the potential purchaser refuses to buy a biting chicken, and then goes his way, my purchaser conducts an inquiry and provides advice. This is a common maneuver that I utilize in the mutual storytelling technique. It is one of the ways in which I provide my therapeutic messages. I wear many guises. Sometimes a passerby stops to watch the action and then, without any invitation on the part of the protagonists, enters into a discussion with them in the course of which he dispenses advice. Sometimes, unbeknownst to the participants, a "wise old owl" has been sitting on a bough of a tree watching the activities below. Then, at some judicious point, he or she interrupts the proceedings and starts pontificating. Again, there is full attention and receptivity to everything the owl says. The protagonists "hang on every word." Sometimes I use a teenager for this purpose. The reader will do well to recognize the value of the teenager in the treatment of latency-aged children. There is no one in the world who possesses more omniscience than the teenager. He knows everything and is in no way modest about his vast knowledge of the world. The reader might be interested to learn that in the 25 years or so that I have been utilizing this technique, not once (I repeat *not once*) has the recipient of such gratuitous advice ever responded with a comment such as: "Listen, Buster, I would appreciate your not butting into our business. If I wanted your advice, I would have asked for it. And until that time comes, I'd appreciate your keeping your trap shut."

Now onward to the second part of my responding story which, as mentioned, directs its attention to the second segment of the child's.

Now, one day this farmer was working in his cornfields and he found a very pretty stone. It was very shiny and very pretty. And he said, "I wonder if this is a magic stone. I'd sure like to have a magic stone. My crops haven't been doing too well lately. So he rubbed the stone and he hoped that the crops would do better. But nothing happened. The crops still were poor.

But one day he was in town and he was in a general store buying provisions and the owner of the store noticed that the farmer was rubbing the stone and holding it in his pocket. And he said, "What are you doing there?"

The farmer said, "Oh, that's my magic stone. That gives me luck."

He said, "Has it ever given you luck?"

The farmer replied, "Well, no, but I'm hoping it will make my crops better."

And the man in the store said to him, "Well, I never heard of a magic stone." He said, "What are you doing with your crops? Are you using any fertilizers and things like that?"

The farmer said, "Well, not really. I really don't believe too much in them. It's a lot of extra work putting in those fertilizers and it costs money."

And the man said, "Well, I think that the reason why your crops aren't doing well is that you're not taking care of them well enough. You're not putting in fertilizers." And he asked the farmer some other questions about what he was doing and it was clear that the farmer was not doing everything that he could. And the man in the store said, "Instead of rubbing a magic stone I suggest you get to work on your farm and start taking good care of your crops. I think there's a better likelihood that they'll do well than if you rub a magic stone."

And the farmer thought about what the man had said and he decided to try him out. So he got the fertilizer and he started to work harder on his crops, and sure enough that year he had a better crop than he had ever had before. Well, although the farmer was impressed with what the storekeeper had said, he wasn't fully sure that the stone still wasn't magic.

In my responding story, the magic stone is not effective in improving the farmer's crops. No matter how much he rubs it, the crops remain weak and malnourished. My advice to utilize more realistic and predictably effective methods is transmitted through the owner of the general store. As I am sure is obvious to the reader, this is another one of the disguises that I utilize in my responding stories. The farmer is receptive to this advice and, although it works, he still does not give up hope that his stone will perform magic. We are generally more attracted to easy and quick solutions than to difficult and complex problems, and the farmer is not immune to this human frailty. It will take a more dramatic proof of the impotency of his stone to convince him of its worthlessness in controlling natural events. (See part three of my story below.)

The above transcript does not provide the reader with information about the boy's facial expressions and gestures while I told my story. While relating the second phase of my story, the patient began to blink his eyes. I considered this to be a manifestation of the tension I was arousing in him with my statement that his fantasies of a magic solution to his problems were not going to be realized. Furthermore, he placed his right hand in a seemingly strange position, namely, as if he were holding a stone in it. His arm was flexed at the elbow and his fingers so positioned in cup-like fashion that he could very well have been holding a stone. I believe that this gesture was unconscious, and it reflected his need to "hang on" to the stone that I was symbolically taking away from him. It certainly provided me with confirmation that my story was indeed "hitting home" and touching on important issues.

I then continued and related the third part of my story:

> And on his farm there was a bridge which was somewhat old and weak, and he used to look at it and say, "I wonder if I should fix it up one of these days. Na, I'll rub my stone. It will keep it going." So he used to rub his stone every time he'd pass that bridge in order to keep the bridge solid. But one day as he was riding his wagon across the bridge a wheel broke and his wagon fell down and sure enough the bridge broke as well, even though he had had his magic stone in this pocket. And there he was in the water—his horse jumping around very scared, the wagon broken even more than it had been, the farmer sitting in the water all wet, and his wagon broken even more, and the bridge completely crushed. And there he was with the magic stone in his pocket! And as he sat there, he realized that this stone really wasn't magic. Finally it took *that* to make him realize and after that he decided to build a new bridge. He threw away the stone and he built a new strong bridge and that was the end of his belief in a magic stone. And do you know what the lesson of that story is?

I interrupt the transcript here before the post-story discussion which begins with the patient's response to my request that he provide the moral of my story. As is obvious, in my story, I again attempt to drive home the point that the magic stone will not work. Just as the patient's third segment is basically a restatement of his second, in that in both the magic stone is used to assuage tension (induced by his parents' threats) and perpetuate his life philosophy that all will go well even if he doesn't put in effort, my third segment is basically a restatement of my second. Here, while I related my story, the patient involved himself in even more dramatic gesturing. Specifically, at the point where I described the farmer sitting in the water, after the bridge had broken through, the patient spontaneously began to rub "water" off his thighs. He then resumed the gesture of holding the stone. However, at the point where I described the farmer's throwing the stone, the patient, without any prompting on my part, engaged in a stone-throwing maneuver. I wish to emphasize to the reader that there was no suggestion, either overt or covert, by me that the patient dramatize or in any way gesticulate the elements in my story. His spontaneous involvement in this way was confirmation that he was swept up in my story and that my message was being incorporated into his psychic structure.

As is my usual practice, rather than tell the moral myself, I generally ask the patient what he or she understands to be the lesson of my story. In this way I can often determine whether my messages have been truly understood because a correct statement of the moral requires a deep appreciation, at some level, of the story's fundamental meaning.

This is the interchange that followed my question:

Patient: Don't count on something else to do your work for you.

Therapist: Right! That's one lesson. That's the lesson with the magic stone. What's the lesson of the part with the chicken and the egg and the biting?

Patient: You should fix your own problems now if you can, or else somebody else will fix them for you.

Therapist: Well, *that* and if you have a problem with someone it's not so easy to get rid of them.

Patient: Try to figure it out.

Therapist: Try to figure it out with them. You can't kill them off, you can't sell them generally. Human beings are not like chickens. You can't just sell them or kill them so easily. If you try to, you know, you'll get into a lot of trouble. So the best thing is to try to work the problem out with the person. The end. Wait a minute. I want to ask you something. Do you want to say anything about this story?

Patient: No.

Therapist: Did you like it?

Patient: Yeah.

Therapist: Any particular part?

Patient: The part where he found the stone and it was pretty and shiny.

Therapist: Uh huh. Any other part?

Patient: No.

Therapist: Did you learn anything from this story? Did this story teach you anything?

Patient: No.

Therapist: Not at all?

Patient: Well, yeah.

Therapist: What does it teach you?

Patient: Well, you should kind of figure out your own problems and don't count on other people to do stuff for you.

Therapist: Okay. What about magic? What does it say about magic?

Patient: Magic—well, if you've got a magic stone make sure it's *really* a magic stone and then go counting on it. (laughs)

Therapist: Do you think there are such things as magic stones?

Patient: No. (laughs)

Therapist: I don't believe so either.

Patient: You can keep them as a good luck charm—as a pretty piece, but not as a magic stone.

Therapist: Do you think a good luck charm *really* brings good luck?

Patient: Hhmmm, not really.

Therapist: I don't think so either. No. Okay. So that's the end of the program today. Good-bye, boys and girls.

It is unrealistic for the therapist to expect that a single confrontation or story, or any other single experience in therapy, is going to bring about permanent change. Those who have conviction for time-limited therapy believe that this is possible, and they will attract patients who are gullible enough to believe this as well. If such rapid changes could indeed take place, Mark might very well say to me something along these lines: "Dr. Gardner, you're right. There's no such thing as magic. You've convinced me of that today. I can promise you that I will never again believe in magic. Now let's go on and talk about my next problem."

There are, of course, patients who say things along these lines. It is one of the more common forms of resistance and/or ingratiating oneself to the therapist. In the real world, the world in which there is no magic, the best one can hope for is to introduce an element of ambivalence regarding the patient's belief in magic. And this is what I believe occurred here. The post-story discussion reveals some discomfort on Mark's part with my message, but also some receptivity to it. In ensuing stories there were statements of negation of magic ("There's no such thing as a magic stone") which is certainly not a manifestation of "cure" of the problem. True "cure" comes when there is no mention of magic at all. Doing and undoing is not the same as never having done at all. Mark did reach the point, however, about three or four months later, in which magic did not appear in any form whatsoever in his stories. It was then, I believe, that he reached a healthier level with regard to this problem.

The Case of Evan
[The Killed Guide
and the Grilled-Cheese Sandwiches]

Evan, an eleven-and-one-half-year-old boy, was referred because of generalized inhibition and withdrawal from peers. His personality structure was schizoid, but he was not schizophrenic. He had trouble asserting himself, and showed little enthusiasm in school. His grades were quite poor although his intelligence was above average. This was the first story Evan told in treatment:

> One day I went up with a group of people and a guide to go mountain climbing in Colorado. It was a big mountain and we were all very tired, but the view was fine. At about 1000 feet I picked up a rock and threw it down. It bounced off the stones and went all the way down. It was a dangerous climb, but we had ropes and a guide and waist chains. He would go up ahead of us on to a ledge. It was a very steep mountain. There were very few grips for our hands and feet. Then we got to the top of one of the ledges, but the guide fell off and he got killed. Then we built a fire and had grilled-cheese sandwiches.
>
> After that it was easier to climb because the mountain wasn't so steep. However, we couldn't get to the top, so we went all the way down and went around to the other side of the mountain. We found a spot that looked good. We got another guide, but he got killed also on the way up. We got to the top and there was a pretty view. It was 5000 feet high and it took us six hours to climb it. We could see a hundred miles in every direction. We stayed up there awhile, enjoyed the view, and then we went down. It was much easier to get down.
>
> *Therapist:* What's the moral of that story?
> *Patient:* I can't think of any moral.

The most striking thing in this story was Evan's total lack of feeling for the guides who fell and were killed. He spoke of their falls with the same emotionless tone used when he described the rock that he had thrown down the mountain. The sentence describing the death of the first one is immediately followed by: "Then we built a fire and had grilled-cheese sandwiches." And the death of the second causes not a moment's hesitation or interference in the journey's progress. The story reveals severe superego deficiencies: an utter lack of sensitivity to the pains of others and an inability to place oneself in the position of someone who suffers.

This is the story I told in response:

One day a group of friends of mine and I decided to go mountain climbing. We were in Colorado and we were in the Rockies. We had a guide who was a very fine person and we all liked him very much. He had many years of experience and we felt very secure with him. He went ahead of us and we all had ropes and waist chains for protection. When we were about half-way up the mountain, he was on a ledge ahead of us and suddenly the rocks slipped from under him and, although he tried to catch on to the ledge, he slipped off and his body plummeted at least 1000 feet to the bottom of the mountain. It was a horrifying experience and we all felt completely helpless. We knew that it was sure death for him.

We were so upset that there was no question in our minds that we could not continue the trip. We were grief-stricken over this man's death, especially since he had died in the process of trying to be helpful to us in climbing this mountain. Well, we all slowly went down the mountain along the path that we had originally taken and when we got to the bottom, there we saw what we all feared and knew to be the case. There was his mangled body on the ground and it was a horrible sight. It was clear that he had probably died in the fall or died at the moment he struck the ground. Most of us cried bitterly. We then went back to the main cabin and notified the authorities. His wife was brought over and it was most painful when we had to tell her the very tragic news. The man had three children who were now left without a father as well. It was, without question, one of the most terrible experiences I have ever had.

In my story I included every ramification of the guide's death that might elicit emotional reactions. The written transcript can only convey a suggestion of the emotionalism which I tried to convey while telling my story. My hope here was to impart to Evan some sensitivity to the agony and torment which others might suffer. It would have been unreasonable to expect that this self-involved boy would, in his first session, respond significantly to an emotion-engendering story, and his overt reaction was minimal. My hope was that Evan might ultimately be reached, and this story was a step in that direction.

The Case of Todd
[The Club of Mean Tigers]

Todd entered treatment at the age of nine-and-a-half because of withdrawal, apathy, and shyness. His parents described him as rarely smiling and "a very unhappy boy." He never reached out for friendships, and few children found him to be a desirable or interesting playmate. He was easily scapegoated because of his fear of fighting back. With regard to this he stated, "I'm afraid I might hurt somebody real badly, so they might die." Although he is described as having been somewhat depressed since he started kindergarten, his depression increased three months prior to referral when he moved into a new neighborhood. At times he spoke of committing suicide, but there was no history of suicidal gestures or attempts.

Todd was the oldest of two sons and was an extremely over-protected boy. Both of his parents pampered him significantly. Although in the fourth grade, and although his school was only six blocks away from his home, he was routinely driven back and forth from school four times a day. Although the vast majority of children remained in school during the lunch break, Todd refused to do so. He wouldn't wait on line at the lunch counter, for fear he might get involved in the usual shoving, name calling, and horse play that typically takes place in that situation. Furthermore, he feared the inevitable teasing and rambunctiousness that took place in the schoolyard when children played there after eating their lunch. His mother would drop him off at school in the morning, pick him up at the beginning of lunch break, serve him his lunch at home, return him to school at the end of lunch break, and then bring him home at the end of the day. Todd had never gone to day camp (not to mention sleep-away camp) because he had initially reacted negatively when his parents proposed the idea a few years previously. In fact there had not been one day in his life that he had been away from his parents.

Todd's father was an extremely domineering man, and his mother was passively dependent on her husband. Her overprotectiveness stemmed primarily from her submission to her husband's dictates regarding indulging Todd. (She was so passive that it would have been difficult to predict how she would have been with another husband, other than that she would have been passive to him.) I believed that an element in Todd's anger was related to the resentment he felt over his father's overbearing manner. However, he was so dependent on both of his parents that he could not dare express his hostility. I considered his pent-up hostility to be a factor in his depression. His inhibition in asserting himself served to protect him from the consequences of hostile expression that would inevitably arise were he to have been more outgoing.

During his second session, Todd drew a picture of a tiger and then told a story that I believe epitomized some of his central problems. I recognized the story as one that would lend itself well to the mutual storytelling game, and so I suggested that he show the picture on television and tell his story again on my "Dr. Gardner's Make-Up-a-Story Television Program." The patient readily agreed:

Therapist: Now our guest has just drawn a picture and he's told me a story and I thought it was such a good story that I suggested that we play the storytelling game. So first he's going to show you the picture. Put it up and show it. Okay. Now what do you want to do, what is that a picture of?

Patient: A picture of a tiger.

Therapist: Okay, now what we want you to do is tell a story about your tiger and then I'll tell a story about a tiger, too.

Patient: Okay. This tiger wants to join this club, but the club has new members.

Therapist: It has what?

Patient: It has people—the tigers are bad in the club.

Therapist: The tigers in the club are bad, yeah.

Patient: And this tiger wants to join, but he's not mean so he's thinking about it in the picture if he should join and then he says, "I'll join the club if I don't have to be mean."

And then he talks to the club leader of the club and he says, "You gotta be mean to join our club."

And then he says, "No, I cannot. I should be myself."

Therapist: I should be myself, yeah.

Patient: And that's all.

Therapist: And so what happens?

Patient: Everybody should be theirself.

Therapist: Okay. So does he get into the club?

Patient: No.

Therapist: Okay. And so the lesson of that story is what? Is that the end of the story? He just doesn't get into the club?

Patient: Yeah.

Therapist: Okay. And the lesson of that story is?

Patient: That you should be yourself.

Therapist: Hmm. Be yourself. You don't want to be mean. Is that it?

Patient: Yeah.

Therapist: What should you do?

Patient: Be yourself.

Therapist: Be yourself. In his case this tiger didn't want to be a member of the club unless they did what?

Patient: Unless he was mean.

Therapist: Oh, they said he couldn't be a member of the club unless he was mean?

Patient: Yes.

Therapist: And what did he say to them?

Patient: He said, "No."

Therapist: Did you say—I remember when you told a story before—did you say something about he told them that they should not be mean?

Patient: No.

Therapist: When you told the story before didn't you say, "I'll only join the club unless you people promise not to be mean?" Didn't you say that?

Patient: He said that if he could be nice. . .

Therapist: If you people in the club.

Patient: No, I said if *he* could be nice then he would join.

Therapist: Oh, you said, "I'll join your club if you let me be nice and let me not bother people." Oh, if you let him not bother people, but the others could bother people. Is that it?

Patient: Yes.

Therapist: I see. He just didn't want—he didn't want to be the one to bother people.

Patient: Yeah.

Therapist: I see. Okay. And the leader said, "You can't join the club because to join our club everybody has to bother people." Is that it?

Patient: Yeah.

I considered the club of tigers who always bother other people to symbolize Todd's view of his peers, namely, a pack of ferocious animals who were ever scapegoating and teasing him. The only way he can gain membership into their club is to become mean himself. This is something Todd is frightened of doing and so he refuses to comply with this provision of admission with the statement, "I should be myself." For Todd to be himself is to be inhibited in asserting himself. His view of his peers as mean tigers stems from Todd's timidity and fear of self-assertion and hostile expression. From his vantage point they appear ferocious. In addition, I believed that the mean tigers were made even more threatening by the projection onto them of Todd's own unconscious anger. He thereby distances himself from his anger by refusing to join the club that requires its expression as a provision for membership. His statement, "I should be myself" makes reference to his determination not to express resentment. With this understanding of Todd's story, I related mine.

Therapist: Okay, I get the idea. Okay. Now, as I've said before, the way it works on this program is that first the guest tells a story and then Dr. Gardner tells a story. And my story may start like yours, but different things happen in my story. Okay?

Patient: Okay.

Therapist: Okay, here we go. Once upon a time there was a tiger, and this tiger wanted to join a club and in this club—this was the mean club. Everybody in the club was mean. And he said, "I want to join your club, but I don't want to be mean. I don't want to bother people ever, and will you let me join your club if I don't bother people?"

And they said, "No, no, no. You can't join this club because here we bother people." So he couldn't join the club.

Anyway, he decided that he would find another club, a club where nobody bothers people. So he looked around and people said, "Well, there are other clubs that don't bother people. In fact, there are two other kinds of clubs. There's one other kind of club where everybody agrees *never* to bother people at all, and then there's another club where the people agree that *sometimes* they will bother people and *sometimes* they won't bother people."

So really there were three clubs. There was the original club where all the tigers always bothered people. There was a club in the middle where sometimes they would bother and sometimes they wouldn't. And then there was the other club where nobody ever bothered people. So which one of the other two clubs do you think this tiger in my story wanted to join?

Patient: He wanted to join the one where he was always nice.

Therapist: Yeah, he said, "That's the club for me, always nice." Nobody ever bothers people. He said, "That's the club for me." So he went to that club and he says, "Can I join your club?"

And they said, "Remember the rule of our club. You must *never* bother anybody. You must *never* get angry at anybody, you must never hit anybody, you must never bite anybody, and you remember that."

He said, "That's the club for me." So he joined that club and he took an oath that he would not bother people. And he said, "I swear that I will never bother people. I'll never bite people, no matter what."

Anyway, that club, the one that never bothered anyone, used to have its meetings, and one day a tiger came along while the club was having its meeting—a lion, excuse me—this is a tiger's club. It was a lion, and an elephant. And the lion and the elephant started coming around and growling and bothering the tigers in the club. And the tigers said, "Oh, please don't bother us. We mean you no harm. We're very nice. We don't bother people. Please don't bite us. Please don't bother us."

Well, that elephant and that lion weren't listening, and they started to make trouble and these tigers all ran way. They didn't want to fight. And then what happened was that the elephant and the lion got a lot of the food that the tigers had collected and a lot of their possessions and stuff. And the tigers felt very sad and depressed about it. And that used to happen from time to time because they made a promise that they would never fight, they would never bother people, they would never bite, even if people started with them. Then they used to be taken advantage of, and that made them feel very bad about themselves.

And finally the tiger decided that maybe he ought to try the second club, the club in the middle. And he went there and said, "What are your rules?"

And the club in the middle said, "Well, our rules are these. Our rules are that we're not going to start fights with other people, but if other people, if other animals start with us, we're going to fight back. So it's not that we never fight. It's not that we always fight. We're in the middle."

And this tiger said, "Maybe I'll try this club and see what happens." So he joined that club of tigers. And one day, as the middle tiger club was meeting, a couple of lions and some elephants came along and some other animals, and they started to make trouble. And the tigers in the middle club said, "Listen, we're warning you. Stay away. We didn't bother you. Don't bother us. But we can tell you this: If you bother us, you're going to be sorry."

Well, the lions and the elephants didn't listen and they started to snarl and bite, and they started to go where the middle club's food was and they started to make trouble. And these tigers in the middle club got together and they started to fight and growl and hiss and jump and claw and there was a fight. Soon the lions and the elephants who came along realized that they were going to get into a lot of trouble. They'd get bitten up and they'd get hurt and so gradually they pulled back and they ran away. And then the tigers in this middle club began talking about the importance of . . . what did they talk about?

Patient: Hm.

Therapist: What did they decide after everybody left, after the lions and the elephants left? What did they decide?

Patient: I don't know.

Therapist: Well, did they think that their plan was a good one?

Patient: Yeah.

Therapist: What was their plan in this club? How did they work things?

Patient: They didn't want to start trouble, but if some other animal started trouble, they would fight back.

Therapist: Right! That was their rule. That was the middle club.

And so after that the animals that came around to bother them, like other tigers and elephants and other animals, realized that these guys wouldn't start up, but that they would protect their rights. They would protect themselves when there was trouble. And gradually other animals realized that that was the best of the three clubs. That was the best thing to do with animals who were always bothering people. Don't start, but if others start up, fight back. Now what about the club of the animals that never bothered people? What was the drawback of that? What was the disadvantage? What kinds of trouble did they get when they never bothered people?

Patient: And then other people would pick on them.

Therapist: Right.

Patient: And they wouldn't fight back.

Therapist: Hh hmm. So which do you think is the best of the three clubs, in your opinion?

Patient: The middle club.

Therapist: Because?

Patient: Because if they starting picking on you, you can pick on them.

Therapist: Right. Right. You defend yourself. You protect your rights. Okay, how did you like this program?

Patient: I liked it.

Therapist: Do you want to see yourself on television?

Patient: Okay.

Therapist: Do you want your parents to come up and watch?

Patient: No.

Therapist: You don't want them to. Why not?

Patient: I'm shy.

Therapist: You're shy.

Patient: Uh hmm.

Therapist: I think it would be a good idea. It's good practice for shyness to do things that you're shy about, and then you find out that it's not so terrible. That's the way to conquer shyness. Do you want to try it?

Patient: Okay.

Therapist: All right, let's call them and have them watch and you'll see that for the person who is shy, each time you do the thing that bothers you, you become less scared of that thing. Okay?

One of the purposes of therapy is to introduce options to the patient that may not have been considered or, if they have, have not been incorporated into the patient's psychic structure. In therapy one helps the patient consider the advantages and disadvantages of the various options, the pathological as well as the healthy ones. *The mutual storytelling technique* provides opportunities for such introductions and comparisons, and this is what I have done here. The story demonstrates symbolically the discomforts and indignities one suffers when one lives by the principle that anger expression under any circumstances is undesirable. It also demonstrates the benefits accrued to those who have a more flexible attitude about anger and use it appropriately.

The patient was deeply involved in my story and readily understood its significance. Although he expressed some hesitation about his parents' viewing the videotape, his enthusiasm more than counterbalanced this negative reaction. I believe this interchange served to catalyze his involvement in treatment.

The Case of David
(The Family with Sixteen Children)

David was referred at the age of nine-and-a-half by his pediatrician. Three months prior to referral, he began suffering with abdominal pains. These began about one month after starting the fourth grade and were so severe that he had not attended school during the six weeks prior to my initial consultation with him. Thorough medical evaluations by three pediatricians revealed no organic cause for his difficulties, and he was therefore referred for consultation.

David was the youngest of six children, the older siblings ranging in age from 23 to 16. Accordingly, there was a 6½-year hiatus between David and his next oldest sibling. During the five years prior to the initial consultation, the older siblings began to leave the household, one at a time. The oldest three had already left the home and the fourth, an 18-year-old sister, was starting to apply to college. In addition, his 16-year-old brother (the fifth of the siblings) had already left the home three years previously for six months as an exchange student in Europe. The family was a tight-knit one, and these losses were painful for David.

Of pertinence to David's disorder was the fact that there was a strong history of appendicitis in the family. Four of his five older siblings had had their appendices removed and appendicitis was under serious consideration during David's hospitalization. However, absolutely no evidence for appendicitis was found. David's father was a highly successful businessman who enjoyed significant prestige in his community. The family members considered themselves paragons of what a family should be. In such an atmosphere the expression of deficiency was strongly discouraged as were crying, depressed feelings, profanity, and any other manifestations that were considered to be deviant. Lastly, David's new teacher had the reputation of being unusually strict and David found this particularly difficult to handle.

During the initial interview I concluded that David was suffering with a separation anxiety disorder. In his case it was not so much separation from his mother that was painful, but the progressive and predictable loss of his older siblings who were serving as parental surrogates. It was as if David had seven parents: mother, father, and five significantly older siblings. As they progressively left the home, he felt increasingly alone and fearful about the loss of his various protectors. The closeness of his family intensified the problem. Had there been a looser family involvement he might not have been so anxious. Furthermore, the family pattern in which everyone was required to present a facade of perfection and imperturbability made it extremely difficult for David to express the anxieties, anger, and depression he felt over these losses. Lastly, the family history of appendicitis provided a model for excused withdrawal. Others were seen to get extra attention and affection in association with this illness, and that probably served to give David the idea that he could enjoy such extra protection by the utilization of the symptom. Of course, the abdominal complaints themselves might also have been a manifestation of his tension and anxiety. During his third session, while playing the mutual storytelling game, the following interchange took place.

Therapist: Good afternoon, boys and girls, ladies and gentlemen. Welcome to "Dr. Gardner's Make-Up-a-Story Television Program." We have a new guest on our program today. Tell me how old are you?
Patient: Nine.
Therapist: Nine years old. What grade are you in?
Patient: Fourth.
Therapist: Fourth grade. Okay, now, let me tell you how it works. On this program we invite boys and girls down to see how good they are in making up stories. Now it's against the rules to tell a story about anything that really happened to you or anyone you know. The story must be completely made up from your imagination. It can't be about anything you've seen on television or read in books. Then, when you've finished telling the story, you tell the lesson or moral of the story—what we learn from the story. As you know, every good

story has a lesson or a moral. And, of course, the more exciting the story is the more fun it will be to watch on television afterwards. Now, when you've finished telling the story, you tell the lesson or moral of your story. Then I'll tell a story and we'll talk about the lesson or moral of my story. Okay, you're on the air.

Patient: It can't be from a book?

Therapist: No, it can't be a story from a book. It has to be completely made up in your own imagination.

Patient: There's this man and a woman, and they lived on top of a huge rock. And they had 16 children and they couldn't find another room. They only had one room.

Therapist: Okay, so there's one room for 16 children. Uh huh.

Patient: And they were all running around and making so much noise that they didn't know what to do. So they called their friend who was really smart. . .

Therapist: So they couldn't handle all the kids? Is that it?

Patient: So the man said if they had any lobster pots. And they said "yes, 16." And he asked them to get the lobster pots. . . .

Therapist: This is the friend?

Patient: Yeah. So he took the lobster pots on his bicycle.

Therapist: He took the 16 lobster pots on his bicycle?

Patient: Yeah, to his home and then at home he got some candy and rope and then he rode back and climbed up to the house, and then when he got up to the house, he said, "Hello . . . " So he tied the lobster pots outside the windows. He had 16 pieces of candy and he put all the candy he had in them.

Therapist: In the lobster pots?

Patient: Yeah, and then the children ran to get their candy . . . and then they jumped into the lobster pots and ate the candy. And the children stayed in the lobster pots.

Therapist: The children stayed there?

Patient: These were big lobster pots. They even had dinner there.

Therapist: They even had dinner there? Who served them?

Patient: The mother and father.

Therapist: So they had more room . . . is that it?

Patient: Yeah.

Therapist: Uh huh. Okay. Is that the end?

Patient: That's the end.

Therapist: Lesson?

Patient: Some people will do anything just to have some privacy.

Therapist: Who's having the privacy there?

Patient: The mother and the father . . . they would do anything just to have some privacy.

Therapist: And what did they do to the children?

Patient: They just lived with them.

I considered this story to represent well the patient's situation with his family. Although his family consisted of six children, he symbolizes it with a family of 16 children. In either case the number is large and both figures share the numeral 6. The story enabled David to gratify his fantasy of entrapping his siblings in such a way that they could not leave the house. Each window contains a lobster pot into which a sibling can be lured with candy. There the child is trapped and cannot flee or leave. Ostensibly, the parents do this in order to provide themselves with some privacy. If that were indeed their motive, they could have allowed all the children to leave the house in such a way that there was little if any link or tie to the home. Accordingly, I considered this reason to be a rationalization. It is the opposite of what the parents *really* want: entrapment of the children in the home. Of course, it is not the parents who want this; it is David who attributes this desire to the parents to serve his own purposes. The story also reflects some ambivalence about closeness with his siblings. On the one hand, he wants them close enough to be seen and ever present (thus he traps them in lobster pots). On the other hand, he puts them outside the window, thereby providing him with a little distance and breathing space (a little privacy after all). With this understanding of David's story, I related mine.

> *Therapist:* I see. Okay, now as I said, when you finish telling your story, I'll tell a story and we'll talk about the lesson and moral of my story. Now, my story will start off like your story, but different things happen in my story. Okay?
>
> Once upon a time there was a family and this family consisted of a mother and a father and 16 children . . . a big family . . . and they lived in one room. Now everyone was getting kind of edgy . . . living on top of one another and things like that.
>
> And finally they decided to consult a friend of theirs who was very wise. And they said to him, "What do you think we can do about this?"
>
> And the father said, "I have an idea. I think maybe I ought to get lobster pots . . . and put candy in them and put them outside the windows and then they'll go into the lobster pots and then there will be less people around the house and I'll have more room."
>
> And the wise friend said, "Well, look, how old are some of your children? What are their age ranges?"
>
> He said, "Well, they range from very little ones to very big ones."
>
> And the friend said, "Well, aren't the big ones getting ready to leave soon? . . . go off on their own and become adults?"

And the father said, "Well, I think that the problem will solve itself as the older ones grow up and leave the house. I think that you want to hold onto these kids too long. If you're going to put them in lobster pots and have them hanging around the house, that tells me that you want to hold them back and keep them in the house forever and not let them grow up and become independent, self-sufficient adults."

And the man of the house realized that the wise man made sense. And he said, the man of the house said, "However, the young ones are going to miss the older ones terribly and maybe we ought to try to keep those older ones there for the young ones' sakes."

The wise friend said, "It isn't fair to the older ones. The younger ones have to accept the fact that the older ones are going to be going. They may feel lonely but you know, they have one another. And they also have other friends they can make."

And the father said, "What about the youngest one? When the other 15 leave, what's going to happen to him?"

The wise man said, "Well, he'll be old enough by then to have his own friends. He'll still have time with the older ones. He'll go and visit them and they'll come to visit him. It's not like they're lost forever. He'll still have some time with them. He'll speak to them on the phone. And then he can make his own friends. He can still be with you people, his mother and father. So it's not the end of his world that he doesn't have that many people around. So. . .

Patient: So they just let them grow up?

Therapist: They let them grow up and then what happened to the younger ones?

Patient: Then they. . .

Therapist: Are they sad?

Patient: I guess so.

Therapist: Uh huh. What happened to them? Anything happen to them?

Patient: I don't know.

It is a well-known principle in treatment that if the therapist is going to attempt to take something away from a person, he or she does well to try to find some reasonable substitute at that point. Even the suggestion that the substitutes be provided at some time in the future is generally not as effective as recommending substitutes in the present. Accordingly, although I recommended in my story that the younger ones resign themselves to the fact that the older ones inevitably are going to leave, I provide definite substitutive gratifications. I recommend that the younger ones involve themselves with one another. The patient still had one younger sibling in the home and so this recommendation was applicable. I also suggested intensified relationships with peers as another way of obtaining compensatory gratification. Last, I reminded David that one can still have frequent and meaningful contacts with older siblings even though they are living outside the home. Telephone conversations and visits are still possible and the awareness of this can help assuage the sense of loneliness one might feel after one's older siblings leave the home. At that point I attempted to engage David in a conversation to ascertain whether he appreciated on a conscious level any relationship between my story and his own situation. As mentioned, I do not consider it crucial for the treatment of the patient to have such awareness. What is important is that the message "gets through" and I am not too concerned whether it is received on the conscious or unconscious level, on the direct or the symbolic level. This is the conversation that ensued.

> *Therapist:* Well, do you think this story I told you has anything to do with you? Has anything to do with your situation?
> *Patient:* Ah, yes.
> *Therapist:* In what way? How?
> *Patient:* My brothers and sisters have gone away.
> *Therapist:* How many brothers and sisters did you have?
> *Patient:* Six . . . five.
> *Therapist:* Five besides yourself. And what are their ages? How old is the oldest? What are their ages?
> *Patient:* Sixteen, 19, 20, 22, and 24.
> *Therapist:* Uh huh. How many live in the house now?
> *Patient:* Not counting when they go to college?
> *Therapist:* Right. If they're off at college, let's consider them out of the house.
> *Patient:* Two.
> *Therapist:* Two. You and. . .
> *Patient:* My brother, Bart.
> *Therapist:* Who is 16? And what year in high school is he?
> *Patient:* Sophomore.
> *Therapist:* Sophomore? So he still has a couple more years at home?
> *Patient:* Uh huh.
> *Therapist:* Uh huh. Now, how does the story I just told relate to yours?
> *Patient:* It's like me. My brothers and sisters are going away.
> *Therapist:* Uh huh. And how do you feel about accepting that fact?
> *Patient:* I think I can.
> *Therapist:* You think you can?
> *Patient:* Yeah.

Therapist: Does it upset you a lot?

Patient: Not a lot.

Therapist: Do you think being upset about them has anything to do with your stomach? With your cramps and your going to the hospital?

Patient: No. I don't think so.

Therapist: Do you think your story has anything to do with your problems or the situation with your brothers and sisters?

Patient: No.

Therapist: I do. I think it has something to do with it. In your story, you put them in cages and keep them around the house. Isn't that right? In your story the mother and father's friend put the boys and girls in cages . . . lobster pots . . . they're kind of cages, aren't they?

Patient: Yeah.

Therapist: And they keep them around the house. They don't go anywhere. They're kind of trapped into staying around the house. I think your story says that you would like to have your brothers and sisters trapped around the house.

Patient (appearing incredulous): Not really.

Therapist: You don't think so. Do you think your story has anything to do with you?

Patient: No.

Therapist: Do you think *my* story has anything to do with you?

Patient: Just a little.

Therapist: Just a little. Okay, Well, anyway, the important thing is that if brothers and sisters stay around the house too long, they don't grow up.

Patient: Yes.

Therapist: And they have to grow up and they have to leave and the other kids left behind have to make friends with others, and it isn't the end of the world.

Patient: Yeah.

Therapist: That's the main message. It's not the end of the world when your brothers and sisters leave. You still have other people . . . other friends. And you can still get in touch with your brothers and sisters too, and still see them. Okay, do you want to watch this for a little while?

Patient: Okay.

Therapist: Do you want to have your mother come up and see it?

Patient: Okay.

As can be seen, the patient did not gain too much insight into the relationship between his story and mine. Nor did he have much insight into the relationship between his story and his situation.

There was some appreciation of some superficial similarity but basically he was unappreciative of the various relationships. He did, however, listen with interest to my story, and I believe that the message got through.

The Case of Harry
[Valentine Day's Candy
from a Loving Mother]

Harry entered treatment at the age of ten because of acting-out behavior in the classroom. Although very bright, he was doing poorly academically. He did not do his homework and would lie to his parents about his school assignments. He did not pay attention in the classroom; rather, he would whisper, hum, shout out, and disrupt the classroom in a variety of ways. He did not exhibit proper respect for his teachers and his principal. At home, as well, he was a severe behavior problem. He was openly defiant of his mother's and stepfather's authority and did not respond to punishment. In spite of this, Harry had an engaging quality to him. Adults, especially, found him "a pleasure to talk to." The parents of the few friends he had also found him a very likable and charming boy, and they often could not believe that he involved himself in antisocial behavior. Harry's mother was married three times. He was the product of her second marriage. He had an older sister who was born during his mother's first marriage. His father was a sales representative for a large corporation and had frequently been away from the home during the first two years of Harry's life, when his parents had still been living together. When the father was with the infant, he tended to be cool, aloof, and disinterested. Harry's mother was a secretary who began working fulltime when Harry was two months of age. He was then left to the care of a series of babysitters, most of whom were unreliable and some of whom were punitive. Unfortunately, both parents tended to ignore the signs of the babysitters' maltreatment.

When Harry was two years old, his parents separated. During the next year he and his sister lived alone with his mother. Following the separation of Harry's parents, there was a custody dispute. Both parents wanted custody, and each claimed to be the superior parent. Harry's father claimed that his wife was promiscuous and, therefore, unfit to take care of the children because she had had a transient affair during the marriage. The trial took place in a rural area in the Midwest, and the judge supported the father's position. After three months with his father, the latter returned the children to the mother with whom they were still living at the time of treatment.

When he was three, his mother's second husband moved into the home and they were married when Harry was four. This was a very stormy relationship, and Harry witnessed many violent battles between his mother and her third husband. In addition, her second husband used corporal punishment in order to discipline Harry. About two years after he moved into the house, Harry's mother's second husband deserted, and neither the mother nor Harry heard from him subsequently.

When Harry was nine, his mother's new husband moved into the house, and he was the stepfather who was involved at the time Harry began treatment. Like his predecessor, Harry's new stepfather was also extremely punitive. He used the strap primarily with the argument, "It was good enough for my father, and it's good enough for me." Harry's mother basically encouraged her husband to use the strap on Harry. When I expressed my opinion that, at ten, Harry was much too old for physical punishment and that I did not believe that corporal punishment was serving any purpose for Harry, both parents disagreed. I emphasized to them that it was my belief that they were making Harry worse, not better, and that there was no evidence that such beatings were reducing his antisocial behavior. In fact, I expressed to them my opinion that it was increasing the frequency and severity of his acting out. Again, they would not listen.

During his second month in treatment, the following interchanges took place while playing the mutual storytelling game:

> *Therapist:* Okay. And now ladies and gentlemen our guest is going to tell us his own original made up story. You're on the air!
> *Patient:* A man was riding his motorcycle on the street and he crashed and eventually he went to the hospital, and when he was in the hospital, his wife came to visit him. While his wife was visiting him the next day would be Valentine's Day. So she brought him on Valentine's Day lots of candy and sweets and the nurse said no candy and sweets for the patient but she did not listen. And so she gave him the candy and sweets he got even sicker.
> So then he had to go for an operation. The operation was successful, but the wife was not allowed in the hospital. So eventually she called the police and she told the police what happened. And she

wanted to speak to her husband and she broke into the window that he was in—the room window and she took him out of the hospital and he couldn't survive on his own and she didn't get him back to the hospital on time almost. So then he had another operation that was not successful and she was not happy because he died.

Therapist: Okay, now were you going to say something else?

Patient: No, that is it.

Therapist: Okay, the lesson?

Patient: Lesson?

Therapist: Yeah. Every story has a lesson or a moral.

Patient: To tell you when something is told to you, to go by it. To go by the rules.

Therapist: To go by the rules! And how did this wife break the rules?

Patient: She kept on giving him things that he was not supposed to have.

Therapist: Like?

Patient: Candy and taking him out of the hospital.

Therapist: Okay, so she broke two rules?

Patient: Right!

Therapist: Why did she break those rules?

Patient: Because she wanted her husband.

Therapist: She wanted her husband. . .

Patient (interrupts): to be with her.

Therapist: She wanted him to be with her even though the doctors had said it was a bad idea?

Patient: Right, he could not handle it.

Therapist: When you say he could not handle it, what do you mean?

Patient: Like he would not even do anything else.

Therapist: You mean he did just what his wife said?

Patient: Yeah.

Therapist: I see. That is when she gave him the candy?

Patient: No, before the candy when he got even sicker.

Therapist: I see, and what was he like when she took him out of the hospital?

Patient: He was really sick, he was coughing and he was weak.

Therapist: What was the nature of his illness? What was wrong with him?

Patient: He didn't have the right type of medicine. Like he was supposed to have every so often, so he could not survive.

Therapist: I see.

I believed that the man, the protagonist of the story, represented Harry and the man's wife, Harry's mother (the only female in Harry's life). Under the guise of being benevolent she is quite malevolent. She does what she considers to be in Harry's best interests, even if what she does is directly opposed to the doctor's orders. Harry is too weak and passive to say no and suffers the consequences of her "benevolence." He eats the candy and knows that it will make him sicker—and this is exactly what happens. He allows himself to be taken out of the hospital—seemingly because of his mother's love and her desire not to be separated from him—and he gets sicker, and ultimately dies.

The story demonstrates well what Harry Stack Sullivan referred to as the "malevolent transformation." This phenomenon is seen in individuals who grow up in homes where a parent professes love and affection; however, whenever such love is dispensed, it most frequently results in pain to the child. Somehow the affectionate maneuver results in a painful experience—always under the guise that love is still being provided. For example, a mother while professing strongly her love and affection will so vigorously hug the child that significant pain is produced. Under such circumstances the child comes to associate professions of love with physical and/or psychological pain. This produces a fear of those who display affection because there is ever the anticipation that the pain will be soon forthcoming. Here, Harry's mother expresses her affection by giving a box of Valentine's Day candy. A more direct and undisguised symbol of love would be hard to find. However, for Harry it is poison because his physical condition is such that sweets are specifically detrimental. Then his mother takes him out of the hospital against the doctor's advice—again because of her love and her strong desire to be close with him. And he almost dies because of her "affection."

This story also had implications for Harry's therapy. The doctors might very well represent this examiner. Harry's mother and stepfather were both beating him with a strap under the guise of affection. It is another example of the malevolent transformation in that Harry could not but experience pain in association with their allegedly well-meaning attempts to help him become a law-abiding citizen. The story also has some prophetic elements in that it implies that if Harry continues to get such "love," it may kill him.

With this understanding of Harry's story, I continued.

> *Therapist:* Okay, now it's my turn to tell a story. Remember I said that I would tell a story? My story may start like your story but different things happen very quickly. Okay, here we go.

Once upon a time there was a man, and he was sick in the hospital and the doctor said to him that he was absolutely not to have sweet things like candy and things like that.

Patient: Oh, too bad, I like that . . . (mumbles) . . .

Therapist: Now, what did you say? Too bad what?

Patient: Too bad. I'm glad I'm not him because I like candy.

Therapist: Well anyway, this man knew that it was important to obey the doctor's orders. Anyway, one day his wife came in, and it was Valentine's Day, and she said "I love you very much dear. Oh my dear husband, I love you very much. You are really my love, and I brought you this big box of Valentine's chocolates."

And he said, "Well, they sure look good, but the doctor said no sweets, no way." And she said, "Just go ahead and eat them."

And he said, "No, no. It's a bad idea. If I eat those sweets I may get even sicker." And he just absolutely refused to eat them, and she realized that he meant what he said and in no way would he eat those candies.

He also said, "If you want to get me something else as a present, something that would not harm me, I would be very happy."

Patient: How about some ice cream?

Therapist: No ice cream! The same thing. It's also sweet. What do you think she came up with?

Patient: A Valentine's card.

Therapist: A Valentine's card, right. Anything else?

Patient: A new car.

Therapist: Well, that is some Valentine's present! How about something more reasonable? Something that costs more than a Valentine's card and less than a car?

Patient: A kiss.

Therapist: A kiss is good. She gave him a big kiss! And he *really* liked that. He said, "That's very nice."

Patient: Did she get him candy then?

Therapist: No, no. She realized that he was right and that he shouldn't eat the candy. Anyway, the next day she said, "I don't like that hospital. I don't like my husband in that hospital because they don't let me do the things that I want, and I'm going to get him out of the hospital." So she came and tried to get him out. She wanted him to get signed out against doctor's advice, and he absolutely refused. So she said, "I love you very much, and I want you at home."

And he said, "If you love me very much, you'll listen to the things that I want. Right now I want to be with you, but I must stay at this hospital and get better. If you really loved me as much as you say, you would listen to what I want and would also do many of the things I want. If you want to spend sometime at home, okay. But if you want to spend some time at the hospital with me, okay. *But I will not go home now.*

Well, after he said that she started to raise a real fuss. She had a tantrum and a fit. And she started screaming, "But I love you so much I want you home!"

Then the doctors and the nurses said, "If you don't cut out that screaming, we'll call the police. You can't have him home and you can't steal him out of the hospital."

And the man didn't want to go with her, and he said, "Right, I have to be in this hospital 'til I'm better." Well, she realized that once again he wasn't going to do what she said just because she said it, and then he said, "If you really love me, you'll listen to the things I want and try to do some of those things, not just the things you want." So she realized that maybe he had a point. So what do you think happened then?

Patient: You said, "They called the police when she set foot in the door."

Therapist: No, no, they didn't have to. They threatened her. They said, "If you don't stop these fits and all this screaming and everything, we will call the police." But you see they didn't have to because she listened to reason.

Patient: I see, and she stopped screaming.

Therapist: Yes, well now what was happening was she was sad about it, but she realized that what her husband said made sense, that it was certainly true that he had to stay in the hospital. (Patient making sounds.) What's the matter?

Patient: Nothing.

Therapist: What were those noises?

Patient: My stomach.

Therapist: Your stomach. Okay. Do you want to settle down? Do you want to hear the rest of the story?

Patient: Yeah.

Therapist: Anyway, she realized that what he said made sense. She realized that he needed to be in the hospital and that getting him out of the hospital early, before the doctors said his time was up, was a bad idea. So what do you think then happened?

Patient: Was his time up?

Therapist: In the hospital?

Patient: Yes.

Therapist: Well, not at the time she wanted him out. But what happened after that?

Patient: He stayed there and he got lonely.

Therapist: And then what happened?

Patient: Then he signed out.

Therapist: No, no. He did *not* sign out. He did *not* break the rules. He listened to the doctors, and he finally got better, went home, and then he and his wife had much more time with one another. And do you think she changed after that?

Patient: Yes.

Therapist: She began to realize that he had a point. And what was the big problem his wife had in my story?

Patient: Not listening.

Therapist: Not listening to what?

Patient: The rules, just like mine.

Therapist: The rules, but something else she did not listen to.

Patient: The rules, just like mine.

Therapist: The rules, but something else she did not listen to.

Patient: Her husband. She wanted her own way.

Therapist: Right, and not listening to what her husband wanted to do. And what should you do with other people?

Patient: Take their thoughts into consideration.

Therapist: Right, take their thoughts and feelings into consideration. You have to compromise. Anyway, that is what happened. They went home. What do you think the lessons of my stories are? Try to figure them out.

Patient: To tell you to listen and you've got to take other people's thoughts into consideration.

Therapist: Right!

Patient: And you have to go by the rules.

Therapist: Very good. You got the lessons. Take into consideration other people's feelings and then compromise. Sometimes you do what they want, sometimes they do what you want. Right?

Patient: Right.

Therapist: And then follow the rules if you think they are important ones and good ones like the rules the doctor makes about getting better. Okay, well, ladies and gentlemen, this is the end of our program today. Do you want to watch this?

Patient: Yeah.

Therapist: Okay, let's turn this off now.

On a few occasions I interrupted my story to ask for the patient's input. The patient's suggestions regarding presents that would be preferable to Valentine chocolates were for the most part reasonable (with the exception of the car). In addition, I periodically interrupted my story to be sure that the patient understood my main points.

Whereas in the patient's story the man is passive (and conspicuously so), in my story he takes an active role in protecting himself from his wife's (symbolizing mother) misguided and coercive benevolence. It is a statement to the patient that, even though he was ten, he was not completely helpless to protect himself from some (but certainly not all) of the indignities he suffers in his home. My story also attempted to help Harry appreciate the basic malevolence behind some of his mother's professions of benevolence. Such clarification can lessen the likelihood that the patient will become involved in pathological interactions. His stomach churning noises were, I believe, a concomitant of the anxiety my message was creating. It is a statement also of the fact that my story was "hitting home."

The Case of Frank
(The Nutcracker and the Three Peanuts)

The last patient I will present exhibited typical manifestations of the Oedipus complex. In order for the reader to appreciate better the way in which I dealt with this boy's oedipal story, I will present first my views of the Oedipus complex.

Freud's Theory of the Oedipus Complex   Freud described the Oedipus complex as a normal childhood psychological phenomenon in which the boy or girl, between the ages of three and five, exhibits sexual-possessive fantasies toward the opposite-sexed parent and simultaneously views the same-sexed parent as a rival. The boy anticipates that his father will castrate him for his incestuous designs on his mother and the girl is said to fantasize that she once did indeed have a penis but lost it or it was cut off. Freud's theory of the Oedipus complex was derived from the analysis of adults— most of whom Freud considered neurotic and some of whom we would today consider psychotic. To the best of my knowledge, Freud only published one article on the treatment of a child, the case of Little Hans (1909), and, as mentioned previously, even here Freud was not the therapist. Rather, the boy's father treated him with Freud serving as the supervisor. In the three-and-a-half month course of treatment, Freud saw the boy only once. Freud believed that Hans' treatment confirmed his theories of infantile sexuality and the Oedipus and castration complexes. Furthermore, Freud believed that sexual attraction toward the opposite-sexed parent and jealous rivalry against the same-sexed parent universally appeared in children between the ages of about three and five.

Freud's Theory of the Resolution of the Oedipus Complex   Freud believed that the healthy child resolves the Oedipus complex at about five years of age and then enters into a six-year period of relative sexual quiescence—the latency period. According to Freud, the resolution of the Oedipus complex comes about partly via natural developmental processes. He compared oedipal resolution to the loss of the milk teeth and the growth of the permanent teeth. In addition, he believed that natural psychobiological processes also contributed to the resolution, specifically that the boy's fear that his father would castrate him contributed to the development of his superego and subsequent suppression and repression of sexual fantasies toward the mother (S. Freud 1924). Freud held that the therapist's role in helping children alleviate oedipal problems was to foster resignation that the boy cannot gratify his sexual-possessive cravings toward his mother. However, he is consoled with the hope that someday he will get a suitable substitute, someone "as wonderful, beautiful, etc." as his mother. In short, the boy is asked to forestall gratification in this area for many years. Last, Freud believed that the failure to resolve the Oepidus complex successfully was a central contributing factor in *all* neuroses.

The Author's View of the Oedipus Complex   My own experience over the 28 years that I have worked intensively with children is that only a small fraction, less than two percent, exhibit oedipal problems. The remainder have difficulties that are unrelated (or only remotely related) to oedipal difficulties. And when oedipal problems are present, there are usually specific factors in the family constellation that are directly contributing to the development of such. They do not arise naturally, as Freud would have us believe, but are the result of very specific family patterns that are conducive to the development of such symptomatology.

To elaborate, I believe there is a biological sexual instinct that attracts every human being to members of the opposite sex. From birth to puberty this drive is not particularly strong. Although weak and poorly formulated during the prepubertal period, it nevertheless exhibits itself through behavior that I consider manifestations of *oedipal interest*. A normal boy may speak on occasion of wishing to marry his mother and get rid of his father. These comments may even have a mildly sexual component such as "and then Mommy and I will sleep in bed together." I believe that the possessive, more than the genital-sexual, interest predominates here. The child is primarily interested in a little more affection and attention undiluted by the rival.

In a setting where the child is not receiving the affection, nurture, support, interest, guidance, protection, and generalized physical gratifications (such as stroking, warmth, and rocking) necessary for healthy growth and development, he or she may become obsessed with obtaining such satisfactions and develop one or more of a wide variety of symptoms that are attempts to deal with such frustrations. One possible constellation of symptoms are the kinds of sexual urges, preoccupations, and fantasies that Freud referred to as oedipal. The instinctive sexual urges, which are normally mild and relatively dormant, have the *potential* for intensive expression even as early as birth. Getting little gratification from the parents, the child may develop a host of fantasies in which frustrated love is requited and the rival is removed. Such fantasies follow the principle that the more one is deprived, the more one craves and the more jealous one becomes of those who have what one desires. Such manifestations can appropriately be called oedipal problems in the classical sense. The foundation for the development of neurosis is formed not, as Freud would say, through the failure to resolve successfully one's sexual frustrations regarding the parent of the opposite sex but through the failure to come to terms with the more basic deprivations from which the child is suffering.

Furthermore, I believe other specific factors must also be operative in order that oedipal paradigm symptomatology be selected. It is not simply the aforementioned deprivations. There must be other factors that channel the adaptation in the oedipal direction. I believe that the most common of these for the boy are sexual seductivity by the mother and/or castration threats (or the equivalent) by the father. It is important for the reader to note that the oedipal paradigm includes two phenomena: 1) sexual attraction toward the opposite-sexed parent, and 2) fear of retaliation by the same-sexed parent. Although the latter is considered to be caused by the former, this is not necessarily the case. A boy, for example, might be threatened with castration without there necessarily being any kind of sexual seductivity on his mother's part. A boy, for example, might be threatened that his penis will be cut off if he plays with it, and this threat might be made in a situation where there is no seductivity on the mother's part (this is what I believe took place in little Hans' case [Gardner 1972b]). Or there might be maternal seductivity without any retaliatory threats by the father. When either one or both of these processes are operative—on a preexisting foundation of parental deprivation—then, I believe, there is the greatest likelihood that symptoms will arise that can justifiably be referred to as oedipal. Of course, one might ascribe "unconscious" oedipal factors to a wide variety of other symptoms, but I am confining myself here to the phenomenological definition, one based on observable or accurately reported symptoms.

My discussion focuses here primarily on boys. I do not believe that this reflects any bias on my part; rather, it reflects the fact that Freud himself elaborated much more on oedipal manifestations in the boy and had great difficulty applying oedipal theory to girls. (It is beyond the purpose of this book to speculate on the reasons for this.) It is also important to differentiate between *sexual seductivity* and *sex abuse*. Oedipal problems may arise when there is sexual seductivity, but not when there has been sex abuse. When there is sexual titillation, the child develops cravings that cannot be gratified, and symptoms may then emerge which are designed to deal with these frustrations and deprivations. In sex abuse, there is no sexual frustration and an entirely different constellation of symptoms may emerge, such as symptoms related to distrust, fear of disclosure of the sexual activity, and generalized fear of involvement with adults who are of the same sex as the abusing parent.

The Author's Approach to the Alleviation of Oedipal Problems Freud used the term "resolution" to refer to the passing of the Oedipus complex between the ages of five-and-a-half and six. I prefer to use the term *alleviation* because I do not believe that oedipal involvements and interests are ever completely resolved. At best, oedipal problems can be alleviated. In fact, I generally go further and use the term alleviation to refer to the therapeutic aim of just about all psychogenic symptomatology. Considering the present state of our knowledge (perhaps the word ignorance would be preferable here), it is premature to use such strong words such as *resolution* and *cure*.

My therapeutic approach to the alleviation of oedipal problems reflects my concept of the Oedipus complex itself. The problems to be alleviated relate to the general problem of emotional deprivation and, if present, parental seduction and/or threats of castration. I attempt to ascertain whether there has been parental seduction. If so, I inform the parents of my opinion that their behavior is seductive and strongly recommend that they refrain from such activities. At times they are consciously aware of the process and, at other times, they are not. In the latter situation, it may be very difficult to impress upon them the seductive elements in their behavior. I also try to learn whether there have been castration threats, overt or covert. Again, if present, I do everything to discourage them. (The case of Frank [below] is a good example of this aspect of the treatment of oedipal problems.)

When addressing myself to the deprivational element I consider the improvement in the parent-child relationship crucial to the alleviation of oedipal problems in children. An attempt is made to improve the boy's relationship with his mother so that he will obtain the gratifications that are due in childhood and will be less obsessed with gaining them in neurotic ways. A similar approach is used with girls exhibiting oedipal problems in their relationships with their fathers. In addition, such children are helped to accept the fact that they cannot completely possess either of their parents and that the affection and attention of each of them must be shared with other members of the family. This sharing concept is an important one to impart. The child must be helped to appreciate that no one can possess another person completely: The father shares the mother with the children; the mother shares the father with the children; and the child has no choice but to share the mother and father with the siblings. In the context of such sharing, children must be reassured that, although they may not get as much as they might want, they will still get something. In addition, they must be helped to gain gratifications from others during the present time. Whatever deficiencies may exist in the parent–child relationship can be compensated for to some degree by satisfactions in other relationships. It is a well-known therapeutic principle that if one is going to take something away from a patient, one does well to provide substitute gratifications at that time, that is, gratifications which are healthier and more adaptive. My approach does not involve suggesting to the child that he wait. To wait for his possessive gratifications may appear to consume an endless number of years. Rather, he has the potential to gain some of these satisfactions in the present and he is given the hope that as he grows older he will have greater autonomy to acquire the more exclusive type of possessive relationship enjoyed by his father. The clinical example I will now present demonstrates how I utilize these principles in treatment.

The Case of Frank   Frank, a seven-and-a-half-year-old boy, was referred for psychotherapy because of generalized immature behavior and poor school performance. Both his teacher and his parents described him as being silly to the point where he rarely took things seriously. He was ever trying to avoid responsibility and typically took the path of least resistance. Most often he would deny responsibility for any unacceptable behavior and was always blaming others. Not taking school work seriously and rarely doing homework, his grades were suffering. He played well with younger children but did not get along with children his own age because of his low frustration tolerance, impulsivity, and inability to place himself in other children's situations to the degree appropriate for his age.

Although there was nothing in the presenting symptoms to suggest that Frank was suffering with oedipal problems, many of the stories he told centered on the theme of rivalry with the father figure for possessive control of the mother figure. In addition, castration anticipations and fears, symbolically presented, were common. As mentioned, when I do see oedipal problems, there are generally specific factors in the family situation that are conducive to the development of this typical reaction pattern. Frank's family situation is an excellent example. His father, an obstetrician, was away for significant periods from the time of his birth right up until Frank began treatment. In the early years this was associated with his residency training and in later years with the building of his practice. Frank and his two younger brothers were left alone with his mother. Although she was by no means seductive, the long periods of being alone with his mother provided Frank with opportunities for intimacy (physical and social, but not sexual) that other boys do not usually have. His father exhibited slightly effeminate gestures, but there were no signs of homosexuality.

Frank was born with undescended testicles which required frequent examination. Often, it was his father who conducted the examinations and reported his findings to the consulting urologist. In addition, at the age of three, an inguinal hernia was found and this, too, was periodically examined by Frank's father. Frank's appreciation that his father's work as an obstetrician and gynecologist involved extensive manipulation of the genital region of people who lacked external genitalia was conducive, I believe, to Frank's viewing his father as a "castrator." Frank's father did, indeed, operate on women in the genital region and it is easy to see how Frank could have viewed his father as having castration potential.

We see, then, three factors in Frank's family situation that were conducive to the development of oedipal problems:

1. The long absences of Frank's father from the home allowed Frank an unusual degree of intimacy with and possessive gratification from his mother.

2. The father's occupation as an obstetrician and gynecologist— an occupation in which the father literally performed operations on the genitalia of people who already lacked a penis and testes—contributed to the father being viewed as a potential castrator.

3. The frequent examination by his father of Frank's own genitalia also could have induced castration anxieties in that such examination was indeed performed to assess Frank's readiness for surgery in that area.

On the Rorschach test, Frank often saw as female those blots traditionally seen by boys as male. In addition, there was some evidence for identification with the stereotyped passive female. This, I believe, was the result of the long contact alone with his mother, depriving Frank of opportunities for more masculine identification models. In addition, the somewhat definite, albeit slight, effeminate gestures of his father probably played some role in this feminine identification problem. However, the Rorschach and TAT did not reveal a complete absence of masculine identification. Rather, a sex-role confusion was evident. Oedipal themes were also apparent. On one TAT card, Frank related this story:

Now his father dies . . . .He and his mother went to the funeral and after to the Greek hall to eat something. He got shrimp cocktail and she ate the same. Then they went home and got into bed and thought about their husband and father. His mother had him before she married his father and so he loves his mother more than his father.

This was the story Frank told during the third month of treatment:

Patient: Once there was three little peanuts and a nutcracker lived down the block. And every day when they went outside, the nutcracker would try to crack them open. So they said they'd have to move from their mother's house because the nutcracker lived right down the block. So they moved. So they found a house that was sold to them and they had a new house. They had a mansion. But the nutcracker moved right across the street from them.

Therapist: Wow.

Patient: And every time they went out in the street to play again, the nutcracker would come out and try to crack them open. So one day the nutcracker came to the door and looked in the window and saw them playing cards. So he shut the window real fast. And then right there was a metal monster eater and he just loved nutcrackers. He gobbled the nutcracker up and there was never a nutcracker again. The end.

Therapist: What did he do?

Patient: He liked metal and especially nutcrackers. He ate the nutcracker whole and there was a happy ending and they never were aware of the nutcracker again. So that's the end of the story. The end. Good-bye.

Therapist: Okay. And the lesson of that story?

Patient: Ah, think smart and you'll be smart.

Therapist: And what was the smart thinking here?

Patient: Uh, they put a metal monster eater right underneath the window.

The three peanuts, as the protagonists of the story, symbolize the patient and his two younger brothers. The nutcracker, who lives down the block, represents Frank's father. He is already out of the home and Frank has gratified his oedipal wishes to possess his mother completely. However, the nutcracker, castrator that he is, is obsessed with the notion of cracking the three peanuts. Their attempts to elude him prove unsuccessful as he pursues them to their new home. Interestingly, it is a mansion—implying that Frank has the wherewithal to live with his mother in "high style." The problem of the nutcracker's relentless pursuit is solved by the peanuts' engaging the services of a "metal monster eater" who "just loved nutcrackers." The story ends with his gobbling up the nutcracker and "there was never a nutcracker again. The End." Finally, "there was a happy ending and they never were aware of the nutcracker again." Now all is well with the world. Frank gains complete possession of his mother and his father is not only removed from the house but is completely obliterated assuaging, thereby, Frank's castration fears.

It was with this understanding of Frank's story that I told mine:

Therapist: Okay. Now it's time for me to tell my story. Now my story may start like your story, but different things happen very quickly. Once upon a time there were three peanuts. And these peanuts lived in a neighborhood where they lived with their mother.

Patient: Yeah.

Therapist: They also lived with their father.

Patient: Yeah, uh huh.

Therapist (looking at patient): In my story, the father is a nut-cracker! (At this point, the patient looks up toward the therapist, somewhat incredulously.)

Therapist: That's my story.

Patient: Uh, huh.

Therapist: And the three peanuts are very upset because they think that their father wants to crack them. So they said to him one day, "Are you going to try to crack us? Are you going to try to crack us open?" (Patient now rolling his kneesocks down.) And the father said, "No, but at times you boys get me angry and I sometimes feel mad at you. But I don't have any desire to crack you or crumble you up or get rid of you that way." (Patient now rolling his kneesocks up.)

Patient: Or throw you out of the window or throw you on the concrete floor or make you smashed. (Patient now laughs nervously.)

Therapist: "No, I'm not going to do that."

Patient (in a reassured tone): Uh, huh.

Therapist: He said, "However, you boys sometimes get me angry." They said, "Yeah, we know that we sometimes get you angry." And (turning toward the patient) do you know when the boys would sometimes get the father angry?

Patient: When?

Therapist: What kinds of things do you think they did that would get the father angry?

Patient (now bends over, puts his elbows on his knees, and supports his chin in his cupped hands): Let's see now. They would do things that the father didn't tell them to do? (Patient now resumes his original position of facing the examiner.)

Therapist: Like what?

Patient: Like, when he wanted them to clean his car and they wouldn't do it.

Therapist: Yeah, that would be the kind of thing that would get him angry. One of the things that would get him angry was when they would want the mother all to themselves, and they wouldn't want him to spend any time with the mother. You know, that would get him angry sometimes, when they would say, "We don't want you around. We don't want you to be with Mommy all the time. We don't want you to be with her. Things like that." He said, "That's the kind of thing that gets me angry." (Patient now tying his shoelaces.) And they said, "Well, that's the kind of thing that makes us think you want to get rid of us. That you want to kill us. That you want to get rid of us. That you want to crack us up and get rid of us, and then have Mommy all to yourself." You see the father and the three boys were kind of rivals. (Therapist now turns to patient.) Do you know what *rival* means?

Patient: Uh, huh.

Therapist: What does rival mean?

Patient: I don't know.

Therapist: They were kind of fighting for the mother to have time with her. Each wanted the mother all to themselves. The father wanted the mother a lot of times and the boys wanted her. The boys wanted to have her to take care of them, to teach them things, and to read books with them, and things. (Patient now stops tying his shoelaces and interlocks the fingers of one hand with the other.) And the father said, "I get angry at you when you want her all to yourself." And they said, "And we get angry at you, because we don't want you around. We want her all to ourselves." They were kind of fighting for her. So what do you think happened?

Patient (now resting hands in his lap): I think the father got so mad that he cracked them open.

Therapist (shaking his head negatively): No way! No. What they decided to do was . . . they realized that the father shouldn't have the mother all to himself, because the boys were still part of the family. And that the boys shouldn't have the mother all to themselves because the father was still part of the family. So they decided to compromise. And they decided that they will *share* the mother. That sometimes the boys will have time with the mother (patient now takes his hand out of his lap and slaps his thighs) and sometimes with the father. (Patient now puts his hands on his thighs.) Now this still made the boys feel a little bit sad, because they didn't have their mother all they wanted to. (Patient now whistling and flapping the palms of his hands on his thighs.) So what did they do then?

Patient: They had a whole day with the mother and didn't let the father have . . . no . . . they had a whole week with the father. (Patient now moving his hands toward his groin area.) No (patient now rubbing his penis), and had a whole week with the mother (still rubbing his penis) and then the father had a whole week with the mother.

Therapist: That was one way. Sharing. That's one thing they can do. (Patient still rubbing himself.) And another thing that made the boys feel better was to spend time with their friends. When they weren't with their. . .

Patient: . . . mother. . .

Therapist: mother, they could spend time with their friends. And also, another thing (patient still rubbing his penis), was they knew that when they grew up they would have (patient now grasps his penis with his left hand and pulls up his shirt with his right hand) a lady. Each one would get married. Or live with somebody, or have a girlfriend. Something like that. (Patient now pulls his pants forward, at the belt level, with his left hand and puts his right hand inside and starts stroking his penis.) And then they would not feel so jealous of the father, you know. (Patient now pulls his right hand out of his pants and strokes his penis from the outside.) Because they would have. . . .

Patient (slapping his both hands now on his thighs with an air of certainty): . . . a lady of their own.

Therapist: . . . a lady of their own. (Both the patient and the therapist's statement, "a lady of their own" was said simultaneously. It was clear that the patient knew exactly what words the therapist was going to say and so they both made the exact statement simultaneously.) Right!

Patient (laughing with a sigh of relief): Uh, huh. (Patient again moves both hands toward the groin and rubs the penis area.)

Therapist: And that's exactly what happened. (Patient still rubbing penis.) And what do you think the lessons of that story are?

Patient: Uh. (Patient still holding penis and laughing nervously.)

Therapist: What are the lessons?

Patient: Let me see. (Patient now removes hands from groin and puts them on top of his head.) Share.

Therapist: Share.

Patient: Share with other people.

Therapist: Right. And is there any other lesson?

Patient (hands now clasped behind his head): . . . and you'll get along together.

Therapist: Share, and you'll get along together. Any other lesson?

Patient (hands on top of head, nodding negatively): No.

Therapist: There's another lesson. What you can't have in one place, you can have in another. Like they couldn't have the mother all the time, but they could have friends: boys and girls that they played with in the street or in the home. . .

Patient (interrupting): Did they have a busy street?

Therapist: Yeah. There were a lot of kids around.

Patient: Were there a lot of cars? (The patient then removes his hands from his head and imitates moving cars with buzzing sounds.)

Therapist: Yeah. But they had quiet streets too in that area. If there weren't friends in their neighborhood, they would go elsewhere. And also, if you can't have something now there's always the hope that you can get it in the future. You know?

Patient: Yeah. (Patient now playing with his wristwatch.)

Therapist: And then they could have a girl all their own. Anything you want to say?

Patient: No.

Therapist: Do you like this game?

Patient (while clasping his hands): Yeah.

Therapist: Do you want to watch this?

Patient (with an excited expression on his face, while still clapping his hands): Yeah!

Therapist: Okay. Let's watch this. Do you want to have your mother come in and see it?

Patient (still excited): Yeah.

Therapist: Let's do that. (Both arise.)

When creating responding stories, the therapist often has a conflict. If the therapist retains the original symbol used by the child, pathological elements may have to be retained. For example, if the child uses a worm or pig to symbolize him- or herself, the utilization of these in the therapist's story implies agreement that the child warrants being symbolized by such loathesome animals. In contrast, to dispense with such symbols entirely may rob the therapist of rich symbolism that significantly enhances the impact of the therapeutic communications. I generally will retain the symbol and make sure, in the course of my responding story, to emphasize the healthy element associated with it and to deemphasize, ignore, or directly negate the unhealthy aspects of the symbol. In my responding story here I purposely retained the nutcracker symbol because I considered the advantages to far outweigh the disadvantages. However, after informing the patient that the father was a nutcracker, I quickly emphasized the point that he has the *potential* for castration but that he does not use his power. Rather, I focused on behavior manifested by the peanuts that might cause the father to be angry and studiously avoided any possibility that the anger could reach such proportions that castration, symbolic or otherwise, could possibly occur.

In addition, at the beginning of my story, I make it quite clear that *the father lives with the peanuts.* This is in contradistinction to the father in Frank's story who has already been ejected from the household. In my story the problem with the father is worked out through discussion rather than acting out. In Frank's story the father is already removed and the father is a castrator. In mine, the father is present, is not a castrator, and engages in meaningful communication to discuss problems with his peanut sons.

The main point that I make in my responding story is that it is not a question of *either* the father or the peanuts having full possession of the mother. Rather, they can *share*. Sometimes the peanuts spend time with the mother, sometimes the father spends time with the mother, and sometimes all of them spend time with her. And, when the father is with the mother, the peanuts can still spend time with others in their neighborhood to compensate for their loss. In addition, they are provided with the hope that when they get older they will have more opportunity for greater possession of an appropriate female peanut.

According to Freud, the Oedipus complex naturally passes like the milk teeth that give way to the permanent teeth. In addition, fears of the father castrating the child contribute to the development of the superego which suppresses and represses the boy's possessive, sexual longings for the mother. Lastly, the boy is consoled with the fact that someday he will have a female of his own. Most therapists agree that it is very difficult to take something away from patients without offering something in return. In Freud's formulation, the boy is consoled with the knowledge that someday he will have a female of his own. For the child of five, this future is like a million years away and is not likely to serve well as a meaningful consolation.

In the kind of oedipal resolution I propose, the boy is not asked to give up entirely his *present* desires for possessive involvement with his mother. Rather, he is advised to share her with his father. It is certainly easier to share a prized possession than to give it up entirely. In addition, the boy is given the consolation that there are opportunities with others at the present time. Last, he is also told about future possibilities.

In the course of telling my responding story, the patient continuously rubbed his genital area and pulled his pants tightly against his penis. It became apparent that he had an erection and that the prospect of possessive opportunities with a female were sexually titillating. Frank's response was clear evidence that my story was indeed dealing with issues that were most important for him and that my message was a most meaningful one. The vignette is an excellent demonstration of a situation in which the therapist knows that his responding story is indeed being received with interest and receptivity and that it is touching on important psychological issues.

The reader who is interested in more detailed discussions of my views on the etiology and treatment of oedipal problems may wish to refer to other publications of mine in this area (Gardner, 1968, 1973c, 1983a).

CONCLUDING COMMENTS

I have described the basic rationale of the mutual storytelling technique. I do not claim to have invented a new method of treatment. The principle is an ancient one, and many therapists have no doubt utilized the method. I believe that my main contribution lies in having written articles on the subject and having formulated more specific criteria for analyzing and creating stories. The utilization of the method in the treatment of a wide variety of psychiatric disorders of childhood is discussed in a number of other publications of mine (Gardner, 1968; 1969; 1970b,c; 1971c; 1972c,d; 1973c; 1974b,c,d; 1975a,b; 1976a; 1979b,c; 1980a; 1981a; 1983a). A comprehensive description of the details of utilizing the technique (with regard to story analysis and the therapist's story creations) is provided in my full-length text on the subject (Gardner, 1971a).

TWO

Dramatized Storytelling

Give a man a mask and he'll tell you the truth.

Ancient Greek aphorism

All the world's a stage
And all the men and women merely players.
They have their exits and their entrances
And each man in his time plays many parts.

William Shakespeare

INTRODUCTION

Children call us "talking doctors." Many of us do not fully appreciate the significance of this epithet, especially with regard to its implication that our therapeutic approach is a relatively narrow one. Let us compare, for example, the following experiences with respect to our involvement in a play. First, we can read the play. Such an experience is purely visual with regard to the reading as well as the visual fantasies that the reading material may engender within us. Compare this to attending a theatrical performance of the play. Here, in addition to seeing the performance, we hear it as well. Auditory stimuli have been added to the visual. With two sensory modalities of communication, acting simultaneously, there is a greater likelihood that the play will affect us. Imagine, then being an actual participant in the play as an actor or actress. Now, added to the visual and auditory sensory modalities are the kinesthetic, tactile, and possibly even the gustatory and olfactory. With these additional modalities of sensory input, it is even more likely that the play will have an impact. However, no matter how skilled and experienced the actor may be, his or her emotions are feigned. No matter how much both the actor and the audience may be swept up by the part, all recognize that everything is basically being dictated by the script: it is "not real," it's "only a play." Compare now play-acting in which there is an actual living experience in which emotional reactions are elicited by real events. Here the linkage between the emotions and the aforementioned sensory modalities is deep and genuine. Nothing is play-acted. Rather, the individual is having an *experience*. And it is the experience that has the greatest affect on us. To the degree that we provide our patients with experiences—as opposed to relatively sterile insights—to that degree we improve our chances of helping them.

Because the therapeutic situation may not allow us to provide our patients with as many natural and uncontrived experiences as we would like, we do best to provide them with every possible encounter that comes as close to them as we can. Although play-acting does not have as much "clout" as an actual experience, it may be a superior form of interaction and communication than merely talking—and this is especially true for the child. Just as the mutual storytelling technique was developed from the observation that children naturally enjoy both telling and listening to stories, the idea of dramatizing them arose from the observation that children would often automatically (and at times without conscious awareness) gesticulate, impersonate, intone, and enact in other ways while telling their stories. I found that when I introduced such theatrics myself the child became more involved in my stories and receptive to their messages.

Whereas originally I introduced the dramatic elements en *passant*, that is, in the process of telling my story (just as the children tended to do), I subsequently formalized the process by inviting the child to reenact our stories as plays following our telling them: "I've got a great idea! Let's make up plays about our stories. Who do you want to be? The wolf or the fox?" At times I would invite the mother and even siblings to join us. (We often face the problem of having a shortage of available actors.) We see here another way in which mothers can be useful in the child's treatment. (A little encouragement may be necessary at times to help some mothers overcome their "stage fright.") Of course therapists themselves must be free enough to involve themselves in the various antics that are required for a successful "performance." They must have the freedom to roll on the floor, imitate various animals, "ham it up," etc. They have to be able to be director, choreographer, writer, and actor—practically all at the same time. They may have to assume a number of different roles in the same play, and quickly shift from part to part. Such role shifts do not seem to bother most children nor reduce their involvement or enjoyment. Nor do they seem to be bothered by the therapist's "stage whispers," so often necessary to keep the play running smoothly.

Younger children, especially those in the four- to six-year age group, who may not be inclined to tell well-organized stories, will often improve in their ability to relate them when the dramatic element is introduced. Others, who may have been initially unreceptive to or too inhibited to freely tell stories, may do so after the enjoyable dramatic elements are utilized. The experience becomes more fun and the child tends to forget his or her reservations. In this younger group, as well, the strict adherence to the pattern of the child's first telling a story and then the therapist's telling his or hers may not be possible or disirable. A looser arrangement of interweaving stories and plays back and forth may be more practical and effective.

Children generally enjoy television (a statement which I'm sure comes as no surprise to the reader). Even more, children enjoy seeing themselves on television (something a child rarely has the opportunity to do). Therapists who have available a camera and video cassette recorder can provide children with an immensely beneficial therapeutic modality. Making a video cassette recording of a therapeutic experience increases significantly the likelihood that children will expose themselves to reiteration of the therapeutic communications. In the 1960s, when I first developed the mutual storytelling technique, the child and I would often listen to the audio tape recording of the mutually told stories. In the late 1960s,

I began encouraging children to bring to the sessions their own audio cassette recorders (a practice initiated by a child) and to listen to these stories at home afterwards.

Around 1970 I purchased a closed-circuit television system and began making videotapes of our stories, both the standard interchanges as well as those that were dramatized. Around 1980 I purchased a standard home video cassette system and camera. This enabled me to lend the videotape to those children who had such an instrument at home. In the last few years, I have added a second video cassette recorder and invite the child to bring his or her tape to the office. This enables the child to watch at home the various therapeutic interchanges that we tape. Of these, probably the most valuable are those in which dramatizations occur because this insures even more that the child will listen to the tape and profit from what is contained therein.

CLINICAL EXAMPLES

The Case of Adam ["Can a Dead Frog Be Brought Back to Life?"]

Adam, an eight-year-old boy with a neurologically based learning disability, exhibited significant social difficulties. It was very difficult for him to place himself in another person's position and this caused him much pain and rejection in social situations. Intellectual impairment (his IQ was about 85) and difficulty in conceptualizing and abstracting resulted in his failing to appreciate and learn many of the subtleties of social interaction. Many of these appear to be learned almost automatically by normal children. Children with minimal brain dysfunction may find this their most crippling problem and it behooves the therapist to appreciate this when working with such children. In Adam's case it was the primary focus of his treatment.

In session one day his mother reported that on the previous day Adam had pulled off the leg of a frog that he had caught in his backyard. I immediately responded with disgust: "Ych, that sounds terrible!" Although I knew that my response was going to lower Adam's self-respect at that point, I felt it was the price that had to be paid for a little superego development. I then asked Adam if he would like to play a game in which I am a frog and he is a boy who wants to pull off my leg. He hesitantly agreed. I lay on the floor and invited him to try to pull off my leg. My moans were immediate: "Ooooh, that hurts! Please stop. Please, my leg is going to come off. Ahhhh—." I asked the patient what the boy then did. He replied that he stopped because he didn't want to hurt the frog any longer. "That's right," I replied. "When the boy realized how much he was hurting the frog, he stopped pulling its leg." I then asked Adam if he would like to play a game in which the boy doesn't stop after the frog screams out and he pulls off the leg and the frog dies. He agreed. This time, in spite of my bloodcurdling cries, the boy pulled off the frog's leg. "Now my leg is off and I'm dead," I mumbled as I lay stiffly on the floor. "Try to bring me back to life," I whispered to the patient as if giving stage directions (a maneuver commonly required in such plays). In spite of the patient's attempts to revive me (these included poking, pulling, artificial respiration, and a little feigned mouth-to-mouth resuscitation), I remained stiff and prostrate, all the while mumbling, "Even that doesn't help. When you're dead, you can never be brought back to life." The game ended (as such games usually do) with questions: "How does a frog feel when someone tries to pull off its leg?" "What can happen to a frog if someone pulls off its leg?" "Can a dead frog be brought back to life?"

One might argue that the above approach is a little too strong and that it might create intense feelings of self-loathing in the child. I can only reply that I do not believe that this has been my experience. Whatever transient lowering of self-esteem the child may suffer in such a game (and I grant that he or she certainly may) is more than compensated for by the ultimate enhancement of self-worth that results from heightened sensitivity to the pains of others and his or her ceasing to inflict unnecessary and wanton pain on others. Last, if such a game is indeed too ego-debasing to the child, he or she can usually be relied upon to refuse to play it or to discontinue it if it gets too "hot." It is grandiose of the therapist to consider to know beforehand whether a healthy communication is going to be devastating to a patient. I tend to try it out and respect the patient's defenses when they exhibit themselves.

The reader should appreciate that I am fully aware that this child's cruel act related to hostility that was being redirected from other sources onto the frog. One cannot focus simultaneously on

many of the multiple factors which usually contribute to a pathological act. Here I chose to direct my attention to the egocentricism
issue (the child's inability to project himself into the situation of
another living thing) and his ignorance of certain aspects of social
reality.

The Case of Frank
[Gonga Wants Too Much More]

Frank's situation demonstrates how a child's feelings about a competent sibling can contribute to the development of an antisocial
behavior disorder that interferes with academic functioning. Frank
was 11 when I first saw him. He had been referred by his school
psychologist because of antisocial behavior. The parents claimed
that Frank's antisocial behavior began when he was three years old,
about the time of the birth of his only brother. He became restless,
distractible, and exhibited frequent temper tantrums. He was evalu-
ated by a child neurologist who diagnosed him as "hyperactive"
and, at the age of four, he was placed on methylphenidate—on
which medication he remained for over six years.

When he began the first grade, things deteriorated significantly. He would not concentrate on his school work. Rather, he
would engage in various types of horseplay in the classroom, tell
jokes, laugh at the teacher, make faces, thump on his desk, and disrupt the class in a variety of ways. Frank was considered to be very
bright but, not surprisingly, received very low grades and did not
learn very much. He was always trying to avoid school responsibilities and rarely did meaningful homework. This behavior continued and he was finally placed in a special educational class in
the third grade, where he still was when I first saw him when he
was at the fifth grade level.

Peer difficulties were also described. He sought friendships
but was not sought by peers. He insisted upon having his own way
and had temper tantrums when thwarted by friends. He did not
respect the rights of others and exhibited little ability to put himself
in other children's situations. He taunted other children and became excessively argumentative. He would cheat while playing
games and generally "didn't know when to stop." He often felt
cheated or gypped and tended to blame others when there were
difficulties.

At home, as well, Frank had many problems. He did not respect parental authority, exhibited impulsivity and low frustration tolerance. He had temper outbursts and, on occasion, would physically abuse his younger brother. He did not seem to learn from punishments that were dispensed in the attempt to control Frank's antisocial behavior.

Frank's parents were very proper, well-to-do, upper-middle-class people for whom everything seemed to be going smoothly. The father, an attorney, was in a law firm that had been started by his grandfather. I viewed them as somewhat "uptight" people but did not consider this enough to explain Frank's severe antisocial behavior. His younger brother was getting along quite well and was viewed by the family as being a "wonderful boy" who excelled in academics, sports, and social relationships. The fact that he was so stable suggested that Frank's parents could not have been significantly deficient in their parenting role—even considering the fact that Frank was their first-born and they might have been more tense with him than his younger brother.

During the first three months of Frank's treatment I really could not say why he was so angry. At the beginning of the session when his mother and/or father was present he would be obstructionistic, used profanities toward them, and at times made himself thoroughly obnoxious. However, although initially resistant to involve himself in the therapeutic activities, I was able to engage him in a meaningful way. The vignette presented here demonstrates how dramatizations enhanced the therapeutic efficacy of doll play. Among the dolls and puppets I have in my office is a small gorilla whose name is *Gonga.* In the show he used this doll as well as a monkey doll that he called *Chip.* He then drew an announcement sign for the program: *Gonga Never Listens.* Prior to the program he requested that I sit on the sidelines and not be within the view of the camera. The dolls were placed on a bridge table and, during most of the performance, the patient hid himself either behind or under the bridge table so that only the puppets were in direct view of the camera.

Therapist: Good afternoon, boys and girls, ladies and gentlemen. Today is Saturday, the 27th of February, 1982, and I'm happy to welcome you once again to Dr. Gardner's program. Our guest today is going to present a show. Now will you please tell us the name of the show?

Patient: Gonga Never Listens. (Holds up sign: GONGA NEVER LISTENS.)

Therapist: Okay, before I turn this off and get ready for the show, is there anything else you want to say?

Patient: This cartoon show is animated.

Therapist: This animated cartoon will be shown in just one minute. We'll be right back.

And now ladies and gentlemen, we are back with you with our show. Our guest has requested that I not be in the picture at this point so I will sit on the sidelines. Okay? You're on the air!

Patient: Hello, my name is Gonga. (Patient holds up gorilla doll named *Gonga*.) And here is my friend, Chip Monkey. (Patient holds up monkey doll.) The show is named *Gonga Never Listens* because that's exactly what I do. I never listen. So here's one of my stories of what I have done. Okay.

Patient (as Gonga): (Patient turns on tape recorder he has brought to the session and plays loud rock music.) I really love that tape recorder. I want to buy it from the store. I'm going to go in there and ask that guy how much it is.

Patient (as man): Yes, what do you want?

Patient (as Gonga): I want to know how much that tape recorder is.

Patient (as man): $97.

Patient (as Gonga): And how much is the tape above?

Patient (as man): $9.50

Patient (as Gonga): Boy, how am I going to get that much money?

Patient (as man): I hope you do because that's a very fine model. I only have three of them left.

Patient (as Chip Monkey): How are you going to get that money?

Patient (as Gonga): I'll find a way.

Patient: (Whispers in therapist's ear.)

Therapist: Now our guest has asked me to play the part of the mother. I'll be the mother's voice and he's told me what lines I say. Okay.

Patient (as Gonga): Mommy, at the record shop today I saw a very neat tape recorder. It's really neat and it's only $97.50.

Therapist (as mother): $97.50!!!!!!! Are you asking *me* for the money?

Patient (as Gonga): Yes, I am but I'll help out with $7.00 of it.

Therapist (as mother): No, you can't have it. If you want to get one of those, you've got to earn the money yourself. You've got to save up from your allowance and you've got to do work.

Patient (as Gonga): But how can I earn enough money for that?

Therapist (as mother): It'll take a long time, but there are things you can do.

Patient (as Gonga): But they only have three of the tape recorders left!!! (Gonga waves hands during conversation.)

Therapist (as mother): Well, you know it's never the case that there are no more. The store may only have three left, but the person who manufactures that tape recorder has thousands that they send all over, and I'm sure that that store can get you more. And when you earn enough money, then you can buy it.

I'll tell you what I will do, though. If you earn $87.50, I'll give you $10 as a present. Because if you earn the $87.50, that shows me that you have worked very hard and then I'll give you the extra $10.

Patient (as Gonga): Gee, that's great. Thanks, mom.

Therapist (as mother): Well, I'm very happy to do that in order to help you work harder and you'll really feel good after you've earned that $87.50, and then you'll get that tape recorder. You'll see.

Patient (as Gonga): Okay, goodbye. I'm going up to my room.

Therapist (as mother): Okay.

Patient (as Gonga): With Chip Monkey. I'm taking him up to my room too.

Therapist: Okay. Now what happens?

As can be seen, I drive a somewhat hard bargain with Gonga regarding the purchase of the coveted tape recorder. I will give him $10, but he must earn the remaining $87.50. Again, I introduce the old work ethic. Although Gonga seems highly committed to the proposition (talk is cheap and it is only a story) it would have been nice if the patient were a fraction as committed as he professed. We then continued.

Patient: The next day, they were playing *The Talking, Feeling, and Doing Game.* (Sets up *The Talking, Feeling, and Doing Game* on the table.)

Patient (as Gonga): Boy, I really like this *Talking, Feeling, and Doing Game.* I'm glad that Dr. Gardner let me use it.

Patient (as Chip Monkey): I like it too. Considering I'm losing, it's still a pretty funny game.

Patient (as Gonga): Well, I'm going to win this game because I'm ahead of everybody . . . naturally. . . .

Patient (as Turtle): Don't brag, Gonga.

Patient (as Gonga): Don't tell me what to do. It's my turn.

Therapist: Do you think Turtle sort of likes Gonga when he brags or is he sort of turned off by Gonga?

Patient: Yeah, turned off.

Therapist: But not enough to stop playing the game. He just thinks he's a drag to play with.

Patient (as Gonga): (Continues to play *The Talking, Feeling, and Doing Game.*) Boy, let me check this card!

Therapist: What does Gonga's card say?

Patient (as Gonga): "Scratch your backside" . . . that's something I'm really good at doing . . . (Gonga scratches backside.)

Therapist: Okay.

Patient (as Turtle): It's disgusting, Gonga.

Patient (as Gonga): But that's what the card told me to do.

Therapist: Yes, but you don't do that in front of other people.

Patient (as Gonga): I know that. Well, I'll move my piece. (Moves piece and purposely knocks Chip Monkey's piece off the table.) Your piece (speaking to Chip Monkey) is always in the way.

Patient (as Chip Monkey): Don't knock my piece on the floor, Gonga.

Patient (as Gonga): Chip Monkey, you can get it yourself.

Patient (as Chip Monkey): Boy, Gonga has been really mean today. (Begins to have a side conversation with Turtle.)

Patient (as Turtle): I'm not playing everything down here. I know.

Patient (as Chip Monkey): Do you want to go home?

Patient (as Turtle): No, I still like this game.

Patient (as Chip Monkey): Well, if he bothers me one more time, I think I'll leave.

Patient (as Turtle): Well, maybe me too.

Patient (as Gonga): So I go 12 spaces, 1-2-3-4-5-6-7-8-9-10-11-12. I landed on "Go back one." No! (Patient slams down hard on the table.) A stupid game! I'm going to my room.

Therapist: Why'd he get so angry? What happened?

Patient: Because he had to go back one.

Therapist: Boy, he really has a temper! So what did the turtle think of that when Gonga messed up the whole game just because he had to go backward one space?

Patient (as Turtle): Let's go home, Chippy.

Patient (as Chippy): Yeah.

Therapist: The turtle didn't want to play with him any more?

Patient: No.

Therapist: I don't blame him.

Patient: Cut.

Therapist: Okay. Cut. (Patient puts away *The Talking, Feeling, and Doing Game.*)

Patient: Later, after Gonga has gotten over his tantrum, "Boy, was I a dum-dum! Well, I don't care about him. Well, I'm going to call Chippy and see if he still wants to play. (Dials phone.) 652-1301. (Bring-g-g-, B-r-rring . . .)

Patient (as Gonga): Hello, may I speak to Chippy?

Patient (as Chippy): This is Chippy.

Patient (as Gonga): Oh, hi, Chippy. This is Gonga, do you want to play? (Sound of phone hanging up and dial tone.)

Patient (as Gonga): I wonder why he hung up on me?

Therapist: Why do you think he hung up?

Patient: Because he was mad at Gonga.

Therapist: Mad at him for what?

Patient: Getting sore, having a tantrum, and knocking his piece on the floor.

Therapist: So what did Gonga do then?

Patient: She went to her room.

Therapist: She went to her room? Is Gonga a *he* or a *she*?

Patient: A he.

Therapist: So he went to his room and did what?

Patient: Sulked.

Therapist: And then what happened?

Patient: He decided to come back down and call Chippy again.

Therapist: Call Chippy again. Okay. So go ahead and call Chip Monkey.

Patient (as Gonga): I can't because Chippy just hung up.

Therapist: That was the first time. Try a second time and see what happens. Maybe if Gonga says that he's *really* sorry and he *means* it, maybe Chippy will listen to him.

Patient (as Gonga): I'll try one more time. (Dials) 652-0210. (Ring-ring.) Hello. Can I speak to Chippy? Okay. Hello, Chippy?

Patient (as Chip Monkey): What do you want, Gonga?

Patient (as Gonga): I'm really sorry about when I threw a temper tantrum.

Patient (as Chip Monkey): I'll bet you are.

Patient (as Gonga): Wait. Don't hang up. I'm sorry. You can come back and play with me if you want to.

Patient (as Chippy): Well, if you won't get so mad over things.

Patient (as Gonga): Okay. Good-bye. (Hangs up.) I want to play more of the *Talking, Feeling, and Doing Game.* I'm going to call Turtle.

Therapist: Okay, he calls Turtle.

Patient (as Gonga): 652-0352. (Ring-ring, ring.) Hello. Hello, Turtle? Can you play?

Patient (as Turtle): Who is this?

Patient (as Gonga): It's Gonga.

Patient (as Turtle): Gonga, why did you get so mad?

Patient (as Gonga): Well, I get mad at things like that. You know I can never listen.

Patient (as Turtle): Well, only if you aren't so mean to me and Chippy. Okay, I'll call Chippy.

Patient (as Gonga): I've already done that.

Patient (as Turtle): He came?

Patient (as Gonga): Yes.

Patient (as Turtle): Okay, I'll be right over. Goodbye.

Patient: I've got to put this telephone away.

Therapist: Mmm. Okay, so they forgave him?

Patient: Yup.

Therapist: So what happened then?

Patient: I can't . . . they're coming.

Patient (as Turtle): I want to play some more of that game?

Therapist: Okay. Why don't you set it up again on the TV and start playing it. Shall I help you?

Patient: Cut it so they can't see you.

Therapist: You don't want me in it, huh?

Patient: So they can't see me either.

Therapist: I'll cut it.

Patient (as Gonga): Boy, oh boy, let me get my dice. Boy, am I doing good at this game! Let's see my card. (Picks card.) That card's no good.

Therapist: What does it say?

Patient (as Gonga): (Puts "bad" card back and takes another.) That's not . . . that's good. "Good Luck! You get an extra turn."

Therapist: No, no, he's not playing fair.

Patient (as Chip Monkey): Wait, Gonga, you can't do that.

Patient (as Gonga): Why not?

Patient (as Chippy): Because you're cheating!!

Patient (as Gonga): I can do what I want to!

Patient (as Chippy): Gonga, you never listen!

Patient (as Gonga): Well, I'll do what I want to.

Patient (as Turtle): Well, you're not going to do what you did last time.

Patient (as Gonga): Okay, jerks. (Picks previously discarded "best" card.) "Jump up and down three times."

Therapist: So Gonga decided to follow the rules now. Huh?

Patient: Uh-huh.

Therapist: What would the guys have done?

Patient: They would have left him.

Therapist: Do you think they would have played with him again this time?

Patient: No.

Therapist: Yeah, he probably realized that.

Patient (as Gonga): Well, I did that. I jumped. Now it's your turn, Chippy.

Using the puppets as players of *The Talking, Feeling, and Doing Game* (a play within a play), Frank exhibits some working through here. A part of him, as represented by Gonga, is the primitive, impulsive individual who acts out his anger. The other part, as played by Turtle and Chip Monkey, represent the civilized superego aspects of his personality. In the end of this segment Gonga becomes somewhat civilized and suppresses his infantile behavior so as not to alienate his friends.

The question must be considered here as to what the therapeutic significance of all this is. It is clear that Frank knows the "right answers." Gonga knows well what is the "wrong" thing to do and his friends know well what is the "right" thing to do. This knowledge is really Frank's. If Frank knows what's right, why is he still doing what's wrong? The answer relates to the fact that without resolution of the fundamental problems that are generating the anger in the first place, it is likely that there will be some acting out or, at least, anger expression in some other way. Here Frank is attempting consciously to suppress the angry impulses in order to protect himself from the alienation of his friends. He is gratifying this desire via his play fantasy.

I believe that something else is being accomplished here as well. The reiterative process serves to entrench the dictates in the superego. Each time the principle or caveat is repeated, it becomes incorporated into the psychic structure. The hope is that such incorporation will ultimately be strong enough to modify behavior even though the fundamental problems have not been dealt with. The superficiality of this process notwithstanding, it is still contributory to therapeutic change. At this point, the play turns back to an as yet incompleted theme: the purchase of the tape recorder.

> *Patient* (as Chip Monkey): Gonga, remember when you wanted to get that tape recorder?
> *Patient* (as Gonga): Yeah.
> *Patient* (as Chip Monkey): Well, they only have one left.
> *Patient* (as Gonga): They do?
> *Patient* (as Chip Monkey): Yeah.
> *Patient* (as Gonga): Well, I'm going to get that.
> *Therapist:* How's he going to get that?
> *Patient:* He's going to get it any way he can.
> *Therapist:* And what way is that?
> *Patient:* He'll do anything he can to get it.
> *Therapist:* Like what, for instance?
> *Patient:* Work as hard as he could. Steal it.
> *Therapist:* Steal it?
> *Patient:* He's crazy. Gonga doesn't listen.

Therapist: Oh, I see. He's going to steal it. . . .

Patient (as Gonga): I might steal it.

Patient (as Chip Monkey): You're crazy, Gonga!!

Patient (as Gonga): Well, who cares. I'm not going to get into trouble.

Patient (as Chip Monkey): You'll get caught and you'll be in the pen. You'll get sent to jail.

Patient (as Gonga): Well, I don't care. It's getting late. You guys ought to go home.

Patient (as Turtle and Chip Monkey): Well, thanks for inviting us. Bye!

Therapist: Well, what happened now with the tape recorder?

Patient: We'll see.

Therapist: We'll see what happened!!

The interchange between Chippy and Gonga is somewhat reminiscent of Jiminy Cricket and Pinocchio. Pinocchio, the "bad boy," is in perpetual conflict with Jiminy Cricket who clearly serves as his conscience. In this part of the story the primitive impulses win out over social dictates.

Patient: (Holds Gonga in the center of the camera field.) "Gonga's Dream." Where am I? (Sounds of "alien" people coming on stage with Gonga.) Who are you people?

Patient (as People): You are in the land of "Don't Listen". . . .

Patient (as Gonga): "Don't Listen???" What is this some kind of joke. Where am I? You move out of the way. (Pushes "alien.")

Patient (as Alien): Gonga, don't touch me or I'll zap you.

Patient (as Gonga): Don't touch me. I'll punch you across the room.

Patient (as Alien): Boy, some specimen this is!

Patient (as Gonga): What are you calling me a specimen for?

Therapist: They're calling Gonga a specimen?

Patient: Yeah.

Therapist: Okay, go ahead.

Patient (as Gonga): I wouldn't talk so much about you guys either. . . .

Therapist: Why are they calling him a specimen?

Patient: These guys are from another planet. . . .

Therapist: Yeah, listen, we have to stop very soon so get to the end of the story.

Patient (as Gonga): Well, what are you people?

Patient (as People): We're moon people. . . .

Patient (as Gonga): Moon people . . . what's that? I'm not going to listen to anything you say.

Therapist: So what do they say when he says that?

Patient (as Moon people): Strange specimen!

Patient (as Gonga): I'm not listening . . . (Tries to put fingers in ears.) Hey, my hands won't go into my ears. . . .

Patient (as Moon people): That's right. We have secret powers.

Patient (as Gonga): Well, I don't know, but I'm getting out of here. I can't move either. . . .

Patient (as Moon people): Yeah, that's why. Well, we are here to talk to you about the tape recorder.

Patient (as Gonga): Tape recorder . . . Oh, rats, well I'm going to get that any way I can . . . I may have to steal it.

Patient (as Moon people): Steal it????

Patient (as Gonga): Oh yeah. You guys haven't been listening to anything I said. . . .

Patient (as Moon people): Yeah. . . .

Patient (as Gonga): Well, I don't care what *you* think. . . . I think you're crazy.

Patient (as Moon people): Well, we don't think you're crazy. We think you never listen. We're trying to teach you a lesson.

Patient (as Gonga): How?

Patient (as Moon people): By getting you with all our creepers.

Therapist: They're going to teach Gonga a lesson for not listening. What are they going to do to him?

Patient: You'll see.

Patient (as Gonga): Hey, where'd you guys go? Hey, you look scary. . . . (Gonga attacked repeatedly by creepy crawlers, little monsters, and a variety of weird creatures.)

Therapist: What are they doing to Gonga?

Patient: Trying to scare him.

Therapist: Why are they trying to scare him?

Patient: So they can teach him a lesson.

Therapist: What's the lesson they're trying to teach?

Patient: To listen.

Patient (as Gonga): Help! Get that spider off me!!! Help me! I'll listen all the time. (Screams as creatures attack him.) And then Gonga woke up from the dream screaming.

Therapist: So did Gonga learn a lesson?

Patient: Yeah.

Psychodynamically, the same process is occurring here as described previously with the rejection of Gonga by his two friends. We see here an excellent demonstration of intrapsychic conflict. There is a conflict between the patient's superego (as represented by the punitive creatures) and his primitive impulses (as represented by Gonga who is the one who threatens to steal the tape recorder). By this process the patient is attempting to entrench and strengthen his superego dictates.

> *Therapist:* I have one question. Why did Gonga not listen in the first place?
> *Patient:* Because he wanted everything his way.
> *Therapist:* Why was that?
> *Patient:* Because he was a snob.
> *Therapist:* Because he was a snob? How did he get to be a snob?
> *Patient:* Well, he just wants everything in the world.
> *Therapist:* He just wants everything in the world.
> *Patient:* It's a she.
> *Therapist:* Okay, I've been a little confused on that point. Okay. How'd *she* get to be that way? How'd it happen that she wants everything in the world? Why is she so different from others who do listen?
> *Patient:* She wanted everybody to do what she wanted them to do.
> *Therapist:* Yeah, but how did she get that way? How did it happen?

I decided not to analyze the reasons why the patient was switching Gonga's sex. Rather, I decided to persist with the inquiry regarding how Gonga got to be so selfish and why she wouldn't listen. One answer had been provided: "Well, he just wants everything in the world." Although this is not a deeply significant comment, it does provide some insight into the feelings of deprivation with which the patient was suffering. I suspected that the change in sex at this point related to Frank's desire to provide further disguise. I say this because of the very important information that was soon to follow. Now, to return to the transcript at the point where the patient is responding to my question: "Yeah, but how did she get that way? How did it happen?"

> *Patient:* Well, a long time ago when she was really young, she had this little brother, and he was getting so much attention that Gonga went crazy. She wanted everything. She wanted all the attention.

I hope the reader shares the excitement I felt at this point. I considered this last statement to represent a real "breakthrough" in Frank's treatment. For the first time, I learned about an important psychodynamic factor in Frank's antisocial behavior. Using

Gonga as the vehicle for expressing his thoughts, Frank is essentially telling us that his anger began a long time ago at the time of the birth of his brother. At that time he suffered a loss of attention that was so painful that he "went crazy." In addition, it tells us something about his insatiable demand to have his own way: "She wanted everything." The revelation demonstrated well the old Greek aphorism: *Give a man a mask and he'll tell you the truth.*

In the ensuing interchange I made an attempt to get Frank to consider an alternative to dealing with the problem of lost attention following the birth of a younger brother. His way of dealing with this situation involved antisocial acting out, insatiable demands for attention, and indulgence of his whims.

> *Therapist:* So what finally happened to her?
>
> *Patient:* She turned into wanting everybody to do everything for her. When they did something for her, she would give them a lot of grief.
>
> *Therapist:* Okay, so how'd it finally end up for her?
>
> *Patient:* The dream taught her a lesson.
>
> *Therapist:* Oh . . . well, what would have been a better thing for Gonga to do after the birth of her brother?
>
> *Patient:* Try to help.
>
> *Therapist:* How? In what way?
>
> *Patient:* Like feeding it . . . by looking after the baby.
>
> *Therapist:* Well, what about the fact that the baby got so much attention. What would have been a better thing for Gonga to do about that? Rather than wanting everything her own way, what would have been a better thing? Instead of wanting everything her own way and getting very angry and not listening, what would have been a better way once the baby's there and the mother and father are giving the baby attention, what should you [sic] have done? To get away from what she did?
>
> *Patient:* Not ignore it.
>
> *Therapist:* The thing is what would have been a better way for Gonga to have dealt with the new baby rather than want everything to herself and never listen?
>
> *Patient:* To help.
>
> *Therapist:* To help is one thing but there's another thing I'm thinking of.
>
> *Patient:* To stay out of the baby's way.
>
> *Therapist:* Well, I would say another thing. To *share* the parents' attention. Can you elaborate on that? What does that mean to *share* the parents' attention?

Patient: To let the baby have someone and Gonga have someone. Not let Gonga have it all.

Therapist: Right! That's the key thing . . . to *share!* So that Gonga would have some attention and the baby would have some attention. Because when Gonga was being so selfish and mean and wanting everything himself, what happened to him? Did he get attention from the parents?

Patient: No.

Therapist: He got a kind of attention, but

Patient (interrupts): Bad attention.

Therapist: Bad attention rather than good attention. So he was worse off. So what did he finally decide to do?

Patient: Stop after the dream.

Therapist: And what did he do?

Patient: He became better.

Therapist: And what kind of attention did he then get from his parents?

Patient: Good attention. He worked really hard and got the $80 . . . $87. . . .

Therapist: $87 . . . and the mother kept her promise and gave him the $10. Okay. Do you want the actors to introduce themselves now that the show is over? (Patient stands, bows.)

Shall I come over and I'll be the person who was the voice. I'll take a bow, okay. So long everybody. Okay, do you want to watch this? Okay, but we don't have enough time to watch it all. We'll watch a little of this now.

Frank's first solutions were not, in my opinion, likely to be efficacious. He suggested trying to help take care of the baby by feeding it. One could argue that via this mechanism he would gratify vicariously his own desires to be an infant and thereby regain in fantasy some of his parents' lost attention. It also might have provided some compensatory enhancement as he assumed the position of the adult who feeds the child. Perhaps, there is an "identification with the aggressor" element here in that feeding the baby is clearly a parental function. Although this mechanism may have provided some compensation, I did not consider it a high priority solution. In addition, I did not consider it warranted to attempt to help Frank analyze this suggestion. I do not think that he was capable of doing so, and I felt that our time would be better spent continuing along other lines.

His next suggestion was that the baby be ignored entirely. Basically, this suggestion involved the utilization of denial mechanisms. These are rarely judicious and are just the opposite of what one attempts to do in the treatment of most people.

His next solution was to "stay out of the baby's way." I believe that this is another statement of the denial mechanism and avoids dealing directly with the problem.

I believed that at that point the patient exhausted all possible solutions that he could think of. Therefore, I introduced mine: for Gonga to *share* his parents' affection with his brother. This is an important point in the treatment of such problems. The patient has to be helped to appreciate that getting parental attention is not an all-or-none situation. He may not be able to get all the attention he wants, but he does not have to settle for no attention at all either. I utilize a similar approach in the treatment of oedipal problems. The boy is helped to appreciate that although he cannot get all of mother's affection, it does not mean that he will end up with none of it. He can share her with father in certain areas.

The reader may have noted that at one point I used the word "you" when I was referring to Gonga. This often happens in discussions in which the symbolic material is being used as a thin disguise for the patient's own behavior. Sometimes the patient may interrupt and remind me that we are not talking about him- or herself. At other times, the patient may actually switch into a discussion of the issues in such a way that he or she is aware that the conversation is self-directed. Here, Frank made no mention of the slip and might have missed it entirely.

The story ends with the patient's appreciation of the difference between "bad attention" and "good attention." Lastly, Gonga decides to earn the $87 rather than steal it. Again, a healthy resolution. One cannot expect dramatic behavioral change following such an interchange, but my experience has been that sessions such as this do contribute to a reduction of antisocial behavior and other psychogenic problems.

Five days later we once again played *The Talking, Feeling, and Doing Game.* Prior to the program he drew a sign for the announcement: "Gonga wants too much." This was held close enough to the camera to serve as a general title of the program.

> *Therapist:* Our guest today is going to put on another show called, as you can see on the screen, "Gonga Wants Too Much." We'll be back with you in just a minute. Do you want to say anything at this point?

Patient: No thank you.

Therapist: Before our program starts, I'd like to introduce our guest. Here he is. (Patient waves.) Do you want to introduce Gonga to us also?

Patient: Here's Gonga.

Therapist: Put him on the screen. Here he is. (Patient holds up Gonga.) Hi, Gonga. Okay let's turn this off and we'll be right back with you. (At the patient's request, the therapist and patient set up a table with Gonga, Chippy, Turtle and *The Talking, Feeling, and Doing Game.*)

Patient: Hi, and here are Gonga's friends, Chippy. (Holds up Chip Monkey.)

Therapist: Hi, Chippy.

Patient (Holds up Turtle.): The Turtle.

Therapist: Hi, Turtle. That's it? Just those two friends? Okay.

Patient: And now we must start the show.

Patient (as Gonga): (Patient now under the table.) Hello. My name is Gonga, and this is another one of my great stories. This is Chippy. (Holds Chip Monkey above table and says "Hi" in a high voice, as if speaking for Chip Monkey.) And this is Turtle. (Holds Turtle above table and says, "Hi, there" in high voice, as if speaking for Turtle.) As you all know, this is my best show yet . . . We're really working on this one. This one is called "Gonga Never Listens." Okay.

Therapist: Our guest has asked me to play *The Talking, Feeling, and Doing Game* with Gonga. Okay? So how do you want to proceed now? What should we do? Shall I roll the dice for Gonga or do you want to roll the dice for Gonga?

Patient (as Gonga): Um . . . you can do it.

Therapist: I'll roll the dice for Gonga. Okay, Gonga got a seven 1-2-3-4-5-6-7. Do you want to read Gonga's card or should I?

Patient (as Gonga): I'll read it.

Therapist: You'll read it. Here's Gonga's card. What's it say?

Patient (as Gonga): "What is the worst problem a person can have?"

Therapist: Okay, Gonga, what is the worst problem a person can have, Gonga?

Patient (as Gonga): Ummm, let's see. I'd say that the worst problem a person can have is probably a bad handicap.

Therapist: A bad handicap. For example, what kind of handicap, Gonga?

Patient (as Gonga): No legs.

Therapist: No legs.

Patient (as Gonga): No arms, or deaf, or blind, or dumb.

Therapist: I see, those are pretty bad handicaps. Which of all those would you say is the worst?

Patient (as Gonga): No legs.

Therapist: No legs. Why would you say that?

Patient (as Gonga): Or blindness.

Therapist: Or blindness. Why would you say that?

Patient (as Gonga): Because you need your eyes for a lot of things. Or no hands, because you need your hands for a lot of things, too. And your eyes you need . . . you can't do many things without your eyes.

Therapist: Uh huh. You know there are some people, Gonga, who have eyes that are good . . . You test their eyes with an eye chart, and they're fine. However, they don't want to see things that they do that are causing all kinds of trouble. And that's a kind of trouble. And that's a kind of blindness, also. Did you ever hear about that?

Patient (as Gonga): No.

Therapist: Never heard about that?

Patient (as Gonga): No.

Therapist: Are you serious?

Patient (as Gonga): Yeah.

Therapist: That's called psychological blindness. Do you understand what I'm talking about?

Patient (as Gonga): No, not really.

Therapist: You don't really . . . try to figure out what I'm. . . .

Patient (as Gonga): They don't see because they don't want to?

Therapist: Right! They don't want to. Why? Why don't they want to?

Patient (as Gonga): They're afraid of what they might see.

Therapist: Right! And what do you think would happen if they were to look at the thing?

Patient (as Gonga): They would get scared.

Therapist: Yeah, but do you think it would be better or worse for them to look at it and not be psychologically blind?

Patient (as Gonga): Better.

Therapist: Why do you say that?

Patient (as Gonga): Well, because then you can do more things.

Therapist: Right! If you make believe there's no problem, then you can't solve it. Did you ever read that book, *Stories About the Real World*?

Patient (as Gonga): Ummmmm. *Stories About the Real World* . . . which one is that? Is that the one with Mack and the Beanstalk?

Therapist: No, that's a different book. That's a book of fairy tales, called *Modern Fairy Tales. Stories About the Real World* has one story in it called "Oliver and the Ostrich." Remember that one?

Patient (as Gonga): The ones I read were *Dorothy and the Lizard of Oz* and "Mack and the Beanstalk" and yeah, the one with "Oliver and the Ostrich" and "The Million Dollar Lie."

Therapist: Right. What did we learn from "Oliver and the Ostrich?" What did we learn from that?

Patient (as Gonga): He didn't want to hear. He made believe there was nothing wrong, but there really was something wrong.

Therapist: Right! What was the trouble?

Patient (as Gonga): He was failing in school.

Therapist: Right! Now how does the ostrich fit into that?

Patient (as Gonga): Well, he thought that the ostrich would poke his head underneath the sand and make believe nothing was there. But really the ostrich would fight as hard as he could . . .

Therapist: The ostrich does what?

Patient (as Gonga): He'd fight as hard as he could.

Therapist: Fight . . . but if the animal who attacked him was too big, what would he do?

Patient (as Gonga): He would run.

Therapist: Yeah, but does he ever hide his head in the sand?

Patient (as Gonga): No.

Therapist: Do human beings do that?

Patient (as Gonga): Well, maybe.

Therapist: Really, or do they act as if their heads are in the . . .

Patient (as Gonga, interrupts): They act. They never really hide in the sand.

Therapist: Right! That's called psychological blindness. Tell me something. Do you do anything . . .

Patient (as Gonga, interrupts): What you can't see can't hurt you.

Therapist: Yeah, but what you can't see *can* hurt you. If the ostrich has his head in the sand, he can't see anything, but can he get hurt?

Patient (as Gonga): Yes.

Therapist: So, is it true that what you can't see, can't hurt you?

Patient (as Gonga): No.

Therapist: It's not true. Tell me something, do you do anything that's like that . . . when you make believe that there's no problem when there really is?

Patient (as Gonga): Oh, yeah.

Therapist: Yeah? How do you do it?

Patient (as Gonga): At school.

Therapist: How do you do it at school?

Patient (as Gonga): Well, I don't listen too much.

Therapist: Uh huh. You don't listen.

Patient (as Gonga): Especially in social studies.

Therapist: Why especially in social studies?

Patient (as Gonga): Because social studies is so boring.

Therapist: So what do you do in social studies?

Patient (as Gonga): Talk about the great explorers.

Therapist: Yeah, but what do *you* do when everybody's talking about the great explorers.

Patient (as Gonga): Play with my fingers . . . (mumbles).

Therapist: Pardon me?

Patient (as Gonga): Play with my fingers sometimes.

Therapist: Uh huh. Why do you do that?

Patient (as Gonga): Because there's nothing else to do.

Therapist: Uh huh. Anything else?

Patient (as Gonga): No.

Therapist: Any other reasons why?

Patient (as Gonga): No, not really.

Therapist: Do you make believe that there's no problem for you there?

Patient (as Gonga): Sort of.

Therapist: Do you think there's a problem that you play with your fingers?

Patient (as Gonga): Yes.

Therapist: Why do you think you do that?

Patient (as Gonga): Because I don't want to listen.

Therapist: How come?

Patient (as Gonga): Because it's sort of boring to listen.

Therapist: Well, so okay. Let's say it is a little boring. What's so terrible about a little boredom . . . hmmm?

Patient (as Gonga): Yeah, well, nothing's so terrible about a little boredom.

Therapist: There's nothing wrong with a little bit of boredom?

Patient (as Gonga): No.

Therapist: You say it's boring; therefore, you're not going to listen. It sounds to me like you have the idea that anything that's unpleasant you shouldn't do. Is that right?

Patient (as Gonga): Well, sort of.

Therapist: But, you know, do you think there's any problem with that way of handling things—that if it's unpleasant you're not going to do it.

Patient (as Gonga): No.

Therapist: There's nothing wrong with that?

Patient (as Gonga): No.

Therapist: I see. I disagree. I think that there are times in life you have to do things that are unpleasant because if you don't, you get into even worse trouble. What do you think about that?

Patient (as Gonga): Well, it's sort of true.

Therapist: I mean everybody can't like every subject in school, and if you decide if you don't like one subject, you're not going to do it or you're not going to push through a little boredom, then you're going to get into a lot of trouble. You fail. So, at times, you have to do things you don't like. What do you think about that?

Patient (as Gonga): Well, that's okay.

Therapist: That's okay? Have I changed your mind on the subject?

Patient (as Gonga): Yeah.

Therapist: Are you sure?

Patient (as Gonga): Yeah.

Therapist: Okay, but what are you going to do now when you go to school.

Patient (as Gonga): I'm going to listen.

Therapist: Well, people don't usually change that fast—I hope you're right—I hope you will listen, but I hope that you'll someday appreciate what I'm saying. Maybe you will now, but people usually take some time to change, and just saying that you're going to listen isn't enough.

By this point, the reader has probably forgotten that this discussion began with the patient's card regarding what is the worst thing that can happen to someone. I used his response about going blind as one of the worst things to embark on a discussion of "psychological blindness," utilization of the denial mechanism. There was some receptivity on Frank's part to accepting the fact that he utilizes denial and "makes believe" that there is no problem when there really is. I also used the opportunity to make reference to my story, "Oliver and the Ostrich" from my book *Stories About the Real World* (1972a) which deals with the same issue via a discussion of the ostrich. Basically, in the story the child learns that ostriches do not stick their heads in the sand when there is trouble ("they would never do such a stupid thing"). Rather, they scrutinize the danger and decide whether to fight or flee (like all the other animals, except the human being).

In the ensuing discussion we touched upon the patient's failure to take seriously his school assignments and other obligations. I believed that Frank, like many children who feel deprived, subscribed strongly to the pleasure principle. Specifically, he had the feeling that he had gotten very little pleasure in life, and he therefore was not going to tolerate any discomforts or frustrations: In Frank's case, the deprivation related to the birth of his brother and the attendant attention that the latter received. In this vignette he appeared to be resolving to tolerate the discomfort of occasional classroom boredom in order to avoid the discomforts of failure, which he agreed is worse than boredom. However, the facility with which he promised to reform was unconvincing and I described my incredulity. At this point, I resumed my conversation with Gonga. The reader should recall that the patient was still under the table during the course of this conversation and that I was continuously speaking with "Gonga," the doll that he was holding above the table in my view.

Therapist: Let me ask you one other question.

Patient (as Gonga): Yeah?

Therapist: Why do you think, Gonga, you don't want to accept anything that's unpleasant. Why do you go around just doing just what you like? Why do you say, "I don't like to do it, I'm not going to do it . . . I'm not going to do what I don't like," when most other people mix it. You know, they have some things they like, some things they don't like and they accept the fact that there are times they have to do things they don't like?

Patient (as Gonga): I give up!

Therapist: You give up? You haven't any idea why you do it?

Patient (as Gonga): No.

Therapist: Just try to guess. Why do you do that?

Patient (as Gonga): Can you say it again?

Therapist: Okay. You go around with the idea that if it's unpleasant you say: "I don't like it, I'm not going to do it."? Do you do that, Gonga?

Patient: Yeah, sometimes.

Therapist: Give me an example of how you do that. When you don't like something, you just don't do it.

Patient (as Gonga): When Chippy and I play *The Talking, Feeling, and Doing Game* at home, when I cheat, he tells me, "Don't cheat or else I'm going to go home." Then I do what I want.

Therapist: You play *The Talking, Feeling, and Doing Game* at home?

Patient (as Gonga): You let me borrow it.

Therapist: I didn't let you borrow it. I don't lend the game to kids to play at home. Is Gonga making that up? Is that it? No, say it, it's all right.

Patient (Gonga): You really did . . . let's say you really did let Gonga borrow it. . . .

Therapist: Oh, you're making believe that I let Gonga borrow it. Because I usually don't let people borrow that game. It's not a game for home. Oh, so you're saying that Gonga is saying I lent it. But I'd like you to make up something that's real . . . that really happened

. . . that Gonga . . . that really happened to Gonga . . . not a made-up thing.

Patient: We play a regular game.

Therapist: You play a regular game . . . then what does Gonga do?

Patient (as Gonga): And I cheat, and Chippy says he'll go home and he won't play with me.

Therapist: So you cheat.

Patient (as Gonga): I don't listen to him.

Therapist: You don't listen to him . . . you just cheat. Why do you cheat?

Patient (as Gonga): Because I want to win all the time.

Therapist: Uh huh, you want to feel good all the time.

Patient (as Gonga): Because I want too much.

Therapist: You want too much . . . uh huh . . . you don't want to hear "no" for an answer, huh?

Patient (as Gonga): That's right.

Therapist: Uh huh. How come? How come you don't want to hear "no" for an answer?

Patient (as Gonga): Because I just like to have a lot of stuff.

Therapist: You just like to have a lot of stuff. And you just want to feel good all the time, huh?

Patient (as Gonga): Yeah.

Therapist: And you never want to feel bad?

Patient (as Gonga): Yeah.

Therapist: Why is that?

Patient (as Gonga): Because I don't like feeling bad.

Therapist: Okay, and what did I say before about bad feelings in life?

Patient (as Gonga): That you have to face them.

Therapist: Yeah, at times you have to have bad feelings. Besides, you have to do things you don't like. What do you think about that?

Patient (as Gonga): I think it's true.

Therapist: And if you don't, what will happen?

Patient (as Gonga): You'll get in trouble.

Therapist: Yeah. You'll feel even worse than you did if you just had a few sad feelings.

Patient (as Gonga): Yeah.

Therapist: Now, why haven't you learned that lesson? Most kids, Gonga, learn that lesson. They know that they've got to do things at times they don't want to do, because they know that if they don't, they'll feel even worse and they'll get left back, or they'll be punished, or they'll be sent to the principal's office, or they'll be grounded, or things like that. Why haven't you learned that lesson yet, Gonga? Why do you think that is?

Patient (as Gonga): I give up.

Therapist: Do you want my guess?

Patient (as Gonga): Yeah.

Therapist: My guess is . . .

Patient (as Gonga): That I don't want to . . .

Therapist: But why don't you want to.

Patient (as Gonga): I don't know.

Therapist: There are many reasons, but I have a guess about one of the reasons.

Patient (as Gonga): What?

Therapist: My guess is that a long time ago . . . like you said at the end of the last program . . . when you were very little, and your brother was born, and before that time, you were like "king of the world." You were the only kid. You were the first grandchild. Everybody doted over you; everybody thought how great you were; and you were really sitting there on the throne. And then, boom, whammo, along came your brother.

Patient (no longer as Gonga): My dumb old [mumbles] brother. . .

Therapist: What did you say? Your dumb little brother?

Patient: Dumb.

Therapist: Dumb, okay. So I say this: You got so mad that you said, "I'm very angry at everybody, because they give him all that attention." That's one thing. And another thing you said was, "I'm not going to suffer any more pain. I'm going to do what I want, when I want, and I've got enough pain with everybody giving him attention. No more pain for me." You see, you say two things: "No more pain for me; I'm just going to get pleasure," and "I'm going to get attention by being bad." What do you think about that?

Patient: That's being greedy.

Therapist: That's being greedy? What did I say? Tell me the two things I said that happened to you when your brother was born.

Patient: When my brother was born, I didn't like it. After my brother was born, everybody paid attention to him and not to me. Then I wanted it all so I took over . . .

Therapist: You wanted what?

Patient: All the attention.

Therapist: So how do you get the attention now?

Patient: By being bad.

Therapist: That's one thing you do. And what else are you doing since your brother was born? You get the attention by being bad and what else did I say you do?

Patient: I don't listen.

Therapist: Yeah, but what happens when you don't listen?

Patient: Well . . .

Therapist: I said that not listening was the same as being bad. I said something else about pleasure. What did I say about that?

Patient: I wanted it all.

Therapist: You wanted it all—why?

Patient: Because I was greedy.

Therapist: Uh huh. And why do you say that you were greedy?

Patient: Because my little brother was born.

Therapist: And . . .

Patient: And I wanted all the good things.

Patient: Yeah.

Therapist: You wanted only pleasure, no pain.

Patient: Yeah.

Therapist: Now, what's this got to do with playing with your fingers in social studies class? Can you link that up?

Patient: No.

Therapist: In social studies, it's boring, right?

Patient: Right.

Therapist: So, that's pain, right? So what do you do? What's the pleasure?

Patient: Playing with my fingers.

Therapist: Right. Do you think that's true?

Patient: Yes.

Therapist: Do you think it has something to do with your brother being born?

Patient: Yeah.

Therapist: How would you link it up?—just so I'm sure you understand.

Patient: I get all pleasure. When my brother was born, I wanted all pleasure and no pain and in social studies I wanted all pleasure and no pain.

Therapist: Right! But what'll happen to you if you live a life in which you only get pleasure and avoid pain.

Patient: You'll be a snob.

Therapist: Anything else? Snob doesn't tell me much . . .

Patient: Be greedy.

Therapist: Yeah. Any other thing that'll happen?

Patient: When you want something and you get it, you'll get a lot of grief.

Therapist: You'll get a lot of grief?

Patient: Yeah.

Therapist: Why will you get a lot of grief?

Patient: Ummmmm. Because . . . well, I don't know!

Therapist: Well, if you don't do your social studies and you just sit there avoiding the pain and the boredom of social studies and just getting the pleasure of playing with your fingers, what's going to happen?

Patient: You can do that all the time.

Therapist: And what'll happen with your social studies?

Patient: You won't learn.

Therapist: And what'll the teacher do?

Patient: Get you in trouble.

Therapist: Yeah, you won't learn anything, so you'll be kind of dumb or ignorant, right? And you'll also get in trouble. So, in my opinion, it's probably worth it to push through the boredom and learn what you have to from the teacher, and then enjoy some of the other subjects more.

Patient: Okay.

Therapist: What was the last thing I said, just so I'm sure you understand it, Gonga?

Patient (as Gonga): I would get in trouble and I would be in trouble instead of learning.

Therapist: Yeah. And what causes more trouble? Which is more painful? The boredom of school or the trouble of failing and getting in trouble with the teacher and not learning and being ignorant, being dumb.

Patient (as Gonga): The second.

Therapist: You say it so I'm sure you understand it. Which is more trouble? Say it, I want to make sure you understand.

Patient (as Gonga): Getting in trouble with the teacher and failing in school and not being able to learn . . .

Therapist: . . . is more trouble than . . .

Patient (as Gonga): boredom.

Therapist: Right, right. By the way, you get a chip for that. That was your question.

I attempted here to help the patient gain some insight into the relationship between his antisocial behavior and the birth of his brother. I had the feeling that some inroads were made here, but I certainly can't say that he responded with the kind of strong emotional response one sees in patients (especially adults) when the therapist has "hit home." Although the insight was at a minimal level, I believe it was nevertheless there.

The reader may have noticed that at the point where I began speaking about the birth of the brother the patient dropped the Gonga disguise and began talking about himself. Near the end of the interchange, I purposely returned him to the Gonga role in order to "preserve anonymity" and thereby assure a freer flow of revelation.

After being awarded the chip the patient requested that Gonga and I discontinue playing *The Talking, Feeling, and Doing Game* and go on to another activity. The reader may note that only one card had been drawn between the outset and the time we went on to another activity.

Therapist: Our guest now has decided that we stop *The Talking, Feeling, and Doing Game* and now he's going to put on a little play about Gonga and his friends and the fire truck. Okay, you're on the air!

Patient (as Chip Monkey and Turtle): Boy, look at that. That's really neat. I love that. Hey, wow, look at that neat thing with the little sprays.

Therapist: What are they looking at?

Patient: The fire engine.

Patient (as Gonga): Hi, guys. (Gonga knocks Chip Monkey.) Oops, sorry, Chippy.

Therapist: So Chippy and Turtle are looking at that fire engine and think it's really neat. Okay, go ahead.

Patient (as Gonga): Boy, that's really . . . Neato . . . Boy, it's neat.

Therapist: Gonga thinks it's neat, too, huh?

Patient (as store manager): Hey, kid, don't touch.

Patient (as Gonga): Shut up. Boy, wow. I really want this . . . look at those pieces . . .

Therapist: He really wants it.

Patient: Those little pieces, those little sprays on the fire engine, everything its got . . .

Patient (as store manager): Kid, you're not supposed to touch it.

Patient (as Gonga): Shut up, mister.

Patient (as store manager): Okay, out of my store.

Patient (as Chip Monkey): Gonga!!

Patient (as Gonga): Who cares about that dumb old guy anyway!!

Therapist: The guy kicked Gonga out of the store because he touched the fire engine?

Patient: Yeah.

Therapist: Okay, and then what did Gonga say?

Patient: Shut up.

Therapist: Who'd he say shut up to?

Patient: The guy.

Therapist: The owner of the store?

Patient: Yeah.

Therapist: And then what happened?

Patient: He left.

Therapist: Gonga left. Okay, now what happens?

Patient: (Whispers to therapist.)

Therapist: You want a cut, okay. Gonga is now home and our guest wants me to play the role of Gonga's father and has told me what to say. Okay, go ahead, you begin.

Patient (as Gonga): Daddy . . .

Therapist (as Gonga's father): Yes, Gonga, what is it?

Patient (as Gonga): There's this fire engine at the store, and I want it very bad. Can I have it?

Therapist (as Gonga's father): Well, how much does it cost?

Patient (as Gonga): $36.00.

Therapist (as Gonga's father): $36.00?

Patient (as Gonga): Well, it's because it's remote control.

Therapist (as Gonga's father): Well, that's a very expensive toy, Gonga, and that's a lot of money for a toy. I'll tell you what I'll do. I'll be happy to give you part of the money, but you're going to have to save up from your allowance and your earnings in order to pay for most of it. I'll pay for $10.00 of it, and you've got to pay the other $26.00.

Patient (as Gonga): No, I want the whole thing!! (Gonga jumping up and down, imitating a temper tantrum.)

Therapist (as Gonga's father): I'm sorry, Gonga . . . I'm sorry you just can't have everything you want when you want it, and you just can't have every toy you want and that's the answer.

Patient (as Gonga): Get you . . . (mumbles) . . .

Therapist (as Gonga's father): What was that?

Patient (as Gonga): No, I want it now. (Gonga has another temper tantrum.)

Therapist (as Gonga's father): Now look, Gonga. If you're going to continue with those tantrums, I'm going to have to send you to your room because I just don't like the noise of those tantrums. So either you're going to stop the tantrums or off to your room.

Patient (as Gonga): If I'm good, can I have it tomorrow?

Therapist (as Gonga's father): Well, I'll tell you . . .

Patient (as Gonga): And then pay you back . . .

Therapist (as Gonga's father): You want to borrow the money?

Patient (as Gonga): Yeah.

Therapist (as Gonga's father): Well, I won't lend you all the money. I'll lend you part of the money, but you'll have a debt. The total amount that you owe for that is $26.00. Now, how much money do you have right now in your bank?

Patient (as Gonga): $11.00.

Therapist (as Gonga's father): $11.00. Okay, so how much do you want me to lend you?

Patient (as Gonga): Could you lend me. . .

Therapist (as Gonga's father): Well, we're running out of time, so I'll lend you $15.00. Fifteen dollars and $11.00 is $26.00, and I'll give you $10.00 toward it. That's $36.00. But remember you owe me $15.00 that you have to earn, right?

Patient (as Gonga): Yeah.

Therapist (as Gonga's father): Okay, so here's the $15.00 and you can buy it.

Patient (as Gonga): Okay. (Patient whispers in therapist's ear.)

Therapist (as Gonga's father): Our guest now has asked me to play the part of the storekeeper. Okay?

Therapist: I'm going to play the part of the storekeeper. Okay. Hiya, Gonga.

Patient (as Gonga): I want that. (Gonga points to fire engine.)

Therapist (as storekeeper): Okay. You got $36?

Patient (as Gonga): Yeah, right here.

Therapist (as storekeeper): Okay. Give me the money. Ten, 20, 30, 35, 36 dollars. Here you are, my good friend.

Patient (as Gonga): Thanks.

Therapist (as storekeeper): Now you have a remote control fire engine. Tell me, how did you get this money?

Patient (as Gonga): My father lent it to me but I had $11.

Therapist (as storekeeper): Uh huh. So your father lent you some money.

Patient (as Gonga): Yeah.

Therapist (as storekeeper): Okay. He lent you money. How much did he lend you?

Patient (as Gonga): Ummmm. Fifteen dollars.

Therapist (as storekeeper): Okay. And that makes $26. Where'd you get the other $10?

Patient (as Gonga): Ummm. He gave it to me.

Therapist (as storekeeper): That was pretty nice of him. I guess you're going to have to work now to earn the $15 to give him back the money, right?

Patient (as Gonga): Yeah.

Therapist (as storekeeper): Good for you. That'll give you a really good feeling when you work off that debt. And then you'll have that all yourself when you know that you worked for it.

Patient (as Gonga): Okay, thanks.

Therapist (as storekeeper): Okay. I hope you enjoy that fire engine.

Patient (as Gonga): Okay. Bye.

Therapist (as storekeeper): Bye. Okay. Now we're coming to the very last part of the show. Go ahead.

Patient (as Gonga): Boy, am I sure glad I earned all that money, and I paid back my debt and I got that money from my father by doing the paper route, mowing lawns, and raking leaves.

Therapist (as storekeeper): Uh huh.

Patient (as Gonga): Boy, do I feel good about myself.

Therapist (as storekeeper): Uh huh. You really feel good about yourself?

Patient (as Gonga): Yeah.

Therapist (as storekeeper): Uh huh. Okay. Now how's it working out with that remote fire engine?

Patient (as Gonga): Great!

Therapist (as storekeeper): Are you really enjoying it?

Patient (as Gonga): Yeah, watch this. You just press the button and it goes.

Therapist: Okay, before we close, I'd like to hear from you, Gonga, what are the lessons of this story? All the different lessons we can learn from this story, which is quite a long one. See if you can figure them out.

Patient (as Gonga): Umm. Don't be greedy . . .

Therapist: Because . . .

Patient (as Gonga): It will never bring you good.

Therapist: Why will it never bring you good?

Patient (as Gonga): Because it's not good to be greedy and nobody will pay attention to you.

Therapist: Well, yeah, they won't like you if you're greedy. They may pay attention if you make yourself a nuisance, you know?

Patient (as Gonga): Yeah.

Therapist: Okay. Go on, why isn't it good?

Patient (as Gonga): Ummm. Because it's not good for you.

Therapist: How come?

Patient (as Gonga): Well, when you grow up, you'll keep wanting stuff.

Therapist: And . . .

Patient (as Gonga): You'll turn into a snob.

Therapist: What is a snob as you see it? What do you mean by snob?

Patient (as Gonga): A jerk.

Therapist: Be more specific.

Patient (as Gonga): You want too much.

Therapist: And then what'll happen if you want too much.

Patient (as Gonga): When you get it, you'll get grief.

Therapist: Why will you get grief?

Patient (as Gonga): You'll give grief.

Therapist: Why will you give grief?

Patient (as Gonga): Because once you get your way. . .

Therapist: How do you give grief when you get your way?

Patient (as Gonga): You misbehave.

Therapist: Uh huh. Okay. And any other lessons?

Patient (as Gonga): Things aren't always as bad as they really are.

Therapist: Say that again.

Patient (as Gonga): Well, we were playing The Talking, Feeling, and Doing Game.

Therapist: What did you learn from that?

Patient (as Gonga): Let's see. Ummm. I think . . .

Therapist: What did we learn in that game?

Patient (as Gonga): We learned that . . . umm . . . that getting in trouble and pain is much worse than boredom pain.

Therapist: Right, right! And what did we learn about how sometimes you have to take a little pain. Huh?

Patient (as Gonga): Yeah.

Therapist: To avoid bigger pain.

Patient (as Gonga): Yeah.

Therapist: Uh huh. And that's part of life, right? And what'd we learn about you and your brother? That's the last thing before we close. What did we learn about you and your brother?

Patient (as Gonga): Ummm. We learned that . . . you can't . . . you mean about me and my brother?

Therapist: Yeah, what did we learn about you and your brother?

Patient (as Gonga): (Patient crawling on floor around table.) We learned that you can't have all the attention all the time.

Therapist: Right. That we share.

Patient (as Gonga): Yeah.

Therapist: And what did we learn about what you're doing? After your brother was born, to get attention, what do you do?

Patient (as Gonga): Get into trouble.

Therapist: And that gives you attention. What did we learn about your feelings about pleasure and pain after your brother was born?

Patient (as Gonga): That I wanted bad pain.

Therapist: You wanted what?

Patient (as Gonga): Umm . . . I don't know.

Therapist: You wanted . . . how did you feel about getting pleasure and pain after your brother was born? What did you want?

Patient (as Gonga): Just pleasure.

Therapist: Right, right. Okay, do you want to come up and say good-bye to everybody, to show your face now? Okay. This is our guest. (Patient stands up and bows.) He's been the guy . . . he's been the voice that you've been hearing. Okay. So long everybody. And now, ladies and gentlemen, we just want to announce that this is The

End. (Patient holds up sign which says *The End.*) We hope you enjoyed this show. Good-bye, everybody. Do you want to say good-bye?
    Patient: So long.
    Therapist: So long. Bye.

Within the few weeks following this session there was a definite reduction in Frank's antisocial behavior. He was much more
compliant in school and cooperative at home. I believe that these
sessions played a role in the behavioral change. I do not believe
that this was simply related to the insight he gained about the relationship between his antisocial behavior and the birth of his
brother. I believe that he gained some appreciation of the fact that
his antisocial behavior caused him more pain than the discomforts
associated with doing what is socially acceptable and desirable. In
addition, I believe he gained some solace from the concept of sharing. He could not have his parents as much as he wanted, but he
could have them to some degree. Unfortunately, this patient's therapy had to be interrupted because his father was required to relo-
cate for business purposes. Arrangements were made for him to
continue therapy with a psychiatrist near his new home. A follow-
up conversation six months later revealed that Frank continued to
improve.

The Case of George
["This Damn Magic Wand Is No Good"]

This eight-year-old boy suffered with a neurologically based learning disability. He was quite immature in many ways and was over-
protected by his mother. His view of the world of magic was very
much like that of the five year old and his magic-cure expectations
were strong. Near the end of his second month in treatment he told
this story.

    Patient: The name that I'm gonna have—I'm gonna have two
    names of the story each.
    Therapist: Go ahead.
    Patient: One name is gonna be "Little Ducklings" and the second
    name is gonna be "One of the Ducklings Turns into a Grown Man."
    There's only gonna be one duckling.
    Therapist: Okay.
    Patient: There's the mother, the father, the brother.

Therapist: Okay. Now do you want to start the first story? Go ahead.

Patient: I said there's going to be two names and that's the story.

Therapist: Oh, just one story with two names?

Patient: Yeah.

Therapist: Okay. Start the story.

Patient: And two lessons.

Therapist: And two lessons. Okay. This is a story, one story with two names and two lessons. Go ahead. Let's hear.

Patient: Once there's a duckling. He said, "Ooh, how did I get changed into a duckling? I was a person all my life. How—how could this happen? How did this happen? I must even act like a duck now so a fairy godmother will come and save me. Quack, quack, quack, quack." But no fairy godmother came. So he said, "Quack, quack, quack, quack, quack" and he was begging for his fairy godmother.

Therapist: Okay, then what happened?

Patient: Then he said, "Quack, quack. Oh, I wish a fairy godmother would come. Quack, quack, quack, quack." And he was quacking so hard that he flew over to the water and fell in.

Therapist: Okay. Then what happened? This is a very good story.

Patient: Then he said, "Caw, caw, quack, quack, coo, coo, quack, quack," and he was . . . (mumbles) . . . up.

Therapist: And he was what?

Patient: Burning up.

Therapist: He was burning up. Why was he burning up?

Patient: Because he said, "Quack, quack, quack, quack, quack!" Like that.

Therapist: Okay. Then what happened?

Patient: Then he said, "Quack, quack, quack." (Patient speaking in singsong manner.) "Oh, I wish a fairy godmother, a fairy godmother." That's a little song the duckling made up.

Therapist: Okay. Go ahead.

Patient (sings again): "Oh, I wish a fairy godmother would come and get me out, would come and get me out, would come and get me out." And he was going, "Quack, quack, quack, quack, quack!" And then he turned into a horse!

Therapist: He turned into a horse! Yeah. Go ahead.

Patient: Then he said, "Boy, what happened with me? I was a duckling before. I used to go heeee, heeee. I hope a fairy godmother comes this time. Heeeeewwwwww, quack, quack." And then he changed back into a duck because he went "quack, quack" by accident.

Therapist: Uh huh. Then what happened?

Patient: And then the fairy godmother *really* came and said, "Huh!

What, what. I thought I heard somebody calling me. I don't see anybody. Hhmm. Must be my magic wand ... (mumbles) ... by accident.

Therapist: Wait a minute. The fairy godmother said, "What, I thought I heard somebody calling me," and then she said what about a wand?

Patient: And then she said, "Hhhmmm! My magic wand probably made him disappear." But the duck was really in the pond under the water.

Therapist (interrupts): She thought that her magic wand made the duck disappear. That's why she didn't see him in the pond. Go ahead.

Patient: "Ooh, oh, oh, oh, I tricked her."

Therapist: Wait a minute. I don't understand that. Who's talking now?

Patient: The duck.

Therapist: And what did he say?

Patient: "Ooh, I tricked that fairy godmother by accident. I'll go get her. Fairy godmother, quack, quack. I'm a duckling. Change me back into a person." But the fairy godmother was in the clouds.

Therapist: So what happened then?

Patient: Then he was there again and when the fairy godmother came again she saw him turned into a horse. And she said, "Hey, what happened, horse? You were quacking before. Don't you know how to make a horse sound? A horse goes, 'Heeehawww, heeehawww.' You went 'quack, quack, quack' and clapping your hands. I'm not gonna help you. Keep this magic wand and try yourself." And then the fairy godmother went away.

Therapist: And then what happened? (Pause) So the fairy godmother went away and wouldn't change him into a person?

Patient: No, because she was so mad at him. He didn't know how to make a horse sound. He changed before the fairy godmother came there.

Therapist: Oh, the fairy godmother was mad because he changed from a duck into a horse?

Patient: Yeah, and she heard him quacking.

Therapist: Oh, she heard him quacking and then he turned into a horse. Okay, and then what finally happened? So the fairy godmother got angry at him and went away. Then what finally happened?

Patient: Then the magic wand worked on him and that's the end.

Therapist: It worked on him. And what happened when the magic wand worked on him?

Patient: It flew back—it was um—it flew back to the fairy godmother.

Therapist: What happened to the duck or horse?

Patient: He turned back into a boy before it went. . . .

Therapist (interrupts): Oh, he turned back into a boy. Oh, I see. Okay. And the lesson of that story?

Patient: Two lessons, remember?

Therapist: What are the two lessons?

Patient: Never (long pause).

Therapist: Never what?

Patient: Never be mad at a duck!

Therapist: Never be mad at a duck? And the other lesson?

Patient: Don't think there's no such thing as fairy godmothers. There's, there's a lesson that goes with that also. And the third lesson is: Don't believe in fairy godmothers because there's no such thing and if you heard a duck quacking and it changed into a horse it was really the duck and don't be mad at it.

Therapist: I see.

Patient: That's the lessons.

Therapist: Okay. Now it's my chance to tell a story.

This story is typical of that told by many children with neurologically based learning disabilities. It is somewhat disorganized and the patient does not concern himself with whether his listener understands what is going on in it. Frequent questioning is required if the therapist is to surmise the story's psychodynamic meaning. In analyzing such a story it is best to think about main issues and general trends and not get bogged down in minutiae. The main event in this story is that a boy is turned into a duck and in that state he has the power to change himself into a horse. Finally, after a few somewhat confusing experiences with the fairy godmother, he is turned back into a boy. George had a speech defect for which he had received some therapy. In addition, his lower lip protruded somewhat and occasionally saliva dripped from it. (Characteristically, his mother was ever at hand to catch the saliva and it was not until I recommended it that she taught George how to use a handkerchief and to think about his tendency to salivate.) His depicting himself as a duck related, I believe, to his speech deficit as well as to his protruding lip. The horse, with his odd vocalization, also lends itself well to symbolizing the patient and his speech defect.

The story also depicts some hostile interchanges between the duck-horse and the fairy godmother: the duck tricks the fairy godmother by making a quacking sound and then changing into a horse; the duck hides from the fairy godmother so that she cannot find him; and the fairy godmother throws her wand at the horse.

To play a trick on someone is a common childhood way of expressing hostility. In this case, the tricks involve hiding from the fairy godmother and fooling her by back-and-forth transformations between a horse and a duck. I suspected that the fairy godmother might have symbolized me (the magic curer) and that the hostility might have related to anger over my not having provided George with a magic cure—but I was not certain.

The story, then, contains two themes: a desire for magic transformation from infrahuman to human status and the expression of hostility (probably toward the therapist). His first lesson: "Don't think there's no such thing as fairy godmothers. There's, there's a lesson that goes with that also." This lesson makes reference to a previous story in which I promulgated the notion that there is no such thing as a fairy godmother. This idea apparently produced such anxiety that he had to negate it with a lesson in this subsequent story. He then continued. "And the third lesson is: Don't believe in fairy godmothers because there's no such thing and if you heard a duck quacking and it changed into a horse it was really a duck and don't be mad at it." Here we see apparent acceptance of my message that there is no such thing as a fairy godmother. Clearly the patient is ambivalent regarding this idea. However, one can't expect immediate receptivity regarding a patient's giving up such an attractive symptom and a phase of ambivalence is a step toward its elimination. Furthermore, the third lesson also makes reference to the hostility issue by advising the listener (? me) not to be mad at a quacking duck that changes into a horse. The request suggests that the patient anticipates that I will be angry at him for his tricks.

I decided not to attempt to create a story that would simultaneously incorporate both the hostility and magic themes. It is generally judicious of the therapist to select one of the themes from the patient's story and use only that for his or her responding story. To try to do more may not only be too much for the child to handle, but the therapist's ability to create a unified story with more than one theme is not as great as the capacity of the child's unconscious to do this. I decided to choose the magic transformation theme rather than the anger. First, I was more certain of its meaning. Second, I reasoned that if I could help the patient reduce his dependency on magic he would rely more on realistic solutions to his problems. Because that goal had a greater likelihood of success, he would then be less likely to be angry at me.

Another problem that I faced in formulating a responding story was that of what to do with the duck. As described, the duck lent itself well as a symbol of the patient because of his speech problem and his salivating, protruding lip. To portray the patient as a duck in my story might entrench this pathological personification and might thereby be antitherapeutic. However, to depict the patient as a boy would then rob me of the opportunity to deal with the magic transformation issue in a manner that was close to the patient's representation of the problem. If the therapist's story gets too remote from the patient's it becomes less therapeutically effective.

In addition, the child's ability to create a fantasy that most efficiently and effectively synthesizes the symbols is far greater than that of the therapist. I believe that we lack the ingenuity not only of our child-patient's unconscious, but of our own unconscious as well. We ourselves cannot consciously create a dream as rich and as efficient as that which can be created by our own unconscious. The efficiency and ingenuity of our unconscious processes to utilize simile, metaphor, allegory, and efficient and innovative symbol fusion far surpasses that of our conscious mind. Therefore, I do not try to reconcile all elements of my story nor do I strive for one-hundred percent consistency. In this case I chose to be a little inconsistent (and even possibly a little antitherapeutic) in order to preserve the duck symbol for the larger purposes of my story, that is, to present a story which focused on the patient's magic cure delusion.

Also, using another symbol would remove us from the scene of the patient's metaphor. This shift would lessen the likelihood of the patient and I then moving along the same psychological track and would lessen thereby his receptivity to my story. However, when I retain the undesirable symbol I am quick to modify it or introduce qualifications that reduce its psychologically detrimental import. When introducing the duck I was quick to point out that the duck was a regular, "plain," and "nice" duck and that his only defect was that he had a speech problem. As will be seen in the transcript, the patient was relieved by this circumscription of his deficits. It wasn't that the duck was totally loathesome; rather he suffered only with an isolated defect. In short, I considered the advantages of retaining the duck symbol to far outweigh the disadvantages and told this story in response.

> *Therapist:* Once upon a time there was a duck and he was just a duck. He was a real duck. He never was a person.
> *Patient:* What's the name of the story?

Therapist: The name of my story is: "The Duck and the Fairy God-mother." Okay? No, excuse me. I'm going to change the name: "The Duck and the Old Lady." Okay?

Patient: (laughs)

Therapist: "The Duck and the Old Lady" is the name of my story. Once upon a time there was a duck. And he was just a duck, a plain duck. He was a very nice duck but he thought it would be better not to be a duck. He thought it would be best to be a person. So he used to go around saying, "Quack, quack, quack, quack, quack quack," hoping he would find a fairy godmother. And he would sing a song and the song would go. How did the song go?

Patient (in singsong manner): "Quack, quack, quack, quack, quack, quack."

Therapist: He'd go, "Quack, quack. I wish I saw a fairy god-mother." He'd go, "Quack, quack, quack, quack, quack, quack, quack. Fairy godmother! Where's the fairy godmother?" No fairy godmother came.

Patient: Talk slow. The duck talks so fast, I can't hear you.

Therapist: He would say, "Quack, quack, quack."

Patient (joins in): "Where's my fairy godmother?"

Therapist: "Where's my fairy godmother?

Patient: And he was shaking his hands . . . (mumbles) . . .

Therapist: But he couldn't find any fairy godmother. Then one day he saw an old lady. She was walking by the river.

Patient: Did that old lady—was that old lady really a wicked witch?

Therapist: No.

Patient: Or a good witch?

Therapist: No, she was just an old lady, but this old lady . . .

Patient (interrupts): Did she have a wand?

Therapist: This old lady used to think that she was a fairy god-mother. She thought that maybe there was such a thing as a fairy godmother and she thought . . .

Patient (interrupts): You told—you told this the other day except it didn't have a duck in it.

Therapist: No. This is a different story. Do you want to hear my story?

Patient: Yes, but the other day you told it about the old woman.

Therapist: Yeah, but this is a different story about an old woman. Okay? Do you want to hear this one?

Patient: Yes.

Therapist: So the duck went over to her and he said, "Quack, quack, quack, quack. Fairy godmother, will you change me into a person?"

And she thought that she had magic powers so she said, "Okay." (Therapist waving imaginary stick over patient's head.) And she had a wand—she had a stick and she said to the duck, "Magic . . . magic . . . duck . . . duck, quack three times and I'll change you into a person. Quack three times." Okay, you make believe you're the duck.

Patient (while therapist rotates imaginary stick over his head): "Quack, quack, quack."

Therapist: And she waved it around and do you know what happened?

Patient: What?

Therapist: The duck still remained a duck!

Patient: (laughs)

Therapist: And she said, "Say quack again. Say quack harder."

Patient (yells): Quack!

Therapist: Harder!

Patient (yells louder): Quack!

Therapist: Harder!

Patient (yells again): Quack!

Therapist: Harder!

Patient (screams): Quack!

Therapist: And he still stayed a duck. And she got very angry . . . "Ooh, this magic wand! (striking the imaginary wand against a table) I'm hitting this magic wand. This magic wand (makes angry sounds) is no good! We'll try it again! Now you say quack again three times. Go ahead. Magic wand. . . .

Patient (while therapist is waving wand again over patient's head): "Quack, quack, quack."

Therapist: And he still remained a duck. And she got very . . . "This damn magic wand!" (Therapist angrily breaks the imaginary wand over his knee.) And she took it and threw it away. (flings the wand away): She said, "Wait, I'll get another magic wand." She came back with another one and she said, "I'm going to say a new thing (waving wand over patient's head). Abracadabra, hokus, pokus, turn this boy (sic, therapist's error) into a person. He's a duck!" What happened?

Patient: He still remained a duck?

Therapist: Right! And she said, "I can't stand these magic wands. Umph!" And she took it and she broke it on her knee (breaks wand on knee) and she threw it away (throws wand away)! She was very mad.

As she was standing there, a man came along and he saw her.

Patient: Who was that man?

Therapist (jumping up and down): And she was jumping up and down screaming and crying, and this man said to her—who was this man? He was just a man walking by, an old man. And he said, "What are you so mad about old lady?"

She said, "My magic wands don't work. I want to turn this duck into a boy, into a person."

And the man said, "There's no such thing as a magic wand."

And she said, "You know, I'm beginning to see that."

Patient (interrupts): In the other story there was a woman with a magic wand like that, but there was no man; there was an owl. There was no duck.

Therapist: Right. In the other story there was a wise old owl. Right.

Patient: And the boy.

Therapist: What's that?

Patient: And in the other story there was a boy who wanted to be turned into a duck, I think.

Therapist: Well, it was a different story, but let's talk about this one. Anyway, so this man said, "There's no such thing as magic wands."

And the old lady said, "You know, I'm beginning to see that. I thought that I would like to be a fairy godmother and do this duck a favor and turn him into a boy."

And the man said, "Well, why would you want to turn him into a boy? He's a perfectly fine duck!"

And the duck said, "No, I'm not! No, I'm not!"

And the man said, "Why? What's wrong with you?"

He said, "I don't speak too well."

Patient (with sigh of relief): He doesn't speak too well.

Therapist: Yeah. And he said, "That's the reason why you want to turn into a person? You can *learn* to speak well."

And the duck said, "No, I can't! No, I can't!"

What did the man say?

Patient: "Yep, you could."

Therapist: And what did the man say as to how he could learn to speak well?

Patient: By going to a speech teacher.

Therapist: Right! So what do you think the duck did?

Patient: Go to a duck speech teacher.

Therapist: He went to a duck speech teacher. He left the old lady who he realized could not really change him into a person. He was a duck. And he went to the speech teacher and then after that, it was very hard and it took a long time, but after that what happened?

Patient: He, he, he—oy, yoy yoy—he . . . (mumbles) . . .

Therapist: He what?

Patient: He, he . . .

Therapist: What happened after that?

Patient: He . . .

Therapist (interrupts): Forget something?

Patient: He . . . uh . . .

Therapist: What happened after he went to the speech teacher?

Patient: He (long pause) . . .

Therapist: Come on, you can . . .

Patient (interrupts): He could talk well.

Therapist: Right! Very good! He could talk well. He practiced very hard and then after that did he keep wishing then he would be a person?

Patient: No.

Therapist: He was happy he was a duck. And the lesson of that story is what? What are the lessons of that story? Can you figure them out?

Patient: How many . . . (mumbles) . . .

Therapist: The first lesson. What's the first lesson?

Patient: Uno (Spanish: *one*) lesson is . . .

Therapist (interrupts): Uno lesson.

Patient: Never think you can change your magic wand into a person or a duck.

Therapist: Right. There's no such thing as magic. There's no such thing as a magic wand. Okay. Come over here. What's the second lesson?

Patient: Number dos (Spanish: *two*) lesson is never cry—eey, yie, yie.

Therapist: Never cry. That's not a lesson. Sometimes people cry. That's perfectly all right. All right. Let me tell you the second lesson. The second lesson of that story is: If you are a duck and you have some trouble speaking, the best thing you can do is to what?

Patient: Is to go to a duck speech teacher or a regular speech teacher.

Therapist: Right. And practice hard and after that you'll be able to speak well.

Patient: The end.

Therapist: The end.

Patient: Could we stay here all day until I want to go home, until I get tired?

Therapist: Well, we'll stay a little while longer.

Patient: Goody!

Therapist: Right. Do you want to watch this program?

Patient (running to turn on TV monitor): Good-bye!

Therapist: Good-bye, everybody.

The purpose of my story is obvious. I attempted to impart the notion that there are no such things as magic cures and that a more practical and predictably effective course toward overcoming one's handicaps is through constructive action. The written transcript

cannot completely convey all the theatrical elements that I introduced in order to enhance the patient's interest in my story and
encourage receptivity to my therapeutic messages. The therapist
who is able to "ham it up" in this manner provides the patient with
a valuable therapeutic adjunct. The child was swept up by my wild
gestures and readily participated in the little play. His statement at
the end: "Could we stay here all day until I want to go home, until
I get tired?" confirms quite well the kind of enthusiasm that such
dramatizations can evoke.

When I started my story I was not completely clear about exactly how I was going to develop it. I did know, however, that it
was going to center on a denial of the efficacy of magic. When a
child asks me to tell the title of a story I generally provide one that
epitomizes the story's primary theme or message. In this case, the
patient's question caught me a little bit off guard because I had not
yet precisely formulated my story. Accordingly, I gave the title "The
Duck and the Fairy Godmother." I immediately recognized that this
title implied that there would actually be a fairy godmother in the
story. Accordingly, I quickly retracted the title and substituted "The
Duck and the Old Lady." Therapists should not hesitate to change
their minds in the course of storytelling if they suddenly realize that
they can do better for the patient by doing so. It is unrealistic to require of ourselves that we create, on the spur of the moment, pol-
ished theatrical performances or cohesively written stories. In the
split second between my stating the first title and then retracting it,
I decided that my story would include an old lady who aspired to be
a fairy godmother but who was unsuccessful. Hence, when I presented the second title I specifically omitted any reference to magic.

In the early part of my story the patient interrupted to point
out that there were similarities between the story I was telling and
a story I had told during a previous session. He was referring to a
story in which a wise old owl was the conveyor of my therapeutic
messages and that story as well dealt with the magic cure theme.
His recognition of the similarities well demonstrates that the messages I communicate in my stories do sink in and are remembered.

This principle is again demonstrated by the sequence presented below which took place nine days later. On this day, instead
of only the patient and his mother appearing for the session, his
father and two younger siblings (his six-year-old brother and four-
year-old sister) also appeared in the waiting room. The father was
about to take the younger siblings out for a walk while the patient
and his mother were in session with me. I invited the father to bring

the children in because of my previous experience that their participation might be useful. The children were quite enthusiastic about the idea because they had heard from their brother such wonderful tales about the exciting things that go on in my office. Also, they had listened to some of the audiotapes that were made during their brother's sessions and had enjoyed what they had heard. George's father, however, was somewhat hesitant to come in because he feared the younger children would be disruptive. Accordingly, I told the younger children that they could come into the room as long as they behaved themselves and that if they did so, they might be allowed to participate in some of the games that George and I played, but I could not promise for certain that they would be invited to join us. The children were quite cooperative and did not interrupt George when he told this story on the television program.

Therapist: Good morning, boys and girls, ladies and gentlemen. Today is Friday, the 20th of April, 1973, and I am happy to welcome you all once again to "Dr. Gardner's Make-Up-a-Story Television Program." Our quest today is now going to tell us another one of his own original made-up stories. You're on the air.

Patient: The name of the story is: "Animals Who Can't Talk and Animals Who Can Talk."

Therapist: "Animals Who Can't Talk and Animals Who Can Talk." Okay. This sounds like a very good title for a story. Go ahead.

Patient: Once there were two animals and they couldn't talk and on the farm and on that farm there were cows who couldn't talk and all animals who couldn't talk. And there was another farm far, far away—there was another farm—and on that farm animals could talk and those animals said to the other animals, "Buh, buh, buh, buh," and the other animals didn't understand those animals.

Therapist (interrupts): Excuse me, the animals who could talk or the animals who couldn't talk said, "Buh, buh, buh?"

Patient: The animals who could talk.

Therapist: Who could talk said, "Buh, buh, buh." Go ahead.

Patient: And the—what am I up to?

Therapist: You're up to—there were two farms. One farm had animals who couldn't talk and one farm had animals who could talk. And the animals who could talk said, "Buh, buh, buh," to the animals who couldn't talk. That's where you're at. Right?

Patient: (nods affirmatively)

Therapist: Now go ahead.

Patient: Then the animals who couldn't talk said (scratches ear)—

didn't say anything, just went like this. (Patient's arms outstretched, shrugs shoulders, palms up, and has wistful expression on face.) That's all. And they—the animals who could talk—didn't know what that meant. And then finally the animals who could talk thought that they were saying it wrong. Instead of saying, "Buh, buh, buh," they said, "How come you can't talk?"

Therapist: Go ahead.

Patient: And then the animals who couldn't talk said (moves lips), just opened their mouths.

Patient's mother: (Gestures that therapist look at patient.)

Therapist: Do that again. I wasn't looking. Your mother said I missed something. What about the animals who couldn't talk? What did they do?

Patient: (Moves lips and mouth without sound coming forth.)

Therapist: Okay. Then what happened?

Patient: And then the animals who could talk said, "Ha! You still can't talk and I was trying to make you talk. I'm going to get a fairy godmother." And he just sat there and he didn't call for a fairy godmother. He didn't wish for a fairy godmother.

Therapist: Who didn't wish for a fairy godmother?

Patient: The animals.

Therapist: Which ones?

Patient: The ones who could talk, to make the ones who couldn't talk, talk.

Therapist: Oh, the ones who could talk wanted to get a fairy godmother in order to make the ones who couldn't talk be able to talk. Is that it?

Patient: (nods affirmatively)

Therapist: Okay, then what happened?

Patient: When he was just standing—sitting on the porch waiting for a fairy godmother . . .

Therapist (interrupts): Who was standing waiting for a fairy godmother?

Patient: Uh (pauses).

Therapist: Who was waiting for the fairy godmother?

Patient: . . . (mumbles) . . .

Therapist: Who?

Patient: The . . . (mumbles) . . . peeg . . . or the giraffe.

Therapist: A peeg?

Patient: A pig!

Therapist: A pig! Was this one of the pigs who could or couldn't talk?

Patient: Who could.

Therapist: Who could talk.

Patient: Or it could be a giraffe.

Therapist: A giraffe who could talk. So a pig or a giraffe was waiting for the fairy godmother. Okay.

Patient: And they just sat there doing nothing. They were looking up in the sky saying, "What happened to my fairy godmother? I probably didn't wish for one or say it out loud." And then he began to scream, "Fairy godmother" so loud that all the animals who could talk and couldn't talk ran away.

Therapist: Why did they run away?

Patient: Because he screamed so loud.

Therapist: Then what happened?

Patient: And then he said . . .

Therapist (interrupts): Who's he?

Patient: And then the pig said, "Oh, wow, I really screamed loud that time. I scared all the animals who couldn't talk away. That's the name of the animals.

Therapist: What?

Patient: Couldn't Talk and Could Talk.

Therapist: Okay. His screams scared away all the animals who couldn't talk. Then what happened?

Patient: Then he said (in singsong manner), "Oh, I wish for a fairy godmother, a fairy godmother," and he sang and sang until he believed, until somebody, until he realized there's no such thing as a fairy godmother.

Therapist: Okay. You mean she never came?

Patient: No.

Therapist: Then what happened?

Patient: The end.

Therapist: Well, I have a question. What happened to the animals who couldn't talk? What happened to them?

Patient: They had to go to a teacher.

Therapist: Hh hmm.

Patient: They went like this (makes grimacing facial expressions) and the teacher couldn't understand what the animals were saying.

Therapist: So what happened then?

Patient: I'm all done.

Therapist: Well, did they learn to talk?

Patient: Yes. They said—they tried hard like this (makes facial contortions) and they made a couple of sounds: "Buh, buh, buh, yup, yup, yup," and then they started talking loud (voice gets louder): "Yup, yup, yup, yup, yup." And they talked so loud that they grew up to be a giant.

Therapist: Uh huh. I see. Okay. Is that the end of the story?

Patient: Yes.

Therapist: And what's the lesson of that story?

Patient: There are two lessons.

Therapist: What are the two lessons?

Patient: Never sit there but if you want a real fairy godmother don't believe in fairy godmothers. My third lesson is: *There's no such thing as fairy godmothers.*

The story demonstrates well how my messages from the sequence of nine days previously had been remembered by the patient and were retold in his story. One could argue that such repeating is not specifically therapeutic and that the child might be doing it merely to ingratiate himself with me. There is no question that this was probably going on. However, there is also no question that such repetition for the purpose of ingratiating the therapist is part of every patient's cure, regardless of age. It is hoped that the patient will reach the point at which new ways of thinking and doing things will be done for their own sake, rather than merely for the therapist's. In addition, I believe that George repeated my story because of his appreciation, at some level, that it had validity and that it offered him more promise for improvement than fairy godmothers.

Because the story had so many healthy elements, I decided not to alter it in my responding story. Rather, I decided to entrench the message by its repetition in the dramatic mode. The presence of George's younger siblings provided me with a source of willing recruits for participation in my planned theatrical performance.

Therapist: Okay. Now I'll tell you what. I think that was such a good story that instead of my making up a story, what I think we ought to do is let's make up a play. Okay? Do you want to make up a play in which we'll make up a play about your story? Do you want to do that?

Patient: What does that mean?

Therapist: Well, what we'll do is we'll act it out. We'll tell your story and we'll play the parts of different animals—you and me. Okay? Do you want to do that?

Patient: (nods affirmatively)

Therapist (points to sister and brother sitting in another part of room): Do you want your brother and sister to be in the play?

Patient: (nods affirmatively)

Therapist (speaking to brother and sister): Would you like to be in a play?

Voice heard from out of camera range: Yes.

Therapist: Okay, come on over here. We'll make a play now. I'll show you how we'll do it. (Sister Sue and brother Bob walk over to where patient and therapist are sitting. Therapist starts moving furniture around.) Let's make a play in which we have two farms. Come over here (motions to Sue and Bob to come closer). These are our two guests on our program today (has Sue and Bob face camera). These two guests are going to be in the play (moves microphone to side).

Patient: But how are you going to be by the microphone?

Therapist: The microphone will pick up our voices. Now here's what we're going to do. We're making believe that there are two farms. Okay?

Patient: (nods affirmatively)

Therapist: On one farm the animals can't talk and on the other farm the animals can talk. Now, let's make believe, first of all, the animals who can talk. Let's make some animal sounds (points to patient). What kind of animal sound do you want to make? What kind of animal sound?

Patient: (just stares in space)

Therapist (to patient while Sue and Bob just remain standing motionless): What animal sound do you want to make?

Patient: What kind of a sound . . .

Therapist (interrupts): Any sound.

Patient: does a giraffe make?

Therapist: I don't know. What kind of sound could a giraffe make?

Patient: (still pondering, while other children are still standing motionless)

Therapist: I don't really know. What's your guess? (after a pause) Well, Pick an animal whose sound you know.

Patient: A pig.

Therapist: Well, how does a pig go?

Patient: Oink, oink, oink, oink.

Therapist: Okay, so you'll be the pig. (turns to Bob) Now what animal do you want to be?

Bob: Dog.

Therapist: You'll be the dog. What sound does the dog make?

Bob: Ruff, ruff!

Therapist (turns to Sue): What animal do you want to be?

Sue (in low voice): A dog.

Therapist: A dog. What sound does a dog make?

Sue: Ruff, Ruff!

Therapist (to all three children): Okay, now, now all the animals make sounds. Let's make believe first we're the animals on the farm making the sounds. Okay, every animal make his own sound! Go ahead. Let's do it, (joins in with them) oink, oink, ruff, ruff.

Patient: Oink, Oink.

Sue: Ruff, ruff.

Bob: Ruff, ruff.

All: Oink, oink, ruff, ruff, oink, ruff, oink, ruff, etc.

Therapist (to Sue): Okay, let's hear you.

Sue: Ruff, ruff, ruff, ruff.

Therapist: Okay, Now those are all the talking animals. Now—turn around (twists Bob around toward camera) so everybody can see you on television. All right? Now (places Sue in one spot) you stand over here. Okay. Now you (places Bob on his left side) stand over here so you'll be seen on television. Now, so those are the animals who *can* talk.

Now, then, there are other animals who can't talk. They just go like (makes strained facial expression), "Mmmmmmmmmmm:" Okay (points to Bob), you do that. (Bob tries to imitate therapist.)

Patient (to therapist): I hear noise out of you.

Therapist: Yeah, but I'm not saying (points to Sue). Go ahead, you try words to do it.

Sue: (just stares at therapist)

Therapist (grimaces and strains face again, trying to evoke some kind of sound): Go ahead (pointing to patient), you try to do it.

Patient: (makes contorted and strained facial expression)

Therapist (joins patient and makes straining expression and sounds again): Now (placing right hand on Sue's shoulder and looking directly at her), you do that.

Patient (interrupts): They should be . . .

Therapist (interrupts while still looking at Sue): Go ahead.

Patient: . . . like this (strains face and clenches hands).

Therapist (again has strained facial expression as he joins in with patient): "Mmmmmmmmm," and they just can't talk. Then the animals — now the other animals come along and say, "Let's get a fairy godmother to help those animals talk." So let's call out for the fairy godmother. (shouts) "Fairy godmother."

Bob (joins in with therapist): " . . . godmother."

Therapist: Go ahead. Call out for her.

All children: "Fairy godmother."

Therapist (joins in): "Fairy godmother. Would you help those animals talk? (looks around at all the children) Go ahead, do it (points to patient). Yell out for the fairy godmother.

Patient (shouts): "Fairy godmother. Will you help those animals talk?"

Therapist (pointing to Sue): You say it.

Sue (in rushed, garbled voice): "Fairy godmother. Will you make those animals talk?"

Therapist (pointing to Bob): What about you?

Bob (shouts): "Fairy godmother. Will you make those animals talk?"

Therapist: All right. Let's look up there. (They all look up at ceiling.) Do you see any fairy godmothers up there?

Patient: No.

Bob: (points toward window): Look up there — nothing!

Therapist: Let's yell louder. Maybe she'll come.

All shouting together: Fairy godmother!

Therapist: Yell louder. Maybe she'll —

All (shouting even louder together): Fairy godmother!

Therapist (showing increasing anguish): Fairy godmother, fairy godmother. (looks all around) Do you see any fairy godmother?

Bob (turning around toward window and holding curtain open in one hand): No, she might be coming.

Patient: Just lights.

Therapist (talking to Bob and then turning toward window and puts hand on curtain): Do you think she may be out the window here? Let's look out.

Bob (as he separates curtain and looks out): She may be coming.

Therapist (to Bob): Well, look out here. Do you see any fairy godmothers out there?

Bob (looking out of window): No.

Patient and Sue: (looking out window from where they are standing)

Therapist (to patient and Sue): Do you see any fairy godmothers?

Sue: (nods head negatively)

Patient: I only see the light but no fairy godmother.

Therapist: Let's try once more. Maybe she'll come.

All (shouting loudly together): Fairy godmother! Fairy godmother. (all look around and up at ceiling)

Therapist: Will you come down and make the animals talk? (with dismayed expression on face) I don't see her. Do you see her?

Children: (seem completely absorbed and interested in what therapist is saying)

Therapist: Now what's going to happen? Now here are all the animals—let's make believe that we're all the animals who can't talk. Okay? (makes strained facial expression)

Children: (imitate facial expression)

Bob: (bends down for a second and pretends he's a dog)

Therapist: "We can't talk." Then what are those animals going to do? (directs attention toward patient) What's going to happen now? What are they going to do?

Patient: I think the other animals will tell where they know a good speech teacher.

Therapist: Right! So all the animals who can't talk go to a speech teacher. (looking at all three children) Who wants to make believe that they're the speech teacher? Who wants to be the speech teacher.

Patient: (raises hand)

Therapist (pointing to patient): You be the speech teacher. Okay, we three are animals. (begins strained facial expression and makes garbling sounds again, and points to Bob) You do it.

Bob: (makes garbling sounds)

Therapist (points to Sue): Okay, you do it.

Sue: (nods head up and down, smiling, tries to imitate garbling sounds)

Patient (looking apprehensive): What should I do?

Therapist: Well, what does a speech teacher do?

Patient: Help people?

Therapist: All right. So what are you going to do?

Patient: Help.

Therapist: Okay, How are you going to help us speak?

Patient: By teaching you how to.

Therapist: Okay, make believe that you're the speech teacher teaching us how to.

Patient: Now say "Moo."

Therapist (pointing to Bob): You try it first. You try to say "moo."

Bob: Moo.

Therapist (all excited): Hey, he said "Moo!" (pointing to Sue) Now you try it. (talking to patient) Teach her to say something.

Sue: Moo.

Patient: Say "Good."

Sue: Good.

Therapist: Okay, now tell me to say something.

Patient: Good, bad, and hat.

Therapist: What is that again?

Patient: Good, bad, and hat.

Therapist: Good, bad, and hat. Okay. (with strained facial expression) G...g...g It's very hard—you see, it's very hard to learn how to speak. It isn't easy. G...g...goo...goo...good. Hey, I said it. Hey, I can start to speak! (talking directly to patient) Now you say to the children, "It takes a lot of practice and you've got to work very hard.

Patient: It takes a lot of practice and you got to work very hard.

Therapist (looking around at all three children): So, all of us, let's say we work very hard for a long time and we're all learning, and we can speak now. Okay?

Patient: (nods affirmatively)

Therapist: Okay. So everybody speak. Speak! Moo, moo.

Bob: Oink, Oink.

Therapist: Oink, moo, meow, oink.

Bob: Ruff, ruff.

Therapist: Ruff, ruff, ruff, meow.

Sue: (seems to be too entranced to join in making animal sounds)

Therapist: Hey, we're all speaking! Thank you very much, speech teacher (shakes patient's hand) for teaching us how to speak. (shakes hand again) Thank you very much. Let's shake this speech teacher's hand.

Bob: (shakes patient's hand)

Sue: (shakes patient's hand)

Therapist: Okay. And that's the end of the program. Let's say good-bye. The end.

Bob and Sue: (wave good-bye)

Patient: So short?

Therapist: So short?

Patient: Yes.

Therapist: Do you want to make it longer?

Patient: No.

Therapist: Do you want to add a part?

Patient: Noooooo!

Therapist: Okay. Do you want to watch this?

All: Yes.

Therapist: Raise your hand if you want to watch this. (patient and Bob raise hands)

Sue: (just looks amused and pensive)

Therapist: Okay, we'll watch.

Again, the written transcript cannot fully convey the children's involvement in the play. They were all genuinely swept up in it and found it exciting and absorbing. The patient's comment at the end, "So short," was only final confirmation that he was having a good time and that the experience was a meaningful one for him. I added nothing new in the way of content; rather, I attempted to entrench the healthy message from his story in a powerful and absorbing manner. This experience marked a turning point in his therapy; following it there was very little talk of magic. This is not to say that there was absolutely no talk about magic; it is unrealistic to expect to remove such an attractive adaptation entirely. In fact, it is probable that none of us give up such hopes completely no matter how old we get. The important thing was that it was no longer a primary mode of adaptation for George.

THREE

Mutual Storytelling Derivative Games

When they're offered to the world in merry guise,
Unpleasant truths are swallowed with a will —
For he who'd make his fellow, fellow, fellow creatures wise
Should always gild the philosophic pill!

William S. Gilbert
Yeoman of the Guard

INTRODUCTION

During the first few years of utilization of the mutual storytelling technique, I found some children to be inhibited with regard to their freedom to create and verbalize stories. Accordingly, I began to think of other ways that could be useful in facilitating children's providing me with such material. Recognizing that children enjoy immensely playing board-type games, especially those in which there is a competitive element, a series of games was devised. These games involve traditional board-game materials such as dice, reward chips, and playing pawns. The introduction of the reward chips serves to enhance children's motivation to provide projective material. Whereas in the mutual storytelling technique no rewards are provided, in these games token chips are given, and the winner (the person who has accumulated the most reward chips) receives a prize.

Although reward chips are given, it would be an error for the reader to conclude that these games represent a kind of "behavior therapy." These games share with behavior therapy the use of reward chips, but the similarity ends there. In behavior therapy one uses rewards in order to change behavior at the manifest level. Behavior therapists differ with regard to their views about the presence or absence of unconscious processes and whether, if present, they play a role in symptom formation. But they are in agreement in not generally giving significant attention to unconscious processes in the therapeutic process. Many take the position that the symptom is basically the disease and its removal represents a cure.

My use of chips here serves an entirely different purpose. I am using them to reward the child for providing self-created free associations and stories, for psychotherapeutic use. My utilization of reward chips is based on the belief that unconscious processes do exist and that the understanding of them (especially by the therapist) plays an important role in the therapeutic process. In short, I am using reward chips for the elicitation of psychodynamically meaningful material, material derived often from unconscious processes. Behavior therapists, in contrast, use the reward chips to change behavior at the manifest level. We share in common the use of reward chips, but we use them for entirely different purposes.

It would be an error, also, if the reader were to conclude that I have absolutely no conviction for behavior therapy. This is not the case. One cannot deny the importance of positive and negative reinforcement in human development. One of the primary reasons why children are "good" is that they hope to gain the affection and love of their child rearers; and one of the main reasons why they inhibit themselves from being "bad" is their fear of loss of such affection. When two-year-old Johnny decides not to run into the street, it is not because he is aware of the fact that he may be endangering his life; rather, he restricts himself from doing so because of his anticipation that significant caretaking individuals will react with strongly negative feedback and even painful physical responses (a slap on the backside or a not so gentle wrenching of his arm) if he does so. The experimental rat presses the bar in order to obtain food pellets and will drop down to the random level of bar pressing frequency if the pellets are permanently withdrawn.

So ubiquitous is this pleasure-pain principle that one could argue that behavior therapy is basically nature's form of treatment. In part, I agree that it is. However, the human brain is so complex and sophisticated that other mechanisms, beyond pain and pleasure, are operative, and so more sophisticated methods of psychotherapy are warranted when psychological disorders are present. This does not mean that we must select between the two. Rather, we can combine both approaches.

Furthermore, I generally prefer to utilize behavioral therapy techniques in the context of my psychotherapeutic program. I consider their isolated utilization to be somewhat artificial and sterile. For example, one could help an agoraphobic woman desensitize herself to her fear of open places by suggesting that she force herself to tolerate increasingly the fears that she experiences when she sets forth from her home. This would basically be the traditional behavior therapy approach. One might even try to quantify the times of exposure on a chart while pointing out to the patient her progressive improvement. My own approach would be to focus on what I consider to be the primary factors that are contributing to the agoraphobia, factors such as excessive dependency on the people with whom she lives and fears of asserting herself as an adult in a world of adults. This would not preclude, however, my encouraging desensitization and some kind of more informal assessment of her progress. Even the most staunch subscribers to the psychoanalytic theory would not dispute the value of desensitization. The crucial question is whether one believes that one can get a significant degree of symptomatic alleviation over a long period by merely focusing on the removal of the agoraphobic symptom. I believe that one is not likely to achieve long-term improvement by the behavior therapeutic technique alone. Even if one does, I would still consider the therapeutic work to have been only partially completed because the underlying factors that have contributed to the formation of the symptom have not been dealt with.

These games also make use of the competitive element. Basically I am using competition to enhance the child's motivation to acquire chips. There are some readers who probably would take issue with me on this point because of their belief that competition is basically a dehumanizing experience that we would do best to dispense with entirely. Obviously, I do not share this view. I think that one must differentiate between healthy and unhealthy competition, between competition that is humane and competition that is inhumane. In healthy competition one strives to win, but one still has respect for one's opponent. In unhealthy competition, the primary purpose is to degrade and destroy for a variety of pathological purposes such as hostility release, compensation for feelings of inadequacy, and self-aggrandizement. At any particular time there are thousands of people working in laboratories hoping someday to win a Nobel prize. Although only an extremely small fraction of these individuals will attain their goal, most would agree that society is a better place for the existence of the prize. And one could say the same thing about a wide variety of other awards in the arts, sciences, and other fields of endeavor—awards that have served to enhance human motivation and striving toward excellence. If not for healthy competition, we might still be living in caves. If not for unhealthy competition, many people who reached premature death might have lived longer lives.

When using the games described in this chapter, the therapist should keep in mind these differentiations and do everything possible to keep the competition at a healthy level. Ideally, the patient and therapist will be so swept up in the game that both will forget whose chance it was and who is to get the reward chip. But even when this ideal is not reached, the therapist should strive to make the game so exciting that the child will frequently forget that it was his or her turn. When the child does appear to be more interested in acquiring chips than providing psychodynamically meaningful material, the therapist does well to discourage such preoccupations with comments such as: "Wait a minute. Don't throw the dice yet. I haven't finished giving my answer." "Hold on, I'd like to ask you a question about what you've just said." and "That's a very good beginning for your story. Now let's hear the middle and the end of your story. Every story has a beginning, a middle, and an end."

The general principle I follow when playing these games is that the child receives one chip for making a statement and two for telling a story. The statement option is introduced for children who are so restricted that they cannot relate a self-created story. As mentioned, the material so elicited should be used as a point of departure for various kinds of psychotherapeutic interchange. Often, the therapist may wish to respond with a story that is created to address itself to pathological manifestations in the child's story. For some children one might want to discuss the child's story at the symbolic level with comments such as: "Why did the cat run away from the rabbit?" and "Was there something else the cat could have done, something better than running away?" The rare child who is interested in an introspective inquiry, might be asked: "Is there anything in your story about the three squirrels that is like what's happening in your house?"

THE BOARD OF OBJECTS GAME

In *The Board of Objects Game*, designed with N. I. Kritzberg, a board of sixty-four squares (a standard checker board serves well) or a larger board of one hundred squares is used. In each square is placed a small figurine of the type readily purchased in most stores selling children's games and equipment (Figure 3.1). The figurines include family members, zoo animals, farm animals, small vehicles (police car, fire engine, ambulance, etc.), members of various occupations (doctor, nurse, policeman, etc.), and a wide assortment of other common objects (baby bottle, knife, gun, lipstick, trophy, lump of brown clay, etc.). A pair of dice is used with one face of each die colored red. Last, there is a treasure chest filled with token reward chips.

The game begins with the child's throwing the dice. If a red side lands face up (and this should occur once every three throws of the dice) the child can select any object from the board. If the child can say anything at all about the object, he or she gets one reward chip. If the child can tell a story about the object, he or she gets *two* reward chips. The therapist plays similarly and the winner is the one who has accumulated the most chips when the alloted time is over. If a person is "lucky" and both red sides land face up, the player can select two objects and gets double rewards. The player may tell one story in which both objects are included or two separate stories. When commenting on, or telling a story about, an object it is preferable for the player to hold it and sometimes even move it about in accordance with what is going on in the story. The child will often do this spontaneously and the therapist should do so as well in appreciation of the enhanced efficacy of the dramatized communication. The therapist's various gestures, animal sounds, vocal imitations, accents, etc. can further involve the child and enhance receptivity to the therapeutic messages. After being used, the figurine can either be replaced on the board or placed on the side, depending upon the preference of the players.

Although the figurines are selected so as to elicit fantasies cov-

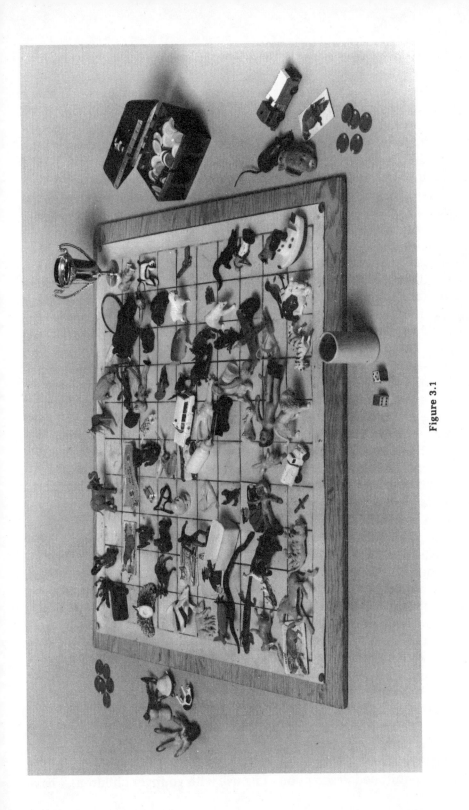

Figure 3.1

ering a wide range of issues usually encountered in most children's therapy, their exact nature, form, and variety is not crucial. The pressure of unconscious material to be released in a form specifically meaningful for the child is far greater than the power of the facilitating stimulus to distort the projected material. Accordingly, the therapist need not be too concerned about the selection of objects if he or she wishes to put together such a game. The usual variety of such figurines found in most toy stores will serve well.

Again, the therapist should try to create an atmosphere in which conversations may take place about the comments made or stories told; rather than one in which there is fierce competition for the accumulation of chips. The therapist plays in accordance with the same rules to create stories of his or her own that are either specifically related to the comments or stories just related by the child or else relevant in other ways to the child's life and problems.

The game is a very attractive one and it is a rare child who does not respond in the affirmative when shown it and asked: "Would you like to play this game with me?" Children below five or six, who have not yet reached the point where they can appreciate meaningfully the rules and organization of standard board games, will still usually want to "play." Some will enjoy throwing the dice until they get a red and will then choose an object. Such younger children may not be able to tell well-organized stories but may still provide meaningful, although fragmented, fantasies—especially because there is a reward chip that can be obtained for such revelations. The therapist must try to select from the disorganized fantasies those threads or patterns that are atypical, idiosyncratic, or pathological, and then use these as foci for his or her own responding comments. Often such younger children will be content to just play, fantasize, and collect chips without giving the therapist his or her turn. Generally, in such situations, I allow the child to tell a few "stories"—by which time I have gotten enough material to create one of my own. I then invoke my right to take my turn to tell stories and use the opportunity to relate my responding messages, either in story or nonstory allegory.

When the allotted time is up, the person with the most chips takes a prize from the box of *Valuable Prizes* (Figure 3.2).

The aforementioned "rules" are those that I have found most useful. However, the therapist may wish to utilize his or her own variations and I, too, at times have modified the game (as in the aforementioned description of its use with younger children). I have

Figure 3.2

found the game particularly useful with children at the kindergarten to second-grade level. At that age their reading ability is usually not great enough for them to play some of the more sophisticated games I describe in this chapter. Yet they do appreciate game structure and so generally become absorbed. At about the age of nine or ten, most children consider the game "babyish" and prefer the more advanced games described herein.

Clinical Example

The Case of Norman (The Cowboy Whose Gun Was Missing)
Norman, a five-and-a-half-year-old boy, presented with a history of lag in his developmental milestones and coordination deficits. He had a tendency to withdraw and to "tune out," especially when an activity might expose his deficits. At such times he seemed to be in another world. A problem that was particularly apparent at the time the interchange below took place was inhibition of self-assertion. He could not fight back when teased by other children; accordingly he was being scapegoated.

The patient often spontaneously told stories about the various figurines on the *Board of Objects* without formally playing the game. The cowboy, which he chose to talk about in the interchange below, had a removable holster belt attached to which were two holsters with guns inside. In order to remove the belt, however, one had to pull the top half of the figurine away from the bottom half, to which it was attached by a small plug. If the holster belt were so removed and then the two halves of the body replaced, a waistline defect was still present where the holster belt had been. This is the interchange that occurred regarding the cowboy.

> *Therapist:* Hello, today is Monday, August 28th, 1972, and I'm here with Norman and he and I are going to play a game with these objects. Norman, can you pick one? The storytelling game. Okay. What is that?
> *Patient:* A cowboy.
> *Therapist:* Okay, that's a cowboy. What are you going to tell me about the cowboy?
> *Patient:* Cowboys have guns.
> *Therapist:* They have guns. Yeah.
> *Patient:* And they shoot.
> *Therapist:* Yeah. Go ahead.

Patient: Make believe he took his pants off.

Therapist: Okay.

Patient: He took his pants off.

Therapist: Yeah.

Patient: If he take his holsters with it only would that be as far as it would be?

Therapist: If you take his holster off what? I'm not clear what you're saying.

Patient: I think I'll try taking. . . .

Therapist: Go ahead. Now what? You took off his holsters. Right?

Patient: Right.

Therapist: Now what did you ask me about that, about taking off his holster? I didn't understand your question. What was your question?

Patient: Is this as far as it goes when you keep the gun on but you take the holsters off?

Therapist: Yep. Right. You mean does the body go together with the feet after you take the holsters away?

Patient: Yeah.

Therapist: No, it doesn't. There's still a space there. What do you think about that?

Patient: Why is there still a space?

Therapist: Because that cowboy was made so he should have guns and when he doesn't have his guns his body and his feet don't go together. That's the way they made him. Do you know why they made him that way?

Patient: Why?

Therapist: What do you think? Why do you think they made him so that the gun should be there? Hh hmm?

Patient: Mmm.

Therapist: Why do you think they made him that way?

Patient: I don't know.

Therapist: Hh hmm?

Patient: I don't know!

Therapist: Does a cowboy need guns?

Patient: Yeah.

Therapist: What does he need them for?

Patient: Shooting.

Therapist: Now do you know why they made him with guns? Why do you think?

Patient: I don't know.

Therapist: What are the guns for?

Patient: Shooting.

Therapist: And why does he do that?

Patient: In case someone starts to bother him.

Therapist: Right, in case someone starts to bother him. Right. So what can he do in case. . . .

Patient (interrupting): Some Indians have bow and arrows.

Therapist: Right. Hh hmm. That's right.

Patient: Did you ever see a bow and arrow?

Therapist: Of an Indian? Sure. What would happen to that cowboy if he didn't have his guns?

Patient: I don't know.

Therapist: What would happen now? You say the guns are good because if someone starts to bother him then he could use them. Right?

Patient: Right.

Therapist: Now what would happen to him if he didn't have his guns?

Patient: If he had a bow and arrow (pauses) . . .

Therapist: Yeah and then what?

Patient: If someone comes along . . . (pauses) . . .

Therapist: Yeah.

Patient: . . . and bothers an Eskimo.

Therapist: If someone comes along and bothers an Eskimo? Is that what you said?

Patient: He said, "If you don't go away, I'll kill you with this spear!"

Therapist: All right. Who says that? Who said that?

Patient: The Eskimo.

Therapist: Is the Eskimo the same as the Indian or is he somebody different?

Patient: He's somebody different.

Therapist: Okay. So what good is the spear then? How does the spear help the Eskimo?

Patient: He hunts with the spear.

Therapist: Right. What else does it do for him? How else does it help him?

Patient: I don't know.

Therapist: What did you say before about what the Eskimo does with his spear?

Patient: Hunts.

Therapist: Anything else?

Patient: Yes.

Therapist: What?

Patient: "If you don't go away I'll kill you with this spear."

Therapist: Right. And what is the person trying to do who the Eskimo says that to—the person to whom the Eskimo says, "If you don't go away I'll kill you with this spear"? What is that person trying to do to the Eskimo? Huh?

Patient: Trying to shoot him.

Therapist: All right. Now what about the cowboy and his gun? What is the good of the guns? What would happen to the cowboy if he didn't have his guns?

Patient (accidentally drops the holster belt on the rug and can't find it): The guns disappear into the rug.

Therapist: Oh my, we can't find it.

Patient: I got a G.I. Joe at home.

Therapist: I want to ask you a question that you're not answering.

Patient: But he's a bigger G.I. Joe. These are smaller G.I. Joes.

Therapist: All right. I want to ask you one question now. What happens to the cowboy if he doesn't have his guns?

Patient: If he doesn't have—if he left his guns at his ranch . . .

Therapist (interrupting): What would happen to him?

Patient: He would have to go back to his ranch.

Therapist: Why would he have to go back?

Patient: To get his guns.

Therapist: What does he need them for?

Patient: He says, "If you don't go away I'll shoot you."

Therapist: Right, if people bother him. Right? Is that right? Huh? Oh, here's the gun. Is that right that if people bother him he'll have the gun?

Patient: Hh hmm.

Therapist: Now why did they make this cowboy with guns then? Why did they make him with guns?

Patient: And then another boy comes along.

Therapist: Yeah and then.

Patient: "Then if you don't go away I'll jump on you." (hums to self) (puts down the cowboy and picks up an airplane)

Therapist: What happened there?

Patient: New airplane and then he flew . . . (makes airplane sounds) . . .

Therapist: Then what happened?

Patient: And then the propeller breaks off.

Therapist: Then what happens?

Patient: And then the propeller broke my—and then his father . . .

Therapist: His father what?

Patient: Glues it back on.

Therapist: Hh hmm. And then what happens?

Patient: So it can never grow, so it cannot, so it can never, so it can't . . .

Therapist: Can't what?

Patient: So it can never—so the propeller can never come off again.

Therapist: Uh huh. Did he watch it himself to make sure that it didn't come off?

Patient: Yeah.

In this interchange I did not directly tell a story; rather, I tried to introduce my therapeutic communications in the context of the discussion about the cowboy and, subsequently, the Indians and Eskimo. I tried to communicate the importance of weapons in defending oneself. It was hoped that Norman would utilize this information in more effectively asserting himself. And this is what ultimately happened. Sequences such as these were contributory toward the patient's ultimately asserting himself more effectively with peers.

Some readers may have wondered why I did not make any comments about the use of guns as lethal weapons and their inappropriateness as a first line of defense (if not a last line of defense). At the time of this interchange (1972), I was not as appreciative as I am now of the insidious influence of gunplay in childhood. Had this interchange occurred at the time of this writing, I would have emphasized that guns are just about the worst way of defending oneself and that they should only be used as a last resort and only then under extreme circumstances. I have come to appreciate that their utilization by children in "war games" contributes to the frivolous attitude that many individuals in our society have toward murder. It would be an error for the reader to conclude that I consider toy guns to play a central role in adult homicide. People who are homicidal generally are so because of severe psychiatric disturbance that has its roots in formidable family difficulties during childhood. Although the influence of childhood war games is small, it is nevertheless operative.

The interchange demonstrates well how many children of this age (including those without neurological impairment) will introduce new figures into the conversation without informing the listener of their appearance in his or her mind. This is what happened here with the sudden introduction of the Eskimo about whom I had heard nothing previously. However, the Eskimo and his spear certainly served as well as the Indian with his bow and arrow and the cowboy with his guns to not only manifest the patient's inhibition in expressing hostility but served as well as excellent objects for my own communications.

At the end of the interchange the patient suddenly put down the cowboy and picked up a toy airplane. While flying it in the air he spoke about how the propeller had broken off and then how his father fixed it so it would never come off again. Classical psychoanalysts might consider this aspect of the child's story to represent a reaction formation or an "undoing" of castration anxiety. Breaking off of the propeller, according to this theory, would symbolize castration and the father's repairing it would represent the boy's fantasy that his father would undo the trauma.

I am dubious about this possible explanation. I think a more reasonable explanation is that it represents the boy's view that his father can correct and/or repair any injuries that may befall him. Another possible explanation is that the boy's father represents the therapist whose story had just served to help him feel more intact and helped him compensate for the feelings of impotence he felt prior to our interchange. Because of my uncertainty regarding the meaning of the story, I chose not to respond to it. Because I had already provided what I considered to be meaningful therapeutic communications, I had no trouble not doing so. Also, I have found that "overloading" can dilute and undermine previous messages that may have been effective.

THE THREE GRAB-BAG GAMES

The Bag of Toys Game

The games described in this section are attractive in that they appeal to the child's traditional enjoyment of the grab-bag game in which the child closes his or her eyes and pulls out an unknown object from a bag. In each, one reward chip is given for a simple response and/or two if the player can tell a story about the object that has been taken from the bag. The therapist enhances the child's curiosity and enthusiasm by occasional warnings not to peek and by exhibiting excitement him- or herself when it is the therapist's own turn. The reward chips are contained in a treasure chest, which serves to further enhance their value. Again, the winner is the player who has accumulated the most chips at the end of the allotted time and he or she selects a prize from the same box of prizes (Figure 3.2) described for previous games.

The *Bag of Toys Game* (Figure 3.3) requires a bag clearly labeled BAG OF TOYS containing about forty to fifty figurines of the kind used in *The Board of Objects Game* (Figure 3.1). When putting his or her hand into the bag, the child is warned against peeking ("Keep your eyes closed. Remember, it's against the rules of the game to peek."), and spending time feeling the objects is also discouraged ("No fair feeling. Just pick out one of the objects."). After the object has been selected and used as a focus for comment and/or story, it is laid aside rather than returned to the bag. Again, the child will often add dramatic elements to the story and it behooves the therapist to do so as well. As is true for the other grab-bag games, the child's comments are used as a point of departure for psychotherapeutic interchanges.

Clinical Example: The Case of Bernard (Let Sleeping Dogs Lie, But Give Them a Bone)   Bernard entered treatment at the age of seven and a half because of significant classroom difficulties. He was disruptive in the classroom, fought frequently with his classmates, was not attentive to his studies, and concentrated poorly. Although very bright, he was not doing well academically. At home he was frequently argumentative and often entered into power struggles with his parents. The parents often used him as a focus for their own marital conflict.

During his third session, the following interchange occurred while Bernard and I were playing *The Bag of Toys Game*.

> *Therapist:* Okay, ladies and gentleman. This is Bernard and the date is April 19, 1974. Okay, you go first. No looking. Close your eyes. You can only open your eyes after you take the thing out of the bag.
> *Patient:* (reaches into bag and pulls out a dog figurine)
> *Therapist:* What's that?
> *Patient:* A dog.
> *Therapist:* A dog. Okay. Now if you can say anything at all about that dog you get one chip. But if you want to tell a story about that dog, a completely made-up story, you get two chips.
> *Patient:* Once upon a time there was this dog. So this dog went away with his master. He was looking for hunting and they were hunting for ducks.
> *Therapist:* Go ahead.
> *Patient:* And when they came back he went to sleep.
> *Therapist:* Hh hmm.
> *Patient:* And after he woke up he got a bone and then he went back to sleep again.

Figure 3.3

Therapist: Excuse me. I'm a little confused. He went hunting with his master for ducks and then he went to sleep and when he got up there was a bone there for him?

Patient: Yeah.

Therapist: What about the—is that the whole story?

Patient: No.

Therapist: Okay. Go ahead.

Patient: And then he went back to sleep.

Therapist: Hh hmm.

Patient: Then he woke up and he went around with a boy.

Therapist: Hh hmm.

Patient: And he was walking him with the leash.

Therapist: The boy was walking this dog. Yeah. Go ahead.

Patient: And the boy hurt the dog.

Therapist: Go ahead.

Patient: He had to go to the, the—he had to go where? Where's the place that dogs have to go to when they're sick?

Therapist: Oh, a veterinarian?

Patient: Yeah.

Therapist: Well, how did the boy hurt the dog? What happened?

Patient: He was pulling on the leash too hard and his neck started to hurt.

Therapist: Go ahead. And they went to the vet.

Patient: And he fixed his neck up. And it took two days.

Therapist: Uh huh.

Patient: And then he went back and he had a bone, another bone.

Therapist: Uh huh.

Patient: And that's the end.

Therapist: Okay. Good.

Patient: I get two chips.

Therapist: Two chips. Right. Now it's my chance.

Patient: I'm winning.

Therapist: What? You're winning. All right. But I go now (reaches into Bag of Toys). Whoops. What do I have here? (picks out a boy figurine) I've got a . . .

Patient (interrupts): It's a boy. Are you going to tell a story?

Therapist: Yeah. Right. I don't have to, but I want to. The same rules hold for me. It's a game. If I can say anything about the boy I get one chip, but if I can tell a story about the boy I get two.

Patient: If it's a tie then you mean we . . .

Therapist (interrupts): Then we both get prizes. Right, if it's a tie. Okay.

The patient's story presents two themes, both of which were relevant to Bernard's difficulties. The dog's main activity appears to be sleeping. Although there is some mention of his going with his master and hunting for ducks, the emphasis is on his sleeping and on his acquiring a bone. The issue of his working for his reward is deemphasized. This quality reflected well Bernard's attitude toward his schoolwork and complying with his parents' requests that he perform chores around the home. He much preferred to shirk responsibilities.

In addition the story exhibits the magic cure fantasy so frequently seen in children during the early phases of treatment. It is especially common among children, like Bernard, who do not wish to apply themselves. The dog is injured, goes to a vet, and is cured in two days. Little is said about any efforts on the dog's part to cooperate or inconvenience himself during the course of his treatment. The way in which the dog got sick is also of psychodynamic interest. We are told that the boy was pulling on the dog's leash too hard and this hurt the dog's neck. I believe that this image symbolized Bernard's relationship with his mother, who was somewhat rigid in her handling of him. Although she nagged, in part, in order to get him to do his homework and household chores, there was no question that her standards were high and she would have been "on his back" even if he were more receptive to her requests. She would insist, for instance, that he finish every bit of food on his plate and was rigid with regard to his bedtime. It was not surprising then that Bernard exhibited this fantasy. Depicting himself as a dog might also have been a reflection of his feelings of low self-worth.

It was with this understanding of Bernard's story that I told mine.

> *Therapist:* Once upon a time there was a boy and he had a dog and this dog went out with him hunting, but instead of—they were going to go duck hunting—and when they got to the place where they were to hunt ducks, this dog suddenly decided to go to sleep. And the boy said, "Hey, come on. I brought you out here to hunt ducks, to help me hunt ducks. You're not doing anything."
>
> And the dog just ignored him completely and went to sleep. And as the dog was sleeping he was dreaming that when he woke up there would be a big nice juicy bone there as a kind of surprise. And when he woke up, he looked around and he smelled around and there was no bone, and he was kind of disappointed. And the dog said to the boy, "Do you have a bone?"
>
> And the boy said, "I would have given you a very nice juicy bone

had you helped me with the hunting for ducks, but you didn't want to do that. Instead you just went to sleep. I'm not going to give you a reward." Do you know what a reward is? What's a reward?

Patient: It's something that you do very good on and you get something.

Therapist: Right. It's kind of a prize or present for doing something. He said, "I'm not going to give you a bone. You didn't help me hunt ducks. You just went to sleep."

Well, anyway, as they were walking home the leash that the boy had the dog on got caught in a bush. It stretched and it injured the dog's neck. The boy didn't want to injure the dog. It was one of these accidents that sometimes happen. Anyway, they had to go to a vet. The vet said to the boy and the dog, "Now look I'm going to give you some medicine. You have to take this three times a day." And also he said to the dog, "You have to do certain exercises with your neck in order to help the muscles get better and the tissues get better."

So they took the bottle of pills and when the boy gave the dog the first pill, the dog didn't want to take it. And the boy said, "Listen, if you want to get better, you'd better take these pills."

The dog said, "Nah, I don't have to take those pills.

Patient: Dogs can talk?

Therapist: Well, you know, in my story a dog can talk. It's a make-believe story. And the boy said, "What about those exercises that the doctor said you should do, you know, stretch your neck and move it in different directions so that the muscles will get strong?"

He said, "I don't have to do that."

Well, a week later the dog had not taken any of the medicine and the dog had not done any of the exercises, and they went back to the vet and the vet said, "It doesn't look very good here. It doesn't look very good at all. Have you been taking your medicine?"

And the dog said, "Ah, I don't need that medicine."

And the vet said, "Have you been doing the exercises?"

And the dog said, "Well, I'm kind of busy."

He said, "Well, it's up to you. If you take the medicine and do the exercises your neck will get better. It's not going to get better on its own. It just doesn't happen like that, by sitting there and doing nothing. The only way that neck is going to get better is if you do the exercises and take the medicine." So what do you think happened?

Patient: He took the medicine.

Therapist: Well, he didn't like it. He didn't like it because he had to think about it three times a day, but he realized that the vet was right. And what do you think he did about the exercises?

Patient: He did them.

Therapist: Yeah. He found that the more he did the exercises, the faster his neck got better. And the lesson of that story is—well, actually there are two lessons to that story. One has to do with the duck hunting. What do you think the lesson of that part of the story is?

Patient: That if your neck gets hurt . . .

Therapist (interrupts): No, the duck hunting part. The story has two lessons. What do you think the lesson is about the duck hunting?

Patient: Hmm. I don't know.

Therapist: Well, what did we learn from that about—remember the boy and the dog and the hunting?

Patient: Oh, yeah, I remember.

Therapist: Okay. Go ahead.

Patient: The boy went duck hunting with his dog and the dog didn't want to go duck hunting, and he fell asleep. He wanted a bone, but in the morning when he woke up the dog found that there was no bone.

Therapist: So what did he learn from that?

Patient: He learned that if you do something the other person will get a bone.

Therapist: Put that in other words. I'm not sure I understand you.

Patient: If you help another person with hunting then you will get something.

Therapist: Right! You don't get something for nothing. If you're just going to sleep you're not going to get any of the rewards or prizes or things that come to those who work at it. That's the first lesson. So if you're going duck hunting, and if you're a dog, and you're helping a boy hunt ducks, he's going to be very unhappy with you if you don't work and he won't give you any presents, prizes, or rewards.

The second lesson is that if you are sick, if you have some problem like your neck is injured, you just can't sit around and wait for it to get better; you have to do the things the doctor says if you really want to get better. Usually things don't get better just by doing nothing. You have to do something about them. The end. Okay. I get two chips. Huh?

Patient: (nods affirmatively)

In my responding story I communicated two messages to alter the unrealistic views of the world that Bernard held. I have found that such communications can be quite helpful in reducing such magical views of the world. I did not deal extensively with the issue of Bernard's mother's nagging him, as symbolized by the boy's pulling the dog's leash too hard. In my story the neck is injured by accident. I attempted here to convey to Bernard a feeling of his mother's psychological blindness with regard to this trait. More importantly, however, I was dealing with this directly with her and she was quite capable of reducing some of her pressures on him. Accordingly, I did not introduce anything into the story encouraging Bernard to handle this problem. In addition, it is unwise to try to introduce simultaneously too many themes into one's story. The child can just absorb so much at a time. When I have tried to introduce too many messages into my story, I have found the child to be overwhelmed and then he or she becomes bored and disinterested and tunes out from the multiple stimuli.

Clinical Example: The Case of Tom (The Bed That Dumped Its Occupants)   Tom, seven years old, was referred because of significant lack of interest in his schoolwork. Although he was very bright, he would spend hours in the classroom dawdling and preoccupying himself with nonacademic activities. Even when given individual attention by both his teacher and special tutors, he would not concentrate and would refuse to apply himself to his tasks.

An older brother, seventeen, had a neurologically based learning disability and was a significant disappointment to Tom's father. Over the years Tom had observed frequent fighting between his father and older brother and this exposure was, without doubt, contributing to Tom's difficulties. In addition, his father was a somewhat aloof man who could not involve himself meaningfully with his children.

During his second month in treatment, the following interchange occurred while we were playing *The Bag of Toys Game.*

> *Patient* (selects bed object): A bed.
> *Therapist:* A bed. What are you going to say about a bed?
> *Patient:* (mumbles)
> *Therapist:* What's that?
> *Patient:* This bed is plastic.
> *Therapist:* The bed is plastic. Okay, you get one chip for that.
> *Patient:* (mumbles)
> *Therapist:* Pardon me.
> *Patient:* I think we're going to have a tie today.
> *Therapist:* We're going to have a tie? Well, maybe.
> *Patient:* Yeah.
> *Therapist:* Hmmm. Who can tell?
> *Patient:* Once there was a bed and it was a very hard bed and it was very mean.

Therapist: It was very mean?

Patient: Yeah, it was a very mean bed.

Therapist: How was it mean?

Patient: If someone laid on it, it would dump—it would tilt itself—and it would dump everybody off and the lady liked it until one day she died. And that's the end. It's short. It's like yours, a little short one.

Therapist: Uh huh. I see. Let me understand something. This bed was mean and it dumped everybody off it who would want to lie on it. Is that it?

Patient: Yeah.

Therapist: And the lady who owned the bed died?

Patient: No, the bed died.

Therapist: The bed died.

Patient: Make believe.

Therapist: Yeah. How did the bed die?

Patient: By doing that when everybody, when . . . when . . . when he tilted himself always he was getting weaker and weaker 'till he died.

Therapist: I see. Okay. You get two chips for that story. Now it's my chance.

I considered the bed to represent the patient's father. In his comment about the bed he stated that it was plastic. And this was reminiscent of his father's personality—especially his lack of feeling. But more important, the bed's practice of dumping everyone who tried to use it is a good representation of his father's rejecting attitudes. Those who would try to get close to his father, as symbolized by getting into the bed, would be rejected. Finally the bed dies. This, I believe, represents Tom's hostility toward his father being released in symbolic fashion. The lady, who owned the bed, represents his mother. Although not stated, the story suggests that even she was dumped from the bed and this too is a good representation of the parental relationship.

With this understanding of Tom's story, I related mine.

Therapist: Now it's my chance. All right. Let's see what I have. (reaches into the Bag of Toys and pulls out a table) A table!

Patient: That's a table?

Therapist: Yeah, what do you think it is?

Patient: Yeah, oh yeah. (patient throws bed onto nearby chair)

Therapist: What are you doing? Do you want to keep your things over there?

Patient: Yes.

Therapist: Okay, Now we'll keep things over there. This table. The table didn't like people to sit next to it. I get one chip. Now for my story.

Once upon a time there was a table and this table, when people would put food on it, it would wobble. It would go (imitates by sound wobbly table) . . . let's say this was food here . . . somebody put a plate on it or something (puts reward chip on table to simulate a plate of food). It would go (imitates wobbly sound while shaking table) and it would knock it off. They'd put it back on and (imitates wobbly sound again and puts back chip) it would knock it off. It just didn't like to have food on it. Once in a while it did. Once in a while you'd put food, you'd put a plate on it and it would let the plate stay. But other times it just didn't want the plates and it would go "oooooohhhhh" and the plates would go off.

So the people in the family decided that the best thing that they could do was to see what the table's mood was. If they saw the table was going to shake they'd put a little something on it. If the table would shake they'd just take it off and then they'd say, "Okay, we'll just use another table. That's all." But if they put something on it and the table let it stay, then they'd all sit around and they would then use it. Now sometimes they would get angry at the table . . .

Patient (interrupts): They should—you know what they should do? Cut it if it shakes all the plates out. Cut it in half.

Therapist: Cut it in half?

Patient: Yeah.

Therapist: Why do that?

Patient: Just do it.

Therapist: Why? Are you saying that—why should they cut it in half if it—you mean when it shook the plate?

Patient: Yeah.

Therapist: Why cut it in half? What would that do?

Patient: They should.

Therapist: But why? What would that accomplish? What would that do if they cut it in half?

Patient: Nothing. It would just, you know, then it would be no good and then they'd be sad about it.

Therapist: It would be no good?

Patient: Yeah, then it wouldn't have—it wouldn't be—then he wouldn't have a lot of fun or anything.

Therapist: Who's that, the table?

Patient: Yeah.

Therapist: Oh, in other words . . .

Patient (interrupts): They would shake it and shake it and everything.

Therapist: You mean they would punish him that way? Is that what you are saying?

Patient: Yeah.

Therapist: I see. Would he still shake things off the table if they cut him in half?

Patient: No.

Therapist: Why not?

Patient: He wouldn't have two legs to do it.

Therapist: I see. Well, now one of the kids in the family thought that would be a good idea to cut the table up in half and to hurt it that way. But one of the teenagers, an older kid, said, "No, that's foolish because that table is still good. Sometimes it stays still and sometimes it lets us put plates on it. We might as well use it when we can and when we can't we'll just use another table and this way we can get some use of the table because it's a very fine table. It's a very good table." So they said it was a good table and there's no reason ruining it or cutting it up. So what do you think finally happened? Hmm?

Patient: Uh, they didn't . . . (pauses) . . .

Therapist: They didn't what?

Patient: They didn't ruin it.

Therapist: They didn't ruin it. What did they do?

Patient: They just left it alone and they wouldn't use it anymore.

Therapist: At all?

Patient: Yeah.

Therapist: Or did they use it when it wasn't rocking around?

Patient: No, they didn't use it at all.

Therapist: No, that's not how my story ends. In my story they use it when it's not rocking around and when it is rocking around they don't use it. That's how my story ends. So I get two chips for that.

Patient: That was a long one.

Therapist: Okay, let's put this table over there. Okay, you go now.

In situations in which a child's mother and/or father have significant inhibitions in involving themselves with a child, one should not encourage the child to attempt to establish a deep involvement with such parents. In fact, it would be cruel to do so because it would only increase the child's frustration and resentment and this could only intensify his or her difficulties. Accordingly, in such situations, I generally try to help the child appreciate that the parent has deficiencies with regard to providing affection, but I try to help the child recognize that such a parent can still provide affection at times. It behooves such children to develop realistic views of their parents and to involve themselves when such involvement is rewarding and to remove themselves and seek gratifications elsewhere when the parent is not inclined to provide it.

In my story I make this recommendation symbolically. The table in my story (like the bed in Tom's story) represents the father. Just as the bed dumps those who would try to sleep in it, my table wobbles and shakes off any food that would be set on it. However, my table is not uniformly rejecting. There are times when it will allow the food to remain. Those who use the table learn to test it first to determine whether the food will be allowed to stay. In this way I encouraged Tom to approach his father and involve himself with him when the latter was receptive and to remove himself when his father was not.

During the telling of my story Tom suggested that the people cut the table in half as a punitive action, as well as a way of preventing it from shaking off the food. Again, he was not only expressing his hostility in an extreme way but also trying to find a method of stopping the rejection. Neither of these represented reasonable adaptations. He could not kill his father nor could he prevent his father from rejecting him. Accordingly, I rejected these alternatives for incorporation into my story in order to maintain what I considered to be the healthier adaptations.

The transcript does not fully communicate the various movements of the table and plates that were utilized to enhance Tom's interest. Although he stated in the end that it was a long story, he did appear to be involved significantly throughout most of it.

The Bag of Things Game

The *Bag of Things Game* requires a bag clearly labeled BAG OF THINGS, in which are forty to fifty objects that are far less recognizable than those in the BAG OF TOYS (Figure 3.3). Whereas in *The Bag of Toys Game* the objects are readily identified (soldier, car, boy, fire truck, etc.), in *The Bag of Things Game* objects have been specifically selected because they are not clearly recognizable. Accordingly, the bag contains various kinds of creatures, monsters, wiggly things, a lump of clay, a few blocks, a plastic ring, an odd-looking seashell, some strange-looking robots, and assorted figurines that vaguely resemble people or animals. Because they are not clearly recognizable they tend to be less contaminating of the child's fantasies than toys in *The Bag of Toys Game*. Often the child tends to anthropomorphize the objects; but their amorphous quality allows their utilization for a wide variety of fantasies. In the course of play, used objects are laid aside and dramatizations are encouraged.

Although *The Bag of Things Game* was designed to circumvent the problem of contamination of projected fantasies, my experience with the game did not prove the instrument to be significantly superior to *The Bag of Toys Game* or *The Board of Objects Game*. In all of these games (and the other projective games described in this chapter), the external facilitating stimuli do not appear to differ with regard to their capacity to elicit meaningful material. I believe that the reason for this is simply (as mentioned before) that the pressure of unconscious processes to express relevant psychodynamic material is far greater than the capacity of the external eliciting stimulus to contaminate such fantasies. Although the objects in this game are more amorphous and less recognizable than those in the other games described thus far, they do not appear to affect significantly the nature of the fantasies that they evoke. However, it would be an error for the reader to conclude that this game should therefore be dispensed with. It is another variation which can serve to facilitate the child's telling self-created stories when other games are losing their novelty.

Clinical Example: The Case of Betty ("Get Off My Back")   Betty came to treatment at the age of eight because of shyness, generalized tension, and poor peer relationships. She was quite tight, restricted, and inhibited in expressing emotions. She feared asserting herself and was easily scapegoated. Her parents were highly intellectualized professional people who were similarly fearful of expressing feelings. During her second month of treatment the following interchange took place while playing *The Bag of Things Game*.

> *Patient* (picking from the bag): I hope I get something good.
> *Therapist:* I hope so too.
> *Patient* (holding up an amorphous creature with a similar smaller creature sitting on its head): What's this?
> *Therapist:* What does it look like to you?
> *Patient:* I don't know what it is.
> *Therapist:* Well, make it into anything you want. People see it differently. Call it whatever you want, what it looks like to you.
> *Patient:* It looks like some kind of monster or something like that.
> *Therapist:* Okay, do you want to call it a monster?

Patient: Okay.

Therapist: Now, if you can say something about that monster you get one chip.

Patient: The monster had a little monster sitting on the top of his head and he was green.

Therapist: Very good. You get one reward chip. Now you can get two more if you can tell a completely made-up story about that monster, one completely made up from your imagination.

Patient: Once upon a time there was this monster. And he had this little monster sitting on the top of his head. And he [the big monster] wanted the little monster to get off because he was heavy and he was bothering him.

Therapist: You mean the little monster was bothering the big monster?

Patient: Yeah.

Therapist: What was the little monster doing?

Patient: He was poking him and he was very heavy.

Therapist: So then what happened.

Patient: So the big monster was walking along one day and the little monster fell off his head, landed on the sidewalk, and he died. The end.

Therapist: Is that the whole story?

Patient: Yes.

Therapist: Okay.

The story is a clear statement of the patient's feeling of impotence regarding effective self-assertion. Just as she cannot effectively defend herself against those who tease her (many of whom were smaller than herself), the monster (who symbolizes Betty) is unable to assert himself and use his own powers to rid himself of the little fellow who is bothering him and is a heavy weight on his head. The problem is solved by the little monster's conveniently falling off and dying. No effort is required of the big monster, no self-assertion, no struggle, no anxiety.

The game continued.

Therapist: Okay. Now it's my turn. I wonder what I'm going to get. I hope it's something good. Let me see. (Pulls out a red creature with large lobsterlike claws. On its head is a little yellow creature with similar, but much smaller, claws.) Wow, look what I've got. What do you think that is?

Patient: It looks like some kind of a lobster or something like that.

Therapist: Okay. We'll call it a lobster. Once upon a time there was this lobster. And on his head sat this obnoxious little lobster. And the little lobster was always poking the big lobster. And he would take his little claws . . . do you see his little claws here?

Patient: Yes.

Therapist: Well, he'd take his little claws and he'd sometimes pinch the big lobster on the ears. And he'd poke him with his claws too. So what do you think the big lobster did?

Patient: I don't know.

Therapist: Well, try to guess.

Patient: The little lobster fell off?

Therapist: Well, that's how it happened in your story but it didn't happen in mine. First, the big lobster kept hoping that the little lobster would fall off and hit his head and even die, but as much as he wished that that would happen, it didn't. He wished it very hard. He would go, "Oooh, oooh, I wish so hard that he falls off." But the little lobster just kept sitting there and poking the big lobster, and biting him with his claws.

And sometimes the big lobster used to cry because it hurt him so when he was poked and bitten. And he'd cry, "Oooh, ooh, you're hurting me." But because he didn't do anything the little lobster just kept on bothering him and biting him.

Patient: Did he bleed?

Therapist: Yes, a little bit. In fact, it was the day that he began to bleed when the lobster's teenage brother was passing by and he saw what was happening. And he said to the lobster, "Why are you letting him do all those terrible things to you? You have very big claws and you could easily get him off your head. Look how tightly closed you keep your claws." (Therapist now talking to patient and pointing to tightly closed claws.) Do you see how tightly shut he keeps his claws?

Patient: Yes.

Therapist: Why do you think his claws are shut so tight?

Patient: Because he's scared?

Therapist: Right! Because he's scared. So what do you think happened then?

Patient: He opened them up?

Therapist: Right! He was very scared to do it and his knees were knocking and his claws were chattering like this (therapist chatters his teeth) and he was scared all over. And the teenager said, "Go ahead, snap at him. You'll see how fast he'll jump off your head." So the big lobster snapped, but it was a very soft and low snap, and so nothing happened. "That's no snap," said the teenager. "Do it harder," the teenager said. Well, the big lobster was even more scared, but he did it.

What do you think happened then?

Patient: The little lobster still stayed?

Therapist: No! The little lobster began crying, "Ooooh, oooh, you've hurt me. Look what you've done to me. I'm bleeding. Mommy, mommy, I'm bleeding." And he jumped off the big lobster's back and went crying to his mother.

And the teenager said, "You see. That wasn't so bad. I knew you could do it."

And how do you think the lobster felt then?

Patient: He felt very good.

Therapist: Right! He felt wonderful. And after that, whenever the little lobster wanted to get on his head to poke him, he would just snap his claws and the little fellow would run away. But at other times, when the little lobster wanted to be friendly and play, they had a good time together.

And do you know what the lesson of that story is? What we can learn from that story?

Patient: If someone bothers you, don't let him do it?

Therapist: Right! If someone bothers you, don't let him do it. It may be scary at first, but if you still fight—even though you're scared—you'll get people to stop bothering you. The end.

The message of my story is obvious. The patient's solution to the problem of dealing with those who bothered her was totally maladaptive. Mine served, I believe, to encourage greater self-assertion, and this is what ultimately happened in the patient's treatment. Stories such as this played, I believe, a role in bringing about such changes.

When rereading this transcript for publication, I realized that I made a therapeutic error in my responding story. The big lobster hopes that the little lobster will get off his head and then wishes very hard that he do so. After that he cries when the little lobster maltreats him. Then, at the advice of the teenager, he asserts himself by using physical force. It would have been better had I had the big lobster *ask* the little lobster to stop maltreating him and then to make various threats before resorting to physical action. The reader does well to note my utilization of the teenager in this story. I often have found teenagers useful as the supreme authorities in my stories. As all the world knows, teenagers are omniscient and omnipotent and are viewed as such, not only by themselves but by younger children. They serve well, therefore, as high authorities in children's stories, and therapists who are not utilizing their services are depriving themselves of valuable sources of wisdom.

Clinical Example: The Case of Ronald (The Robot Baby Who Receives Unconditional Positive Regard)   Ronald, age seven, exhibited many social perceptual difficulties as a manifestation of his neurologically based learning disability. He was of at least average intelligence and did not have significant visual-perceptual or auditory-perceptual problems. However, he did behave differently from other children, mainly because of his impulsivity, angry outbursts, and insensitivity to the nuances of appropriate social interaction.

While playing *The Bag of Things Game* he drew an object that closely resembled a robot. There was a slot in the back enabling one to use the figurine as a bank. This is the interchange that took place.

> *Therapist:* Just stick your hand in and take whatever one you want. One thing, please.
>
> *Patient* (taking figurine out of bag): Ooh, what's that?
>
> *Therapist:* I don't know. What does it look like to you?
>
> *Patient:* Bank.
>
> *Therapist:* A bank? I guess it can be used as a bank.
>
> *Patient:* But how would you get the money out of it?
>
> *Therapist:* I think it's more than a bank—well, what does it look like?
>
> *Patient:* A bank because of that (points to a slot in the back).
>
> *Therapist:* Right. You can put money in it. But what is the bank? I mean there are things like piggy banks. What is that? What kind of a bank is that? This is a treasure chest bank here we're keeping the reward chips in. What kind of a bank would you call that? What does that look like?
>
> *Patient:* Maybe a robot bank.
>
> *Therapist:* Now if you want to say something about the robot you get one chip and if you can tell a story about it you get two.
>
> *Patient:* Once upon a time there was a robot and it had one little baby and everybody loved that little baby. Everybody came to visit him. And they loved that little baby so much. The end.
>
> *Therapist:* I have a question about that. What was there about that baby that they loved so much?
>
> *Patient:* Uh, his eyes. They liked to play with that baby.
>
> *Therapist:* Hh hmm. What else made them like the baby?
>
> *Patient:* Everything.
>
> *Therapist:* Is that it?
>
> *Patient* (whispers): Yeah.
>
> *Therapist:* Okay. You get two.

The story is typical of those told by many children with minimal brain dysfunction. Having few assets that they consider worthy of gaining them the affection of others, they hope to be loved for innate qualities. In this case the baby is liked because of his eyes. In addition, we are told that people like to play with the baby; but again, no specific ingratiating qualities on the baby's part are described. Last, when I specifically asked the patient, "What else made them like the baby?" he replied, "Everything." Again, this is an avoidance answer and does not provide specifics.

With this understanding of Ronald's story, I related mine after choosing a somewhat nebulous little wiggly creature from the bag.

> *Therapist:* Now it's my chance. (holds up figurine) What does this look like?
>
> *Patient:* I don't know.
>
> *Therapist:* Okay, let's just call him a baby. Okay?
>
> *Patient:* Okay.
>
> *Therapist:* Once upon a time there was this baby and everybody looked at this baby and everybody said, "Ooh, what a cute little baby. Isn't that a nice little cute baby? Ooh, how cute." (pretends he's kissing baby while making kissing sounds) They used to coo with him and they would hold him and hug him. "Ooh, what a cute little baby."
>
> This little baby, as he grew up, he found that people weren't cuddling him so much and weren't saying, "Ooh, what a cute little baby." And he thought that just by sitting there and doing nothing that people would continue to love him. Well, that's how it is with babies. Babies can sit and do nothing and everybody will love them, or most people will love them. But as you get older, if you want to get people to like you, you have to be doing things. You have to be nice to them or make things that they may like or do things for people and you just can't sit there and smile and expect everybody to love you.
>
> But he didn't know this, so when he became five, six, seven years old and he would just sit there and do nothing he found out that people weren't going over and saying, "Ooh, how lovable you are. Ooh, we like you so much." And he got kind of lonely because they weren't loving him like they used to when he was a baby. But then when he started doing things—when he started being nice to people, being friendly, and he started learning a lot of things that made him interesting to talk to—then people started liking him more and he wasn't so lonely.
>
> And do you know what the lesson of that story is?
>
> *Patient:* No.
>
> *Therapist:* Try to figure it out. What do you think the lesson is?

Patient: (silent)

Therapist: Well, do people like you for sitting there and doing nothing?

Patient: No.

Therapist: Do they like little babies when they sit there and do nothing?

Patient: Yeah.

Therapist: Yeah, but when you get older what happens?

Patient: They don't like you anymore.

Therapist: Right. And what do you have to do when you are older in order for people to like you?

Patient: Be nice to them, make things that will make a person happy.

Therapist: Right. Right. And that's how you will get friends when you're older. The end. Okay. I get two chips for that. Right?

Patient: Right.

Therapist: Okay. Your chance.

The purpose of my story is obvious. I attempted to help the patient appreciate that one is loved for assets and qualities which attract people, and that if he is to be liked by others he must apply himself. Children with neurologically based learning disabilities must be strong adherents to the work ethic if they are to overcome their deficits. And it is the purpose of therapy to help bring about such commitment. Elsewhere (Gardner, 1973b) I discuss in detail this important aspect of self-esteem development.

The Bag of Words Game

The Bag of Words Game requires a bag labeled BAG OF WORDS. In it are approximately four hundred words, each of which is printed with thick ink (a "Magic Marker" or "Flair" pen will serve well) on a 2"× 3" card (Figure 3.3). Different colored cards and inks can be used to make the game more attractive. Words have been chosen that are most likely to elicit comments and stories relevant to issues commonly focused on in therapy, e.g., *breast, anger, mother, father, boy, girl, foolish, doctor, love,* and *hate.* A full list of of the words I have found most useful is shown in Tables 3.1–3.3; however, readers are likely to think of a number of words on their own and may find some of my words less useful than I have found them. In accordance with the aforementioned principle of the pressure of unconscious material being more powerful than the con-

Table 3.1

accident	bird	Christmas	dollar
adult	birthday	cigarettes	draw
afraid	birthday party	circus	dream
airplane	black	clay	dumb
allowance	blame	clean	early
alone	blood	climb	egg
ambulance	boast	clothing	enemy
anger	boat	clown	escape
animal	body	club	eyeglasses
annoy	book	cockroach	fail
ant	bottle	compliment	fall
ape	bowel movement	conduct	famous
apple	boy	cookie	fat
ashamed	boy friend	cop	father
automobile	Boy Scout	counselor	fear
ax	brag	cow	feeling
baby	brat	cowboy	fight
baby-sitter	brave	cripple	finger
backside	bread	crook	fire
bad	breast	cruel	fire engine
bad habit	bug	cry	fireman
bad luck	build	crybaby	fish
bad thoughts	bully	cuddle	fix
ball	calf	curse	flour
balloon	cake	dad	food
bang	camera	danger	fool
bare	camp	daughter	foolish
bath	camp director	dentist	forget
bathroom	candy	die	fox
bathtub	car	dinosaur	freak
beat	care	dirty	friend
beautiful	cat	dirty trick	frog
beaver	catch	dirty words	fun
behavior	cheat	discover	funny
belly button	chewing gum	disgusting	game
best	chicken	doctor	garbage
bicycle	child	dog	garbageman
big	children	doll	gift

Table 3.2

girl	invisible	mean	peacock
girl friend	jail	medal	penis
Girl Scout	jerk	medicine	pet
God	job	mess	phony
good	joke	message	pick on
grab	joy	milk	picture
grade	judge	mirror	pig
grandfather	kangaroo	mistake	piggy bank
grandmother	kill	model	pill
grown-up	kind	mom	plan
gun	king	money	play
hamster	kiss	monkey	playground
happy	knife	monster	please
harm	lady	mother	poison
hate	lamb	mouse	poke
healthy	large	mouth	police car
hear	late	mucus	policeman
heaven	laugh	mud	polite
hell	lazy	nag	pony
hen	leave	naked	poor
hide	letter	nasty	praise
hit	lie	naughty	pray
hole	like	new	present
holiday	lion	nice	president
homework	lipstick	nightmare	pretty
honest	little	nipple	prince
hope	lollipop	note	princess
horrible	lonely	nurse	principal
horse	lose	old	prize
hospital	love	operation	proud
house	lucky	ostrich	psychiatrist
hug	mad	owl	psychologist
hungry	make	paint	punish
hurt	make believe	parent	pupil
ice cream	magic	parrot	queen
ill	man	party	quiet
Indian	manners	pass	rat
insult	matches	pay	refrigerator

Table 3.3

respect	sleep	stone	train
reward	slob	story	treat
rich	sloppy	strong	tree
right	sly	student	trick
robber	small	stupid	tricycle
rotten	smart	suck	trip
sad	smell	surprise	truck
scaredy-cat	snail	sword	try
scary	snake	talk	turtle
school	sneak	teacher	ugly
scold	soap	teacher's pet	upset
scoutmaster	soldier	tease	vagina
scream	son	teenager	vomit
secret	song	telephone	water
secret plan	sore loser	television	weak
see	sorry	temper tantrum	weep
selfish	spanking	thank	whip
share	spear	therapist	whisper
sheep	spend	thief	win
shoot	spider	threaten	wish
shout	spit	thumb	wipe
shy	spoil	tickle	wolf
sick	sport	tiger	worm
silly	steal	toilet	worry
sissy	stick	tooth	worst
sister	stingy	touch	young
skunk	stink	toy	zoo

taminating effect of the eliciting stimulus, the specific choice of words is not vital. Occasional cards provide the child with extra reward chips ("You get two extra reward chips"), and these increase the child's excitement while playing the game. Used cards are laid aside and dramatizations are encouraged. Again, the child's responses are used as points of departure for therapeutic interchanges.

Clinical Example: The Case of Marc (The Man Who Picked the Big Coconuts Off the Palm Tree) Marc came to treatment at the age of seven because of tics, excessive tension, and agitated behavior in the classroom. His mother, a very buxom woman, was quite seductive with him. Near the end of his first month in treatment the following interchange took place while playing *The Bag of Words Game.*

Patient: I've got the word *tree.* Once there was a tree and it was a talking palm tree.

Therapist: A talking palm tree. Go ahead.

Patient: It was so full of coconuts that he couldn't even move or talk. He was too heavy. So one day it decided that it would quit and just try and make all the coconuts come off, but they wouldn't come off. So he looked around until he found somebody with a gun shooting birds, and he asked him if he would . . .

Therapist (interrupts): Who is he now?

Patient: He was just looking—the palm tree was looking around and he just found someone.

Therapist: Oh, the palm tree wanted to get his own coconuts off?

Patient: Yeah.

Therapist: Okay. It was a *he* palm tree?

Patient: Yeah.

Therapist: And then he finally found someone with a gun.

Patient: Yeah.

Therapist: Okay.

Patient: Who was shooting birds with a shotgun. But it wasn't easy because he just had to look around because he couldn't move. So he called him and he asked him if he would shoot them off. And he [the man] said, "I won't shoot them off, but I'll pick them off. I love coconuts." The end.

Therapist: So what happened?

Patient: And the lesson was if you're a palm tree and you have coconuts on you, you shouldn't just try and take them off, but if you're a palm tree there's nothing you can do.

Therapist: Wait a minute. The lesson is if you're a palm tree, what?

Patient: There's nothing to do except stay where you are just like other trees.

Therapist: And don't do what?

Patient: Don't try to take your coconuts off.

Therapist: Why not?

Patient: Because they're supposed to come off theirselves.

Therapist: I see. So what was the trouble? Did this palm tree get into any kind of trouble by having this man shoot the coconuts off?

Patient: The man said that "I wouldn't, um, I won't shoot them off but I'll pick them off because I love coconuts."

Therapist: So he picked them off.

Patient: Yeah.

Therapist: The man picked off the coconuts. I'm not clear what the lesson is.

Patient: The lesson is that if you are a palm tree you shouldn't want to make your coconuts come off because they'll come off themselves and all that you should do is stay where you are just like other trees.

Therapist: Hh hmm.

Patient: They don't move.

Therapist: Okay. Now it's my chance.

Although Marc represented the tree as male, I considered it to represent his mother. The coconuts, being round and filled with milk, well serve as a breast symbol. They are high up on the tree and inaccessible. The central theme of the story is whether or not the coconuts will be made available to those on the ground. We are told that the tree was so full of coconuts "that he couldn't even move or talk." This, I believe, represented Marc's view of his mother as being buxom and that her breasts were the most prominent part of her anatomy. Marc's mother was well-endowed in this area and was a very seductive woman, as well.

The man with the gun, I believe, represents Marc's father. He has a powerful phallus which somehow enables him to gain access to the coconuts, that is, the mother's breasts. There is some ambivalence on Marc's part regarding whether or not the coconuts should come off the tree. The tree asks the man to take the coconuts off (with the help of his powerful weapon), but the man refuses to shoot them off. Rather, he decides to pick them off stating, "I love coconuts." Although Marc's presentation is somewhat confusing, the main element that comes through is that the tree is advised not to encourage premature removal of the coconuts; rather, it should wait until they come off naturally.

In essence, I considered this story to reflect Marc's wish that his father not have such ready access to his mother's coconuts, that is, her breasts. He would prefer that she withhold them from access to him as long as possible. However, he sees his father as having the power to get them at his will; but he gets his father to take them by hand, rather than with a gun. Possibly, this represents Marc's fear that his father might destroy the coconuts and then they would be completely unavailable to him. If his father has to get the coconuts he might as well preserve them. However, Marc would much prefer the tree to be less receptive to the father's ready access to them. The story reveals, as well, his appreciation that his mother wishes to provide the father access, and this is symbolized by the tree's wishing that the coconuts would come off. It was with this understanding of Marc's story that I related mine.

Therapist: Okay. Now it's my chance. (picks card from bag) I've got the word *boy.*

Once upon a time there was a palm tree and this palm tree had many coconuts on it, and there was a boy who lived next door to the property where this palm tree was. He used to look up at that palm tree and he would say, "Boy, those would be great coconuts to have. That would be terrific if I could have those coconuts. I'd like to get them off that tree. I'd like to split a couple open and eat the coconut and drink the milk that's in the inside and . . . "

Patient: (gestures to speak)

Therapist: Do you want to say something about that?

Patient: I just wanted to say that I hate coconut trees.

Therapist: You hate coconut trees. Anyway . . .

Patient (interrupts): Coconut juice!

Therapist: Anyway, in my story this boy liked coconut juice and he liked those coconuts, and he used to eye those coconuts every day. And one day he thought, "Gee, it would be great to get those coconuts." But he knew they belonged to the man next door.

So one day—he knew that if he went on the property there or tried to climb the tree to pull down those coconuts the man would get very angry. So one day he thought he would get a gun, and probably shoot down some of those coconuts. Anyway, as he was taking aim to shoot down a coconut, just at that moment, the owner of the house—the owner of the coconut tree—came out and he saw the boy and he said, "What are you doing, Sonny?"

He said, "Oh . . . I . . . uh." He was really trying to think of some kind of a lie but he really couldn't because it was obvious what he was really doing and he sort of had to confess that he was going to try to shoot down the coconuts.

Patient (interrupts): I know what he could say.

Therapist: What could he have said?

Patient: He could have said that he was trying to shoot down birds.

Therapist: Well, the man could see that he was aiming directly at the coconuts and he wouldn't have gotten away with that story. So he had to kind of confess that he was trying to shoot down the coconuts.

And the man said to him, "I'm very sorry. Those coconuts are mine. I'm not letting you shoot them down. But there are two things that we can do. One, I'll give you one of the coconuts because there are lots of coconuts on my tree. However, my suggestion to you is that you plant your own coconut tree or save up some money and buy some coconuts from a store or buy some coconuts from someone else because I'm not selling any." What do you think the boy did?

Patient: He did what the man told him to.

Therapist: What did he decide to do?

Patient: He decided to save up his money and buy more coconuts or buy it from somebody else.

Therapist: Right. He got a job as a newspaper delivery boy and saved up some money and bought some coconuts. In addition, every once in a while the man let him have some of his coconuts and let him know that those were really his and he couldn't have them, but that he could have a little bit. But the main thing was that the boy learned that he couldn't get them from the man so he had to get them elsewhere.

And the lesson of that story is: If you like coconuts and the coconuts you like are owned by another person, ask him. Perhaps he'll give you some or a little bit. But if he won't give you all, which is usually the case, because nobody is going to give you all the coconuts he owns, then try to get them elsewhere, like earning some money and buying some, or planting your own coconut tree. That's the lesson of that story. Anything you want to say about that story?

Patient: (nods negatively)

Therapist: Did you like that story?

Patient: (nods affirmatively)

Therapist: Good. What was it about the story that you liked?

Patient: Well, the coconuts.

Therapist: What was the main thing about it that you liked?

Patient: When he was trying to shoot down the coconuts.

Therapist: Hh hmm. Okay. When he was trying to get down the coconuts. Okay.

In my story I tried to communicate to Marc the fact that his mother's breasts were his father's possession. However, he could have some physical gratifications with her, but only to a limited extent. The father, however, does not react punitively. Rather, he is willing to allow Marc some of these physical gratifications, but encourages him to seek them elsewhere through his own efforts, both in the present and in the future. This is typical of the kinds of story I utilize in helping youngsters resolve oedipal problems.

When I see oedipal problems in boys, they are generally the result of maternal seductivity, with or without paternal castration threats (overt or covert). In Marc's case, his mother was extremely seductive. She wore low-cut blouses, tight-fitting clothing, invariably used perfume, and spent significant time at beauty parlors. In addition, she undressed in front of Marc up to the time he began treatment. In my responding story, I introduced the element of sharing. As mentioned, this is a central factor in the resolution of oedipal problems. My telling Marc that the man (equals father) will occasionally allow him to have some coconuts, but he must get most of those he wants elsewhere through his own efforts, is a way of giving Marc some oedipal gratifications, but to a limited degree. It was not that I was going to actually encourage Marc to caress (pick) his mother's breasts; rather, I was only suggesting with symbolism that he could get some kind of physical and possessive gratifications in his relationship with her. I do not recommend, however, that Marc wait until he is an adult; rather, I suggest that he obtain at that time substitute gratifications elsewhere. And these are important elements in my helping boys deal with oedipal problems.

SCRABBLE FOR JUNIORS

Whereas in the standard game of adult *Scrabble** the players form their words with letter tiles on a blank playing board, in the child's version, *Scrabble for Juniors*,† simple words are already printed on the board and the child attempts to cover the board letters with his or her own letter chips (Figure 3.4). In the modification of the *Scrabble for Juniors* game devised by N.I. Kritzberg and myself, all the letter tiles are first placed face down along the side of the playing board. The patient and the therapist then select seven letter tiles each and place them face up in front. The game proceeds with each player in turn placing two letters over those on the board. The patient is advised to try to so place the letters that he or she will be working toward the completion of a word. The player who places the last letter necessary to finish a word (this need not be the final letter of the word, it can be anywhere in the word) receives a reward chip. If the player can say anything at all about the word, he

---

*Manufactured by Selchow & Richter Co., Bay Shore, New York.
†*Ibid.*

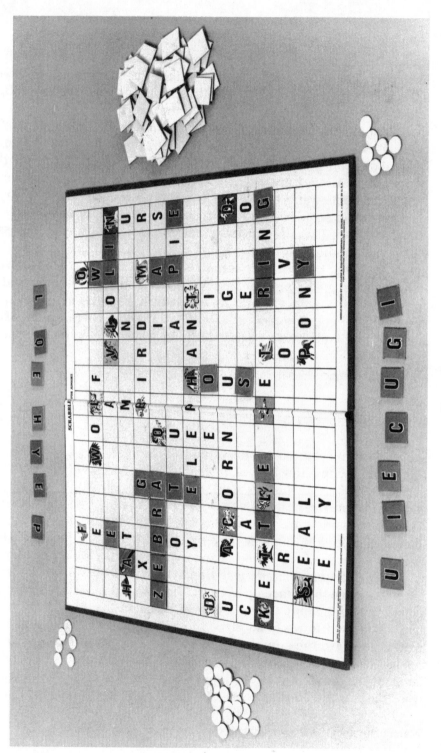

Figure 3.4

156

or she gets a second reward chip. And if the child can tell an original story about the word, he or she gets two extra reward chips. (Accordingly, the maximum number of chips obtainable for completing a word is four.)

Generally, I try to let the patient be the first to complete a word in order to learn those issues that are uppermost in the child's mind at that time. This information enables me to relate more meaningful communications when my turn comes to comment on or tell a story about a word that I have completed. Because the players' letter tiles are placed face up, I can see what letters I can place on the board that would make it most likely for the patient to complete his or her word first. In addition, I may fail to complete a word that I am capable of and "by mistake" use the letter elsewhere. Although I, like most therapists, am a firm believer in being totally honest with my patients, there are times in child therapy when a little duplicity is justified because it serves the purposes of the child's treatment.

Sometimes children will focus on a particular word on the board and try to complete it because they are especially eager to tell a story about it. In such situations the therapist can be fairly certain that the word has triggered significant associations. More often, however, the child's choice of a word is dependent upon the letters he or she happens to choose. In addition, most children tend to favor words that are closest to their side of the playing board. In spite of the drawbacks implicit in these determinants of the words chosen, my experience has been that the completed word will generally be used in the service of expressing those issues most pertinent to the child at that time.

Again, the winner is the player who has accumulated the most chips at the end of the allotted time. A slow pace is encouraged so that the words, comments, and stories can serve as points of departure for discussion. Dramatizations are also encouraged during the course of play. The game is useful from the late first-grade to about the fourth-to-fifth-grade level. Older children find the words too "easy."

My attempts to use the standard adult *Scrabble* game with older children have not worked out well. They tend to get much too involved in the point values of the various letters and so swept up in the strongly competitive elements in the adult version that comments and storytelling tend to take a secondary role. Accordingly, I do not have adult *Scrabble* available in the office as one of the games the child can choose to play. Also, the child is no match for the adult because of the latter's larger repertory of words. If the therapist then plays with full conviction and honesty, the child will be demeaned. If the therapist feigns ignorance to equalize the game, the strongly competitive factors intrinsic to the game will still serve to contaminate it for therapeutic purposes.

Clinical Examples

The Case of Cary (The Frog and the Seal)   Cary entered treatment at the age of ten because of a number of difficulties—mainly interpersonal. He refused to fight back when teased or picked upon and so was easily scapegoated, even by younger children. The only way he was able to attract friends was to beg them to come to his house where his parents had always made sure there was a plethora of toys and attractive games. He was very fearful of new situations and would often be unable to fall asleep for two or three nights prior to an anticipated event.

During his third session we played *Scrabble for Juniors.*

Therapist: Now Cary has finished the word *lily* for which he gets a chip. Now, wait a minute, hold it; don't go on yet. If you can say anything at all about the word *lily*, you get a second chip—anything at all.

Patient: What do you mean?

Therapist: Just say anything at all about a lily, any sentence which includes the word *lily*.

Patient: A lily grows on a pond.

Therapist: A lily grows on a pond. Okay, so you get a second chip. Now, if you can make up a story about the word *lily*, any story at all, but it must be completely made up from your own imagination, then you get two more.

Patient: Once a frog sat on a lily in the swamp and then the frog jumped off onto another lily.

Therapist: All right, that's a good beginning of a story, but that's not a whole story. A story has a beginning, a middle, and an end.

Patient: Hhmmm. I can't think of one.

Therapist: Well, try. See, if I can tell a story about a lily I can get two as well, although you end up with four, I can end up with two. So, you know, the person who has the most chips wins, so if I can tell a story about a lily I can get two and then we'd be even.

Patient: What I said was a beginning. Right?

Therapist: Okay, well, say it again. The frog jumped . . .

Patient: A frog jumped on a lily in the swamp and then it jumped off to another lily.

Therapist: Okay.

Patient: And then—and then the lily started floating down the pond.

Therapist: Okay.

Patient: Then there was this waterfall and the lily fell right into the waterfall.

Therapist: The lily fell into the waterfall?

Patient: Hh hmm.

Therapist: And the frog was on it?

Patient: (nods affirmatively)

Therapist: Then what happens?

Patient: The frog died.

Therapist: Okay, you get two for that. Now . . .

Patient (interrupts): I still have one more letter to go.

Therapist: Okay, yeah, but now it's my chance to tell a story. You put it down later. I can get two for telling a story about a lily.

I considered the frog to symbolize Cary. His being on a lily pad is a reflection of Cary's feeling that his situation is an unstable one and that he could easily "sink." Worse, he could meet his doom and be helpless to prevent his demise. Floating down the river and being killed by being thrown over the waterfall is a poignant statement of his feelings of impotence with regard to the destructive forces of the world.

It was with this understanding of Cary's story that I related mine.

Therapist: Once there was a frog and he jumped on a lily pad and he noticed that the water was kind of moving, that it wasn't just a stagnant pond. The water was kind of moving and he saw that the water was moving kind of rapidly. It became more and more rapid and then he heard some noise and it sounded like a waterfall, and he realized that the lily was moving toward a waterfall. So he leaped off onto another pad and then leaped to another one, and leaped from pad to pad until finally he got to shore. He went along the shore and there he saw that there really was a waterfall and he was glad that he had looked around and was careful and had avoided the catastrophe of going over the waterfall.

And the lesson of that story is: Look around you and listen. It may help you avoid trouble.

In my story I tried to impress upon Cary the fact that he has the capability to protect himself against the dangers of the world; that if he uses his senses and utilizes foresight he can prevent many of the calamities that may befall him. Cary was clearly not trying very hard to deal with his difficulties and my hope was that my story might contribute to his taking a more active role in solving his problems.

The game continued.

Therapist: You got the word *seal.* You get one chip for the word *seal* and another one if you can tell something about the word *seal.*

Patient: I once saw a seal.

Therapist: Okay. Two more for a story.

Patient: There were two seals swimming in the Atlantic Ocean and they were swimming really far out and they would have fun. They were playing around and one time the seal—there was this big fish and the seal saw it and started to swim away and the big fish saw it and went and tried to eat it.

Therapist: Tried to eat one of the seals? Yeah, go ahead.

Patient: And then they went over a rock and then the fish hit a rock and the seal got away.

Therapist: Wait a minute, now. There were two seals. Right?

Patient: Right.

Therapist: And were any of them hurt by the big fish or what?

Patient: No, the big fish was hurt.

Therapist: Oh, the big fish hit a rock and that's why the seals got away?

Patient: Right.

Therapist: And they weren't hurt at all?

Patient: Right.

Therapist: I see. Okay. Now it's time for me. Did you take your two chips?

Patient: No.

Therapist: Take two chips for that.

In this story the seals, who represent Cary, are confronted with a big fish who tries to eat them. The latter represents, I believe, Cary's tormenting peers and all others who may be hostile to him. The problem of their attacking him is readily solved without any effort on Cary's part. The pursuing fish conveniently hits a rock and the seals get away. The story reflects Cary's wish that his problems will be neatly solved by external events favorable to him, with no effort on his part necessary to bring about the desired changes in his situation.

With this understanding of Cary's story, I responded.

Therapist: Once upon a time there were two seals. They were out in the ocean there swimming and all of a sudden this big fish came along and the fish started to attack them. Now that was kind of foolish of that fish because these were two seals against one fish, and they were very good friends and they started to fight this big fish. And the first seal was really happy that he had such a good friend because this good friend helped him fight the big fish. In addition, all of a sudden they saw a rock near the shore and they took this rock and they threw it right at the big fish—they threw it right at the big fish. And this hit the big fish right on the head and that big fish then swam away and they got rid of that guy, and they were glad that they had fought him.

One of the fish would have hoped that the big fish might swim into a rock or something like that and in this way they would be able to avoid a fight, but the second one said, "Listen, that's not going to happen. Those big fish don't swim into rocks. He has eyes and he has fins and that's not going to happen to him. If we want to get rid of him we've got to hide and throw some rocks at him." And that's exactly what happened.

And the lesson of that story is: If you are a seal and if a big fish is trying to bite you, there are two things you can do, among other things. You can have a friend and the two of you can fight the big fish or you can do some things, like throw rocks at that fish. But don't just sit back and hope that the big fish will swim into a rock and hurt himself and then go away. Things like that just don't happen. The end.

Okay, I get two chips for that.

In my story I attempted to impress upon Cary the fact that his somewhat magical solution to his problem of being scapegoated was unrealistic. The seal who hopes that the fish will hit a rock and thereby cease his pursuit is dissuaded from this passive and dangerous way of handling the situation. Rather the seals fight, and are successful in driving away their tormentor. In addition, they make use of the strength they have in numbers. In this way I hoped to provide Cary with the motivation to make friends, in part, that they might serve as his allies against those who bullied him.

The Case of Timothy (The Seal and the Cat)   Timothy entered treatment at the age of nine and a half because of severe behavior problems in school. He was disruptive in the classroom and irritated both his teacher and other children with his antics. A mild neurologically based learning disability was present; however, this was only a small contribution to his academic difficulties. In addition, his parents had been separated but did not get divorced and had been living apart for two years. His father, although consistent in providing for his family's financial needs, was erratic with regard to his visits. When he did come to the home, his relationship with Timothy was poor in that he had little interest in those things that involved Timothy.

After about a year and a half of therapy Timothy exhibited significant improvement in his classroom behavior and, in addition, was able to handle better the angry feelings he felt toward his father. Specifically there was far less displacement of such anger toward classmates and a healthier adjustment to the reality of his relationship with him. It was during this period that the following interchange took place while playing the *Scrabble for Juniors* game.

> *Therapist:* Okay, you finished the word *seal* for which you get one reward chip. If you can say anything at all about the word *seal* you get a second chip.
> *Patient:* Once upon a time there was a seal . . .
> *Therapist (interrupts):* No, no, no. That's a story. First, just say anything at all about the word *seal*—just a statement about the word *seal*.
> *Patient:* The seal is an animal that lives in the cold.
> *Therapist:* Okay, you get one for that. Now, you can tell a story about the word *seal*.
> *Patient:* Once upon a time there was an Eskimo hunter who was going to catch a seal and there was a couple of the seals. This one seal said, "I'm too smart for that guy." And like he, um, uh—so he put some bait, you know, kind of like fishing, you know, fish and he got the bait and he caught the seal, and the seal was, you know, he killed the seal or put him in a zoo, more or less, put him in the zoo.
> And in the zoo he didn't have as much fun. He was in the zoo, you know, bored.
> *Therapist:* Hh hmm.
> *Patient:* He couldn't catch his own fish and stuff so he was bored. That's where I quit. That's my story.

Therapist: That's the whole story. Lesson?

Patient: That don't think you're so smart on catching in traps.

Therapist: Don't think you're so smart . . . ?

Patient: Don't think—don't be so sure in traps.

Therapist: Can you be a little bit more specific?

Patient: Like, um, don't . . . that's what I really mean . . . don't, uh . . .

Therapist: Don't what?

Patient: Just because you see a little piece of bait lying out you don't just get it.

Therapist: Hh hmm.

Patient: Because it might be led to a trap.

Therapist: Hh hmm. Okay, you take two chips.

Patient: I got two chips already.

Therapist: You got one for completing the word *seal* and saying seals live in the cold. Take two more for the story. Okay.

I considered the seal to represent the patient and the Eskimo trapper those around him whom he considers to be malevolent. There is a healthy element in the story in that the seal's wise-guy attitude is being criticized. However, the seal does get caught and this, I believe, is a statement of the patient's feeling that he is somewhat helpless to protect himself from those who would be malevolent to him. Being put in the zoo symbolizes, I believe, the patient's feeling that he is entrapped by overwhelming forces.

With this understanding of the patient's story, I related mine.

Therapist: Now wait a minute. It's my chance to tell a story now. Okay, you want to wait.

Patient (proceeding with the game): Yeah.

Therapist: Just hold up. Now I tell a story about the word *seal* and I can get two chips for it. Once upon a time . . . actually you get one for getting the word, one for saying something about it, and two for the story. Okay?

Patient: (nods affirmatively).

Therapist: Now I go. I get two if I can tell a story.

Once upon a time there was a seal and this seal lived up north where it was cold and there were Eskimos who were constantly trying to capture seals. So this seal's mother and father said to him, "Now listen, you know the Eskimos are out to catch us and we have to be very careful. We have to watch out for their traps and watch out for their bait."

Well, this seal was kind of a wise guy and he said, "Ahh, I don't have to watch out for their bait. I don't have to watch out for their traps. I don't have to watch out. Nothing is going to happen to me."

So whereas the other seals listened very carefully to their teachers and their mothers and fathers regarding the kinds of traps the Eskimos used and the kinds of bait that they used, this seal didn't. And sure enough, one day he got caught in a trap, but fortunately only his fin got caught. He was able to pull himself out of it and he got away. And he had his fin, his little paw—I don't know what they call them—the seals have little flappers. His flapper was . . . (to patient's mother) what do they call it?

Patient's mother: Flipper.

Therapist: Flipper. His flipper had a little piece of flesh nipped off, but otherwise he was all right. And he came back to his parents and he was bleeding, leaving a kind of trail of blood, but they managed to fix him up.

And for the rest of his life he remembered that little experience and every time he looked at his flipper and saw the scars there it reminded him to be careful. And, of course, after that he learned very much about the kinds of traps that Eskimos have and how to avoid them.

And what do you think the lesson of that story is?

Patient: It's your story, not mine.

Therapist: Okay, the lesson of that story is that often it pays to learn about the things that can be useful to you in life and that can often save you a lot of trouble. The end.

Patient: You can see the scar on his flipper. Nothing was . . . nothing was . . . he didn't have anything cut off.

Therapist: No, no. Just a . . .

Patient (interrupts): . . . scar.

Therapist: A scar and a little piece of tissue was taken out, but the scar filled that up. Okay, I get two chips.

In my story, I confirmed the healthy element in Timothy's story by reiterating the inappropriateness of the wise-guy attitude. However, in my story the seal, although scarred, learns that one can avoid certain dangers by considering their possibility in advance. The scar serves as an ever-present reminder of his trauma and helps him remember to avoid difficulties throughout the rest of his life. My main message here, of course, was that one need not be helpless with regard to dangers that may be present; one has the power to avoid them if one wishes to attend to them. I was referring here not only to the patient's classroom difficulties but to his problems with his father as well.

Subsequently, the following interchange took place.

Therapist: Okay, you completed the word *cat.* Wait, you get one chip for the word *cat.*

Patient: A cat is an animal. It's a smaller animal related to the lion.

Therapist: Okay, now you get. . . .

Patient (interrupts): Then there's tigers; zee, um, chet . . . cheetahs and jaguars are all cats.

Therapist: All right, now if you can tell a story about the word *cat* you get two more.

Patient: Once upon a time there was a cat and the cat really liked these people, you know. They didn't think—they didn't like him, you know. They. . . .

Therapist (interrupts): Wait. The cat liked the people, these people?

Patient: Yeah.

Therapist: Go ahead.

Patient: And it kept on . . . (mumbles) . . .

Therapist: What?

Patient: And the cat didn't like the people . . . the cat liked the people, you know. The people didn't like the cat and the cat's an old bugger.

Therapist: Wait. The cat liked the people, but the people didn't like the cat.

Patient: Yeah.

Therapist: Okay.

Patient: And, um, they'd tell the cat, "Get lost, you old cat." The cat came back the very next day. The cat would not stay away. Hey, that rhymes!

Therapist: Okay, go ahead.

Patient: And they did it again. They kept on doing it and doing it because the cat like was abandoned and he wanted someone to own him, you know, love him.

Therapist: Hh hmm.

Patient: And the cat . . . they'd kick it out and it kept on doing it and this cat came back (sings) the very next day. The cat would not stay away.

Therapist: Okay.

Patient: And, um, so the cat . . . so the cat foretold them, "Don't think that . . . " the cat . . . well, they looked around the place where there were rats, you know, rats and mice.

Therapist: Yeah, I'm not clear. What's that about rats and mice?

Patient: Well, the people lived around a place where there were rats and mice and stuff.

Therapist: Yeah.

Patient: And the cat killed them all, you know.

Therapist: Yeah.

Patient: The cat was hanging around and when the cat was hanging around there weren't any mice, so they decided, "Hey, that cat's really helpful. He gets rid of the rodents and stuff." So they got the cat and the moral of the story is like you don't just kick around someone because you don't like them, like they might be very useful and they like you. That's the moral of the story.

Therapist: Hh hmm. Okay. Okay. You get two for that. That was a very good story.

I considered the cat to represent the patient himself and the owner, his father. At first, Timothy is abandoned; however, when he proves that he has a worthwhile skill he is then reaccepted into the household. The story reveals the patient's lingering feelings of rejection; however, it also reveals his appreciation that one way that one can counteract rejection is to exhibit useful and ingratiating qualities. The fantasy, therefore, is a reflection of a healthy adaptation. However, it does reveal the fact that Timothy has not given up completely his hope to regain his father's affection. With this understanding of the patient's story, I related mine.

Therapist: Okay, now it's time for me to tell my story. Once upon a time there was a cat and he lived with this man and this man decided that he didn't like this cat too much. The cat was all right in some ways, but he decided that he didn't want him. So he told the cat to leave. And the cat went out and he was very unhappy. He said, "Aw, come on, let me come back and live with you."

The man said, "Ah, you're no use."

And the cat said, "I'll show you. I'll show you that I can be useful. You don't like me anymore and you won't let me live with you anymore. Okay, we'll see."

Anyway, the cat went to a nearby house and there were some people there who were really having a lot of trouble with mice and rats and things like that. And he said to them, "You know, I can be very helpful to you in killing off these mice and rats."

And they said, "You can? Would you come to live with us?"

And he said, "You people look like you'll appreciate me." So he went to live with these other people and he was very useful, and they gave him a good home, they gave him good food, and they gave him a good place to sleep.

And then the other man that he had left realized that he had made a mistake in sending this cat off, but it was too late. The cat had already lived with these other people, but he saw his first owner once in a while. He would see the old owner once in a while and the old owner realized that he had made a big mistake in sending this cat off, but it was too late. The cat had another home. And the cat realized a very important lesson, which was what?

Patient: It's your story!

Therapist: Okay, the lesson is that if someone doesn't like you or, you know, may like you very little, it doesn't mean that no one else in the whole world will like you. There are always other people in the world who can appreciate the good things in you. The end.

Anything you want to say about that story?

Patient: (nods negatively)

Therapist: Okay.

Whereas in Timothy's story, his father's appreciation of him and reconciliation with his father are accomplished, in my story there is no reconciliation. To foster such reconciliation would have been unrealistic because of the long period that the patient had been separated from his father and the fact that there was absolutely no reason to believe that the father was going to return to the home. However, I did emphasize the ingratiating qualities that the patient possessed so as to reinforce this element from his story.

More significantly, however, in my story the cat finds love and affection in another home but still maintains some relationship with the previous owner. My attempt here was to help Timothy appreciate that others can show him affection in compensation for the deprivations he suffers in his relationship with his father. This need not mean, however, that he has to break completely his relationship with his father; rather, he can maintain gratifying relationships with a number of individuals.

THE FEEL AND TELL GAME

In the three grab-bag games, the bags are open at the top and the child merely retrieves an item from the bag. In *The Feel and Tell Game* (Figure 3.5) objects are placed in a double canvas bag bound at the top. On the outside of the bag are written the words FEEL

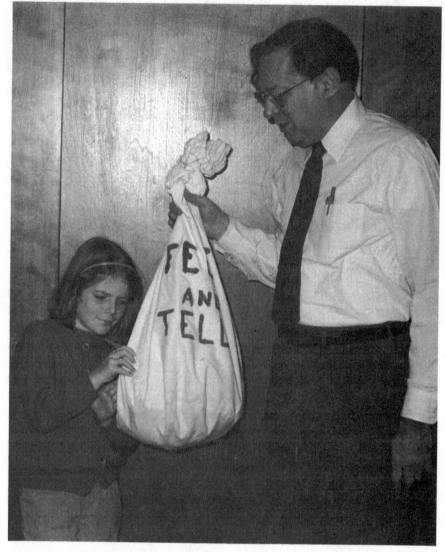

Figure 3.5

AND TELL. The child is merely asked to feel an object through the double canvas bag and state what he or she believes the object to be. Because the bags are bound at the top, the child cannot stick his or her hand inside the bag in order to identify the object. A chip is given for merely stating what the child guesses the object to be. It is not necessary for the child to identify accurately the object; it is only necessary for the child to make a guess regarding what the object *might* be. Because the objects have been selected for their amorphous shape or unusual configuration, it is not likely that the child will identify most of them correctly.

The child obtains one chip for making a guess (any guess will do), a second for making a statement about the object, and a third for telling a story about the object. The game, in a sense, can be considered a "tactile projective game." The more successful the examiner is in utilizing objects that are amorphous, the greater the likelihood the child's projections will be the primary determinant of what he or she considers the object to be. Accordingly, the examiner does well to select objects that are not easily identifiable while being felt through a double canvas bag. Often, junk items that should have been thrown out long ago serve well for this purpose. In Figure 3.6 the reader is shown those objects that I utilize in my *Feel and Tell Game.* I am sure that most people have similar collections of junk objects that can now be put to good use.

Clinical Example

The Case of Mary (The Kangaroo in the Mother's Pouch)   Mary was referred for treatment at the age of nine because of fear of going to school. She was significantly dependent on her overprotective mother and presented with a typical picture of separation anxiety disorder. As is often the case in such families, her father was passive in his relationship with her mother and viewed the mother's overprotectiveness to be a manifestation of superior maternal capacity. Each morning, when Mary's mother would prepare her to go to school, she would complain of a variety of somatic difficulties: headache, stomach ache, nausea, fever, pain in the joints, and so forth. Typically her mother would indulge these complaints and often kept her home from school, even though there was rarely evidence for bona fide illness. During her second session, the following interchange took place:

> *Therapist:* Okay, Mary, here's how this game is played. I'll hold up this bag. What does it say on this bag?
> *Patient* (looking at the bag): Feel and Tell.
> *Therapist:* That's right. Now the way this game is played is that you have to try to figure out what's in the bag by just feeling it. Actually, it's a double bag and there's a string on the top so that you

Figure 8.6

can't put your hand inside. And you can't look inside either. You have to try to guess what's in the bag, or the two bags, by feeling through them. Okay, let's see you do it.

Patient (feeling the bag): I don't know what this is. What is it?

Therapist: As I told you, you're supposed to try to guess what you think is in there. There's no right answer. Just saying what you think is in there will get you a chip. Then you'll get another chip if you can say something about that thing. And then you'll get two more chips if you can tell a story about that thing. Okay, let's see you make a guess.

Patient (feeling different objects in the bag): I don't know what these things are. This one feels like a kangaroo. Yes, I think it's a kangaroo.

Therapist: That's a very good answer. You get a chip for that. (therapist gives the patient a chip) Now you can get another chip if you can say something, anything at all, about the kangaroo. Let's see you do it.

Patient: The kangaroo was in his mother's pouch.

Therapist: That's a very good answer. The kangaroo was in his mother's pouch. You get a chip for that. (therapist gives the patient another chip) Now let's see you tell a story about a kangaroo. It must be a completely made-up story. It can't be about anything that really happened to you or to anyone you know. It can't be from television or books. It has to be completely made up. Okay, let's see how good you are at making up a story about a kangaroo. If you can, you get two more chips.

Patient: Well, once there was this baby kangaroo. And he was in his mommy's pouch. He liked it there. The end.

Therapist: What you've said so far is a very good beginning for a story. But every story has a beginning, a middle, and an end. Now tell us the middle of your story. Go ahead.

Patient: I can't think of anything else. That's all I can think of.

Therapist: You know, if you want to get two chips, you have to tell a whole story.

Patient: That's all I can think of.

Therapist: Okay, you get one chip for that story, because it's only a part of a story. I hope that you'll be able to tell longer stories next time and then you'll get more chips.

Patient: Okay.

The fact that the patient envisioned a kangaroo is in itself of significance. The object she was feeling (a small, somewhat round teddy bear) in no way had the configuration of a kangaroo. The fact that she felt it to be a kangaroo is a statement of the power of the projective process. And this is an important principle for the therapist to appreciate when utilizing this game. The greater the disparity between the objects and the child's fantasy regarding its identity, the greater the likelihood that powerful forces are distorting the item for the purposes of satisfying unconscious needs. A kangaroo, of course, lends itself well to symbolizing a maternal figure. I consider it to be equal (if not superior) to the cow in this regard. The baby in the pouch (of course) symbolizes the patient and the kangaroo her mother. Although the story is a short one, it is, in essence, a complete story. The little baby kangaroo wants to stay in the pouch and remain indefinitely in a dependent state. That is essentially the whole story and when the patient initially said that it was the end of the story, I was basically in agreement with her. However, in the hope that I might get more material and elaborations, I encouraged her to add more to the story—but I was unsuccessful. With this understanding of the patient's story, I told mine:

Therapist: Okay, now I'll tell my story. Once upon a time there was a kangaroo. And this kangaroo liked to stay in his mother's pouch. It was nice and warm in there and the nipples of her breasts were always next to him. Whenever he wanted to suck on the warm milk, he could do so. And his mother didn't mind his staying there, even though other kangaroos his age were already outside and not spending so much time in their mothers' pouches.

Well, one day, while this kangaroo was resting comfortably in his mother's pouch, he suddenly heard some noises outside. They got louder and louder and he began wondering what they were. He stuck out his ear, above the edge of his mother's pouch, and he could hear other children kangaroos laughing, singing, and dancing, and having a lot of fun. Then he pulled himself up above the edge of the pouch and looked down to see what was happening down there. Then he saw all the kangaroo kids having a good time. The children kangaroos were jumping up and down and they were having a grand time, laughing, singing, and dancing, and things like that.

Well, he wanted to join in the fun but he was scared to leave his mother's pouch. He was frightened that something terrible would happen to him out there. His mother was always telling him to play near her or to stay inside because there were rough kangaroos outside who might hit him. Also, she had warned him a lot about getting hit by cars, getting drowned, getting taken away by strangers, and even such things as getting stabbed and shot. And so, when he was thinking about leaving the pouch, he began to think about all these things his mother said could happen, all these terrible things that he didn't want to happen to him.

Well, as he was thinking about these things, the other kangaroos outside started calling up to him and asked him to come out of his pouch and play with them. The kangaroo told them that he was very busy and that he would come out some other time. But they could see, by the look on his face, that he was frightened. And so they started calling him "scaredy cat" and other names like that. They started yelling up, "Hah, hah, hah, the baby's afraid to go out and play" and other things like that. This made the kangaroo feel very embarrassed. He also felt very sad. He really wanted to go out and play and he really wanted the other kids to stop calling him names like that. (therapist now turning toward patient) So what do you think he did?

Patient: He just stayed in the pouch and didn't listen to the other children.

Therapist: Well, a part of him wanted to do that because he was scared to go out, and he wanted to remain in a safe place in his mother's pouch. However, another part of him wanted to go out and play with the other kids and join in the fun. Also, he didn't want the kids to be teasing him that way and calling him all those terrible names. So, he decided that he was going to try to go out of the pouch, even though he was very scared. And so, little by little, he pulled himself out of the pouch and little by little, more and more of him came out. As he was doing that, the little kangaroos outside were all cheering him for trying. And this gave him more confidence that he could do it. But, the more he was outside the pouch, the more scared he became. A few times he went back in, and then the other kangaroo children started laughing at him and calling him names. But, when he pulled himself out, they cheered him and that made him feel better. (therapist again turning to patient) So what do you think finally happened?

Patient: Well, I think that he was still too scared to get out.

Therapist: Do you think that's a good thing?

Patient: I don't know.

Therapist: Well, would you like to hear my opinion about that?

Patient: Yes.

Therapist: Well, in my opinion, it would have been better for the kangaroo to go out, even though he was scared at first. And that's exactly what happened. He finally got out. It took some time, but he finally did it. He was scared at first, but, after a while, he got used to being outside and he found that it was a lot of fun to play with the other kangaroos. And each time he did it, it was easier and easier, and that's how he got over being scared to play with the others and being scared of being out of his mother's pouch.

My story obviously needs no explanation. It encourages desensitization to a fearful situation and is part of the treatment of any child with fears.

THE ALPHABET SOUP GAME

The Campbell's Alphabet Soup Game* is packaged in a container that closely resembles a very large can of Campbell's tomato soup (Figure 3.7). The container is quite attractive and therefore readily appeals to the child who is looking over the toy shelves for a game to play. The equipment consists of a plastic bowl filled with plastic letters and two spoons. The modification that I have found most useful therapeutically is for both the patient and therapist to each scoop a spoonful of letters from the bowl and form a word with them. The patient (whom I generally allow to go first) gets a reward chip for having been able to form a word. If the child can say anything at all about the word, he or she gets a second reward chip. And if the child can tell a story about the word, he or she gets two extra reward chips. I then similarly respond to my word. The responses, of course, are used as points of departure for psychotherapeutic interchanges.

The game can then proceed in a number of ways. One variation is for the players to attempt to form other words from the same batch of letters in order to obtain more reward chips. When the player is no longer able to, he or she can take a second scoop by "paying" two chips to the bank. These can be added to the original group of letters (the preferable alternative because there are then more letters with which to form words), or serve as a replacement for them. Sometimes trading letters with one another adds to the enjoyment of the game. Or the two players can decide to trade their whole batch of letters with one another to see if they can form other words, not previously used. Whatever the variations utilized (and I am sure the reader can devise his own) the basic principle holds that a player gets one reward chip for the word, a second for a comment, and two more for a story. Again, the winner is the player who has received the most reward chips at the end of the allotted

---

*This game is no longer being manufactured. The interested reader, however, should be able to put together a reasonable facsimile. All that is necessary are two spoons, a soup bowl, 1″ plastic letters available in most toy stores, and a treasure chest of reward chips.

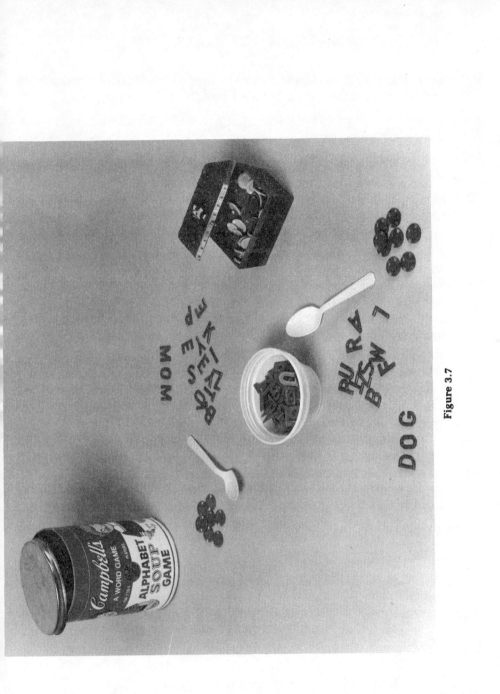

Figure 3.7

time. He or she, of course, receives one of the *Valuable Prizes* from the previously described box of prizes.

Clinical Example

The Case of Larry (The Boy Who Felt His Mother's Breasts) Larry entered treatment at the age of seven and a half because of compulsive touching of walls and furniture. He was a very tense boy and intermittently exhibited tics of the neck and shoulders. On occasion his tics took the form of yawning and throat-clearing sounds. However, the verbal tics were not that prominent that one could justifiably consider him to have a Gille de la Tourette's syndrome. Excessive masturbation was also described by the parents. At the end of the initial interview, while I was standing and talking with the parents and Larry, he began to caress his mother's breasts. She continued to talk to me as if nothing were happening. When I brought this to the family's attention the father stated that he had not noticed that anything was happening and the mother said that Larry caressed her breasts on occasion, that it was an innocuous practice not associated with sexual excitation by either of them, and that she did nothing in response.

In my subsequent evaluation I found the father to be a man who compulsively spoke about sexual matters—especially in a humorous way. The mother was coquettish and undressed frequently in front of Larry. On one occasion, early in treatment, Larry wrote the following note to his mother: "Fuck shiter old god damn mommy. Happiness is watching mommy pull her god damn fuckin pants down."

I considered Larry's tensions to be related to pent-up sexual excitation which could not be released directly. As expected, many of his stories revealed sexual and oedipal themes. My responding communications attempted to help him resolve his oedipal conflicts. During the second month of treatment the following interchange took place while playing *The Alphabet Soup Game*.

> *Therapist:* What word do you have?
> *Patient:* Jug.
> *Therapist:* Okay. Now you get one chip for completing the word jug. Now if you can say something about jug you can get another chip, and if you can tell a story about jug you can get two more chips.
> *Patient:* Don't you get—um, oh yeah.

Therapist: Go ahead.

Patient: Okay. I'm going to tell a story and. . . .

Therapist (interrupts): . . . and say something. Go ahead.

Patient: Okay. A jug could hold flowers.

Therapist: Okay, that gets another chip. A jug could hold flowers. All right. Now a story can get you two more chips.

Patient: Okay. Once there was a girl and she was picking flowers. She was cutting off flowers on one of her trees and . . . (pauses) . . .

Therapist: Yeah. Go ahead. And . . .

Patient: And she was putting it in her mother's jug. So . . . (pauses) . . .

Therapist: Go ahead.

Patient: And so when she was putting it in she brought the jug over so she could put in all the flowers that she got and it broke because she dropped it.

Therapist: What broke?

Patient: The jug.

Therapist: Okay. She dropped the jug, yeah, as she was putting the flowers in?

Patient: Yeah.

Therapist: Yeah. Go ahead. You don't have to wait for me. Go ahead. You tell your story.

Patient: And . . . (pauses) . . . she—so she—so she stopped to think and her friend and her friend's mother were going out to the flower shop and she—and that was the same flower shop where her mother bought the jug so the girl asked her friend's mother if she could go. And she said, "Why?" And she told her the story and then she went to buy her a new one. And so when they got back her mother was just coming back and then she put the same kind of flowers—she just—since she broke that one she cleaned it out and then the flowers that she picked out of the dirt she put in so that . . .

Therapist (interrupts): Oh, did they bring her another jug—this friend and the mother?

Patient: Yeah, but she went.

Therapist: She went with them. And she got another jug.

Patient: Yeah.

Therapist: Go ahead. And then what happened?

Patient: That's the end.

Therapist: And she put the flowers in?

Patient: Yeah.

Therapist: Okay. And the lesson of that story? What do we learn from that story?

Patient: That you should tell your mother if you do something or something bad happens. Or you shouldn't take a jug or a vase and, um, and bring it in the front but in the back you could just take another vase or make your own. You don't have to take your mother's vase or jug.

Therapist: You don't have to take your mother's vase or jug, or, or—

Patient: jug.

Therapist: —or jug. You can get another one. Is that it? I'm not clear what that last part is.

Patient: You can make one of your own or you can buy one, or if you have your own you should use your own.

Therapist: Hh hmm.

Patient: You shouldn't use your mother's.

Therapist: Hh hmm. You should use your own.

Patient: Yeah.

Therapist: Okay. Very good.

I understood the jug to represent Larry's mother's vagina. The flowers, which were taken from a tree, in this case I felt were phallic symbols. Although flowers are traditionally a female symbol, in this situation I considered them more likely to represent male genitalia in that they were inserted into a jug. In addition, their being taken off a tree suggests that Larry is acquiring his father's genitalia for his own purposes.

Although Larry represented himself as a girl in this story, I did not consider him to have a sexual orientation problem. Children will often represent themselves as a person of the opposite sex to disguise the figure and prevent realization that they are talking about themselves. As the girl consummates the sexual act, that is, as she inserts the flowers into the jug, it drops and breaks. I felt that this represented Larry's basic feeling that his mother's genitalia were "too hot to handle." By dropping the jug he avoids getting "burned," that is, suffering various anticipated repercussions for this "transgression." In addition, the jug's dropping represents his ambivalence about consummating the sexual act. Dropping the jug prevents the flowers from remaining in it.

He then acquires a jug on his own. I considered this to be a healthy step in the alleviation of his oedipal problems. By getting his own jug he gives up the quest for his mother's. I believe that this story revealed, in symbolic form, an appreciation of messages that I had communicated in previous sessions in which I advised Larry to consider alternative sources of gratification, both in the present and in the future. This, of course, is an intrinsic part of helping a child resolve oedipal difficulties.

With this understanding of the patient's story, I attempted to form a word from my own letters that would enable me to respond appropriately. This is the interchange that followed.

Therapist: Now it's my chance. Okay?

Patient: (nods affirmatively)

Therapist: Now I've got the word *box*, (spells) b-o-x. Now I get a chip for the word *box*. All right?

Patient: (nods affirmatively)

Therapist: And, let's see now, if I can tell something about the word *box* I can get a second chip. I'll say that a box—there are some boxes that are very pretty, very fine boxes. So I get a chip for that. Okay?

Patient: (nods affirmatively)

Therapist: Now if I can tell a story about the word *box* I get a third one. Right?

Patient: (trying to form new word with his letters)

Therapist: Listen, do you want to hear my story or do you want to try to make your word now? What do you want to do?

Patient: Hear your story.

Therapist: Okay, then leave this and then you'll try to make another word from your letters after I finish. Okay?

Patient: (nods affirmatively)

Therapist: Okay. Once there was a girl and she wanted to take some flowers off a tree and her mother had a very beautiful box— and this box had been given to the mother by the father—and the father told the girl that she could look at the box once in a while and she could use it once in a while, but that she couldn't have it for herself. It wasn't hers, that it was the mother's. It was a very fine, beautiful box.

Now one day the girl wanted to put the flowers in that box—the flowers that she had picked—and she was kind of scared about that. She was afraid that if she put the flowers in that box, that her father would really get very very angry at her and he might beat her, hit her, or punish her very severely. And so as she was putting the flowers in the box—and her hands were shaking—in fact, it was so much so that she almost dropped it, her hands were shaking so.

Her father came in and he said, "What are you doing?"

And she said, "I'm oh, I'm just using this box for some flowers." She had to tell him what she was doing. It was clear what she was doing.

And the father said, "You know what I told you about that box. That's not your box. That box belongs to your mother. You can use it a little while, but if you want to really keep those flowers, you'd better get your own. And you can use that box for a while to keep those flowers in, but I want you to go to a store with your own allowance and buy your own box and then you can transfer the flowers to that box from the one I gave your mother."

The girl wasn't too happy about it because she thought the box was quite beautiful and she said, "Gee, I wish I had a box like that someday."

And the father said, "Well, someday you may. There's no reason why you shouldn't and when you're older you may get one like that. At any rate now you can't have it. You can only use it a little bit once in a while."

And so she put her flowers in the box and then she went to the store. She took some of her allowance and some money she had saved and bought herself a box, and then put the flowers in that.

And do you know what the lesson of that story is?

Patient: (nods affirmatively)

Therapist: What is the lesson?

Patient: If somebody has something and you want it, you can't have it.

Therapist: Or they may let you use it a little bit, but you can go out and get your own. Do you know what the other thing is called when you get your own?

Patient: No.

Therapist: It's called a substitute. Do you know what the word *substitute* means? What does *substitute* mean?

Patient: Well, is it the kind of person who like when the teacher is absent a substitute comes in?

Therapist: Right! You get a substitute teacher. Right. Okay. So I get two chips for that one. Right?

Patient: Right.

Therapist: Okay.

Patient: I get 50¢ allowance.

Therapist: Who gets 50¢?

Patient: Me, and my brother.

Therapist: Yeah. What do you spend it on?

Patient: . . . (mumbles) . . .

Therapist: What?

Patient: I save it.

Therapist: Uh huh. Are you saving up for something?

Patient: Yes.

Therapist: What?

Patient: At Woolworth's they have a motor that I want to get.
Therapist: Hhmmm. Good. Okay. Let's turn this off.

In my story the box is very much the mother's. However, the girl (again representing Larry) was permitted to use it once in a while, that is, share mother's affection with father. I emphasized the fact in my story that the box is the mother's and that it was given to her by the father. In my story I introduced the element of Larry's fear of paternal retaliation if he were to take his mother's box and use it for himself. Although this issue did not come up specifically in Larry's story about the jug, I knew it to be one of his problems and a significant element in his tension. Because his story contained what I considered to be part of a healthy resolution of the oedipal conflict (namely, acquiring a substitute gratification), I decided to focus on what I considered a still-to-be-resolved element in Larry's oedipal difficulties.

In my story the father does not react punitively to Larry's "transgression." He does allow him to use the box once in a while. He encourages Larry, however, to purchase his own box with money saved from his own allowance. Here, I introduced the notion that Larry will have to apply himself if he wishes to get the same kinds of gratification from a woman that his father enjoys.

In helping a boy resolve oedipal difficulties I try to help him appreciate that his mother's affection must be shared with the father. He can get some physical contact with his mother but cannot enjoy the intense degree of intimacy that his father does. The younger the child, the less likely he is to appreciate that such intimacy involves sexual intercourse. However, the young child is generally not particularly interested in that kind of experience; rather, he is more interested in generalized physical contact, sole possession, and occasional physical pleasure.

We continued to play the game and it was now Larry's chance to form a word.

Therapist: Okay. Now what word did you make?
Patient: Gun.
Therapist: Okay. You get a chip for the word gun. Now you can get a second one if you can tell a story with the word gun.
Patient: Okay.
Therapist: Or you can say something about the word gun. Do you want to say something about. . . .

Patient (interrupts): You need a license to have a gun.

Therapist: Okay. You need a license to have a gun. That gets a chip. Now a story.

Patient: Um. Once there was a man who had a gun and he found a spaceship—part of a —when he was in the ocean on a boat by himself 'cause he was fifteen years old. So. . . .

Therapist (interrupts): Did you say he was on a spaceship or he found a spaceship?

Patient: He found part of a spaceship in the ocean when he was on a boat because he's old enough to have his own boat.

Therapist: He found a spaceship in the ocean?

Patient: Part of it.

Therapist: It was floating in the ocean or it was underneath the ocean?

Patient: Floating.

Therapist: Okay.

Patient: Do you know, when a rocket blasts off if it has three stages the stages fall off them?

Therapist: Oh, so he found one of the stages.

Patient: You don't have a capsule, just a stage.

Therapist: Okay. So he found one of the stages floating in the ocean. Go ahead. Then what?

Patient: And he wanted it so he had a rope. So he took the rope and he tied it onto the boat and he tied it on to that part and he got on and he took the motor off of his motorboat and put it on the rocket ship, the stage of the rocket ship.

Therapist: Oh, he took the motor off his boat and he put it on the rocket ship.

Patient: Yeah.

Therapist: Okay.

Patient: So that would move and pull the boat. So when he was moving along he found he went deep, deep, deep into the ocean, all the way in. Out there there were sharks and whales and it was very rough. It was so rough that he fell off the rocket ship. So there was a shark in the water coming toward him; so there was only one thing that he could do. There was an island and the only problem was that it was full of snakes. So the rocket ship went down. So quickly he took the motor off and put it back on his boat. He started it up and he went past it, but he just got a little bite in his foot, and he went back home and he didn't want to go back in the ocean again. That's the end.

Therapist: Okay. And the lesson of that story?

Patient: If you have your own boat or if you're in the ocean and see something that you want, like something big, you can't have it unless it's like a toy gun or something. You can't take something big.

Therapist: Oh, you can have a toy gun, but you can't have a big rocket stage. Is that it?

Patient: Yeah.

Therapist: Because? Hhmm? Because?

Patient: Because it's too big and anyway there's nothing more you could do with it and there's no room for it.

Therapist: Uh huh. Okay. Very good. You get two chips for that. Okay. Let's turn the tape recorder off while I try to get a word, and then I'll tell a story about my word.

Patient: Turn it off.

In this story we again see strong oedipal themes. The patient wishes to hook his boat up to a rocket ship stage that is floating in the ocean and to be pulled around by it. He would take the motor off his own boat and attach it to the rocket ship stage. I believe that the rocket ship capsule probably represents Larry's father and that the stage that fell off it, Larry's mother. In essence, he has his father discard his mother and she is then available to him as she floats in the ocean. Larry's motor, as a symbol of his genitalia, is hooked up to his mother. However, it is she who pulls him around, and this, I believe, symbolizes his dependency rather than his sexual ties to her. However, the father once again appears—this time as a school of sharks and whales. He immediately "fell off the rocket ship" and tries to find safety on a nearby island. However, "the only problem was that it [the island] was full of snakes." Again, the punitive retaliating paternal figure appears to be ubiquitous. Accordingly, he flees from the scene suffering only a "little bite" in his foot. The story ends with his not returning to the ocean again.

This story is a dramatic statement of Larry's oedipal fears. The retaliating father is ever-present. However, his "bark seems worse that his bite" in that Larry suffers only a "little bite" in his foot. I believe that this represented an appreciation of my message given in the previous story that father will not be as punitive as Larry anticipates. In addition, in the "lesson" Larry sets his sights on smaller prey, namely, a toy gun—in other words, something closer to Larry's size and his ability to handle. One could argue that the rocket ship stage represents Larry's father's penis and that the story reveals Larry's desire to acquire his father's penis and his fear that such acquisition will be met by powerful and dangerous retaliation. This interpretation does not preclude my original. Rather, it is probable that both are operating simultaneously here. And, they are not inconsistent with one another in that they both serve the purpose of Larry's desire for a more intimate involvement with his mother. In short, if the rocket ship represents Larry's mother, the story reveals his attempt to "hook on" to her. If the rocket ship represents Larry's father's penis, the story reveals Larry's desire to acquire this large penis for the purposes of becoming more attractive to his mother so that he can "latch on" to her.

It was with this understanding of Larry's story that I responded as follows.

> *Therapist:* Now I've got the word *pet.* Okay?
>
> *Patient:* (nods affirmatively)
>
> *Therapist:* Now I get a chip for the word *pet.* I can get a second chip if I can tell a story about pets. Okay? Or a second chip if I can say something about pets. People like their pets and sometimes they don't want to share their pets, or they don't want to share their pets all the time. And now if I can tell a story about the word *pet*, I'll get two more chips.
>
> Once upon a time there was a man and he had a boat and he was riding his boat in the ocean—it was a motorboat—and he saw a stage of a rocket that was floating in the ocean. And he said, "Boy, it would be great to have that great rocket and then I could really zoom around the ocean here, zoom around the water, zoom around the island, and everything else."
>
> Well, he didn't know that the sharks who lived in that water and the snakes who lived on the islands had kind of adopted that stage—that rocket stage—as a pet. They liked it and they would swim around it. They would play in it and they would go inside it. The sharks would swim through it; the snakes would swim through it. And when this man put his motor on that stage, they got very upset and they said to him, "Listen, that's ours, that rocket stage. You can't have it. We'll let you play in it a little while, but you're going to have to get your own."
>
> Well, he said, "No, I want it all my own."
>
> And they said, "Listen, you can't have it all your own. It's ours. You can play with it a little bit." And he realized that the sharks meant business and the sharks and snakes were really kind of powerful.
>
> But he said, "Well, what can I do?"
>
> And they said, "Well, look at this ocean—we're near Cape Canaveral here and they fire off these rockets every once in a while and there are other stages here which fall into the ocean. Now we suggest you go over there and find out when they're going to shoot off the

next rocket and then you just take your boat out into the ocean along the path of the rocket, and I'm sure you'll be able to get a stage."

So what do you think happened?

Patient: He got one.

Therapist: He got one! How did he get it?

Patient: He found out when the next rocket was going off and then one that fell.

Therapist: Right! That's exactly what happened.

Patient: Are you finished?

Therapist: Did you think I was finished?

Patient: Yeah.

Therapist: Yeah, I was finished, but I was just trying to talk about the lesson of it. That's what I was trying to do. What do you think the lesson of that story is?

Patient: Same as mine.

Therapist: What's the lesson?

Patient: In my story it was that if you want something, you can't have it if it's too big or something, like if it's very big and you just want it, like the rocket stages there's no use for it. You take it out of the water or something and there's no place to keep it.

Therapist: Hh hmm.

Patient: Or back in the water if you have a dock.

Therapist: Hh hmm. Well, in my story what does the man do when he finds out that the sharks and the snakes won't let him have that rocket, except that they'll let him play with it for a little while?

Patient: He has to get his own.

Therapist: Right, so that if you want a rocket stage and it's already adopted as a pet by sharks and snakes, then go and get another one. There are usually others around. The end.

Okay. Now I get two chips for that story. Look, I'll tell you. Would you like to watch some of this now?

Patient: Yeah.

Therapist: Okay, let's watch some of it now.

Patient (counting the reward chips): It's even.

Therapist: It's even. Right. So we both get prizes.

In my story the sharks and snakes do permit Larry to spend some time with their rocket ship stage. However, they are firm in not permitting him full ownership of it. However, they suggest that he acquire his own and inform him that there are many other rocket ship stages that fall into the waters because they are quite close to Cape Canaveral.

The post-story discussion revealed that Larry did appreciate my message. On the clinical level Larry did subsequently enjoy an alleviation of his tics and touching compulsion. I believe that interchanges such as those presented here played a significant role in the alleviation of his difficulties.

As mentioned earlier in this book, I consider less than one percent of all the patients I have seen to be suffering with what could justifiably be referred to as oedipal problems. All of the rest have problems which are better explained by other mechanisms. However, when I do see oedipal problems, very specific family problems are operative. As discussed in Chapter One, I consider oedipal difficulties to rest on a foundation of parental deprivation of affection. The child's preoccupation with possession of the opposite-sexed parent is related to the desire to compensate for the frustrations felt over not being given the affection, love, attention, guidance, and protection that it wants. Furthermore, there is usually some seductivity by the opposite-sexed parent but no sexual fulfillment. The child is titillated but not given sexual gratification. Accordingly, we are not dealing with sexually abused children; rather, we are dealing here with children who have parents who are sexually seductive, but not to the point of providing gratification. When the seductive parent is a mother, there may be castration threats (overt or covert) by the father. These are not necessarily present and are not, as Freud believed, an intrinsic part of the paradigm.

Larry's mother was very seductive with him. She allowed him to play with her breasts (through clothing) but denied that there was any sexual excitation for either her or him. Larry's father was observer to this practice and considered it innocuous. I believe the excitation so produced contributed to his tics and generalized tension. His father's compulsive talk about sexual matters also contributed to Larry's excitation, but I could not find therein specific evidence for castration threats. I did not consider Larry's problems to be the result of normal sexual cravings; rather, I considered them to be the result of specific family factors that engendered the development of the oedipal paradigm.

THE PICK-A-FACE GAME

Creative Playthings manufactured wooden plaques depicting various facial expressions (Figure 3.8). Although not designed specifically to be utilized as a therapeutic game, they lend themselves well to this purpose. Unfortunately, Creative Playthings is no longer

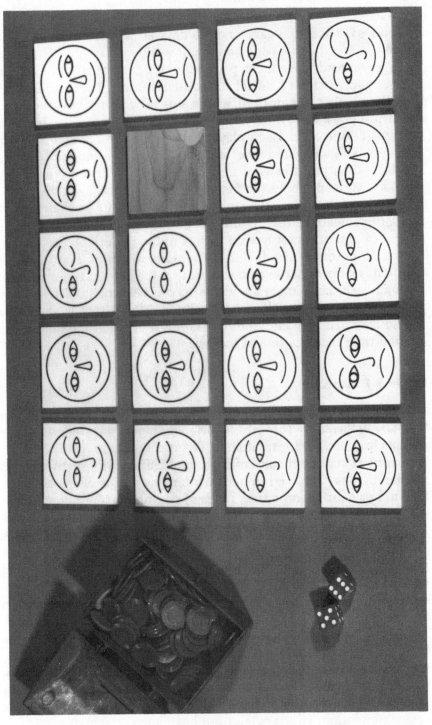

Figure 3.8

187

in business. The same game can be devised by mounting pictures of various facial expressions on small wooden plaques.

I have used these faces primarily as a mutual storytelling derivative game, which I call *The Pick-a-Face Game*. For this purpose, I use the plaques, a pair of dice (one side of which is covered), and a treasure chest of reward chips. The tiles are placed on the table face up (Figure 3.8). Each player in turn throws the dice and if a die lands with a covered facet up, that player is permitted to select any face. One point reward chip is then given. If the player can make a statement about the face, he or she receives another chip. And, if the player can tell a story about the face, he or she receives two more reward chips. Again, the material so elicited is used as a point of departure for a wide variety of therapeutic interchanges. Although these specific facial expressions might be restricting of free fantasy, my experience has been that they are not. A child will generally ascribe to them a wide variety of emotions that are likely to be present in most self-created stories. After a face is used, it is turned over. The person who has the most chips at the end of the allotted time receives one of the prizes.

Clinical Example

The Case of Gloria (Make Believe There's No Trouble, and You Won't Be Bothered By Things)   Gloria was eight years old when her parents brought her for treatment. The main problem was poor performance at school in spite of high intelligence. She spent most of the day in class involved in her own fantasy world. She was oblivious to her poor report cards, notes of complaint sent home by her teacher, and threats of parental punishment for her lack of commitment to her education. Gloria's father had his first heart attack at the age of 38 and his second at 44. Two years prior to the beginning of treatment, he had undergone a bypass operation. Both parents had made every attempt to cover up the import of the father's illness and had used a wide variety of ploys to protect her from the knowledge of his condition. In the first few months of treatment, I impressed upon them the importance of giving her accurate information. Although they complied with my request in this area, they did so without full conviction. The result was that Gloria continued to utilize the denial mechanisms she had learned from her parents. I believed that if they had had greater conviction for my recommendation, Gloria would not have been so denying.

In her fifth month of treatment, while playing *The Pick-a-Face Game*, the following interchange took place:

Therapist: Okay, the dice say you can pick a face. Which face are you going to pick?

Patient: I'm going to pick this one here. It's a smiling face.

Therapist: Okay. You get one chip for picking that face. (therapist gives patient a chip) Now you can get another chip if you can say something about that face.

Patient: He's smiling.

Therapist: What's he smiling about?

Patient: He's smiling because he's happy.

Therapist: What's he happy about?

Patient: He's just happy. He's not happy about anything. He's just happy.

Therapist: You can't just be happy about nothing unless you're a retard or something like that. You have to be happy about something.

Patient: Okay, he's happy because his mother bought him some ice cream.

Therapist: Okay, you get a chip for that. (therapist gives patient a reward chip) Now you can get two more chips if you can tell a story about that boy and his smiling, happy face.

Patient: Okay, let me think. . . . Once upon a time there was a boy. And he was a happy boy. He was a very happy boy. He was the happiest boy in the whole world. He got good grades in school. He got all As. He got As in conduct. The teacher said that he was a "pleasure to have in the class." And he was happy at home. Everything was good at home and he was happy there. And he had lots of friends who liked him very much. One day the family went on a picnic and they had a good time. They went home and the children watched television and then they went to sleep. The End.

Therapist: That was a fairly good story, but I've heard better ones. It didn't seem to have very many exciting things happen in it. Can you jazz it up a bit? Can you add things to make it more exciting?

Patient: I can't think of anything else.

Therapist: You know, in every family, both good things and bad things happen. What about this family? Did only good things happen to them? Or were there some bad things that happened also?

Patient: Only good things.

Therapist: Only good things? Nothing bad at all? Never at all?

Patient: Never at all.

Therapist: You know, in any family, things can happen like people getting sick or things like that. Didn't that ever happen in their family?

Patient: Well, once one of the children got the flu and had to stay home from school for a few days. But the parents were always okay.
Therapist: Anything else you want to say about that story?
Patient: No, I'm finished.

I considered the story to represent Gloria's significant utilization of denial mechanisms. The child in her story is doing well in school; Gloria was doing abominably. The family of the child in Gloria's story are all happy; all is going well with them; and neither of the parents is sick. This, of course, is opposite to what was the situation in reality for Gloria. With this understanding of Gloria's story, I proceeded as follows:

Therapist: Okay, it's my turn. The dice show that I can pick a face now. I'm going to pick this one. (therapist selects a face with a smile) Once upon there was a boy, named Jack, and he was always smiling. I didn't say that he was always happy; I only said that he was always smiling. In fact, he was the kind of a person who would smile even when he was sad, even when he was unhappy, even when he was very unhappy, even when he was very, very unhappy. In fact, Jack thought that the best thing to do about bad news was to make believe that it didn't exist, to make believe that it just wasn't there. Of course, that doesn't help anything because when you make believe that a problem isn't there—when it really is—then you don't do anything about the problem. Did you ever read any stories of mine that tell about people who do that kind of thing, people who don't talk about problems when they really have them?
Patient: No.
Therapist: Try to think hard. Don't you remember the stories I gave you?
Patient: No.
Therapit: Think again. When you first came here, I gave you a book and I told you to read the stories either by yourself or with your parents. Do you remember that book?
Patient: . . . Oh, yes.
Therapist: You remember the name of that book or what it was about?
Patient: There was some stories in it, but I don't remember.
Therapist: Do you remember one about an ostrich?
Patient: Oh, yeah, it was about an ostrich who put his head in the sand.
Therapist: No, it was just the opposite. Do you remember what it said about the ostrich and whether or not it put its head in the sand?

Patient: I don't remember. I thought he did when there was trouble.

Therapist: No, he does just the opposite. He wouldn't do such a stupid thing. When there's danger, the ostrich either looks at it and thinks what to do or runs away, but never makes believe that there's no danger. Only people think that way. And they think that ostriches do it that way also, but they don't. They're wrong. Do you remember that now?

Patient: Yes.

Therapist: Do you do that?

Patient: No.

Therapist: What about in school?

Patient: I don't think so.

Therapist: Well, I think you do. I think you make believe that there's no trouble in school, when there really is. What do you think about that?

Patient: Well, maybe I do it a little bit.

Therapist: Well, give me an example of a time when you do it, a time when you say you do it a little bit.

Patient: I don't remember now.

Therapist: Okay, I'll continue with my story about the boy Jack who was always smiling. One day Jack learned that his mother was sick and that she would have to go to the hospital. She was very sick and they thought she might die but they didn't know for sure. When Jack first heard the news, he was sad for a short time. Then, he pushed the whole thing out of his mind and began smiling. He just smiled and made believe that there was no trouble. His teenage brother, Fred, however, came up to him one day and asked him what he was smiling about. Jack said that he was very happy. His brother Fred said, "I don't know what you're so happy about, Mom's very sick."

Jack answered, "I don't want to talk about it. I don't want to think about it."

The big teenage brother Fred then said, "Well, I think you'd better think about it, because it's really going to be terrible around here if something bad happens to her, like if she dies."

Jack then began to scream and shout and said, "I told you, I don't want to talk about it."

Again, Fred told him that it was important to talk about it. Jack then ran off into his room and began to cry. As he lay in bed, he thought of himself out in the cold snow, starving and freezing, and that made him even more upset. Finally, his older brother Fred came into the room and heard him mumbling, "I'll freeze to death. I'll starve to death. No one will take care of me."

Fred then said, "I see now why you didn't want to talk about things. You think that if something happens to Mom that you'll freeze to death or starve to death, and there'll be no one to take care of you. But you've forgotten one important thing.

And Jack said, "What's that?"

And Fred said, "We still have a father. If something happens to Mom, we still have Dad."

As soon as Jack heard that, he felt better. He realized then that he had forgotten that his father would still be around and could be a *substitute* if anything happened to his mother. Do you know what a *substitute* is?

Patient: Yes, like a teacher, a substitute teacher.

Therapist: That's right, when your teacher is sick, you get a substitute teacher who takes over for her. And a father can be a substitute for a mother if the mother gets sick. Well, anyway, when the boy heard that, he realized that he had been stupid for not talking more about it and making believe that there was no trouble. And his teenage brother too helped him realize that it is important to talk about problems and that if you do, you can often do something about them and that if you don't, then they often get worse. Do you know what the lesson of my story is?

Patient: Talk about things.

Therapist: Right!

I cannot say that this was one of the most successful interchanges I've ever had with a child who exhibits denial mechanisms. However, a little progress was made. It takes many bricks to build a house and every brick contributes.

THE MAKE-A-PICTURE STORY CARDS

The *Make-a-Picture Story Cards* (MAPS) (Schneidman, 1947) is a valuable instrument. In fact, I consider it to be one of the most useful diagnostic and therapeutic instruments in the child therapist's armamentarium. First, I will discuss its standard use as a diagnostic instrument and then the modifications that I utilize for therapeutic purposes.

Diagnostic Utilization

The instrument consists of 22 cards (Figure 3.9) on each of which is depicted a scene, e.g. a doctor's examining room, the attic of a house, an empty street, a stage, an empty raft floating on the ocean,

Figure 3.9

193

a forest, and so forth. In addition, there is a blank card. No figures, either animal or human, are present in any of the scenes. In addition, there is a collection of figurines, both human and animal. Some of the human figures appear to be typical family members, but others are readily identified as a pirate, clergyman, soldier, doctor, nurse, Santa Claus, superhero, and maid. A few animals are also included, such as a snake and a dog. The patient is asked simply to look through the pictures and select one. Next, the patient is asked to review the figurines, select one or more, place them on the selected scene, and then create a story. I consider the stories to be valuable sources of information about underlying psychodynamics.

As a diagnostic instrument, I consider *The Make-a-Picture Story Cards* (MAPS) to be superior to *The Thematic Apperception Test* (TAT) (H. Murray, 1936) and the *Children's Apperception Test* (CAT) (L. Bellak and S.S. Bellak, 1949), which it resembles. In the TAT and CAT the scenes, although designed to be somewhat vague, still include figures that are definitely recognizable. In the TAT one can state easily whether the depicted people are male or female, young, middle-aged, or elderly. In the CAT there is even greater specificity with regard to the activities of the various figurines (invariably animals). Accordingly, although there is a universe of possible responses to the TAT and CAT cards, there is still a certain amount of contamination of the child's fantasies by the eliciting stimuli. The MAPS pictures, however, are created by the child. Thus, there is less contamination than one has with the CAT or TAT instruments, and so there is a larger universe of responses that may be elicited. For this reason I consider the MAPS instrument to be superior to the TAT and CAT.

However, there is one major drawback to the utilization of the MAPS cards. Specifically, the facial expressions on all of the figures appear to this examiner to be somewhat grotesque, macabre, and hostile. At best, they are poorly drawn; at worst, they are morbid. My experience has been that one gets more hostile and morbid fantasies than would be obtained from more neutral and/or benevolent figurines. Accordingly, in order to offset the contaminating effect of this drawback of the instrument, I generally present the child with both the figurines provided by the manufacturer and my own set of small play dolls that I traditionally use in my work with children. When the instrument is used in this way, I have found that I get a better balance of fantasies.

Therapeutic Utilization

The MAPS cards lend themselves well to therapeutic utilization (Figure 3.10). All one needs to do is add the treasure chest of reward chips to the aforementioned equipment and one has what I consider to be an extremely valuable therapeutic game. The game begins with the child's being told that he or she will receive one chip for creating a picture by placing one or more figurines on the selected card. An additional chip is given for a statement about the picture and two more for a self-created story. Again, the therapist plays similarly and the material so elicited is used as a point of departure for a wide variety of psychotherapeutic interchanges. The winner is the person who has accumulated the most chips at the end of the allotted time.

Of the various mutual storytelling derivative games described in this chapter, I consider this one to be the most valuable. One of the problems with the other games is that the unconscious well appears to run dry quickly after four or five stories, and the material then elicited tends to be more stereotyped and less idiosyncratic. Somehow, the MAPS cards and figurines appear to give the unconscious "new ideas." However, with the MAPS these are less likely to be contaminations than with the other instruments; they are more likely to be catalysts for the expression of important psychodynamic themes.

Clinical Example: The Case of Ruth (The Army of Babysitters)   Ruth entered treatment at the age of six, when she was in kindergarten, because of "hyperactivity and poor attention span." Because of these symptoms the school considered her to be suffering with a neurologically based learning disability. Although the school authorities were aware that both of her parents were suffering with serious physical illnesses, they still considered Ruth to be neurologically impaired, and the question was raised about her repeating kindergarten and possibly entering a class for learning-disabled children. In addition, Ruth exhibited manifestations of depression, withdrawal, apathy, disinterest in play, and generalized sad affect.

My own evaluation revealed absolutely no evidence for the presence of neurologically based deficits. There were, however, definite family problems that provided a much more likely explanation for Ruth's difficulties. When Ruth was three her father de-

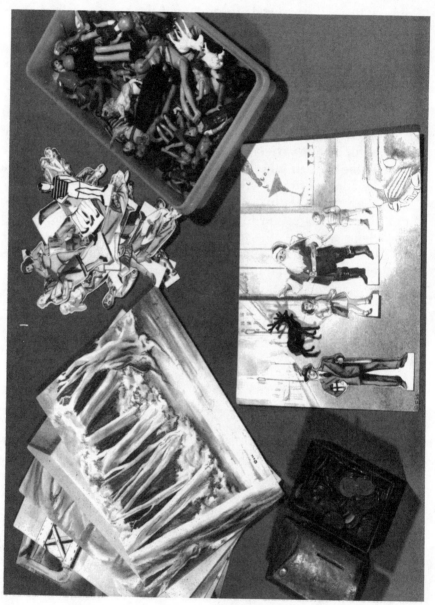

Figure 3.10

veloped signs and symptoms of a brain tumor. This was diagnosed and removed; however, his prognosis was considered guarded. When I saw her at six, her father exhibited mild neurologically based sensorial deficits—deficits that were probably not apparent to the unsophisticated observer. However, because he was bald and did not wear a hair piece, his operative scars were readily apparent. He was back at work and, I suspected, was not functioning at the same level of performance that he was at prior to his illness.

About one year prior to her initial visit, when Ruth was five, her mother exhibited various sensory and ocular changes that were ultimately diagnosed as multiple sclerosis. During the subsequent year she suffered with a number of significantly severe exacerbations, some associated with sight loss (bordering on bilateral blindness) and intermittent weakness in both lower extremities (that required the assistance of crutches or a cane).

In her projective play Ruth routinely cluttered every scene with as many humans and animals as were available. When administered the MAPS cards, Ruth covered every card with as many figurines as she could find. I considered such utilization of the play dolls to be a manifestation of her separation anxiety and the desire to compensate for the potential loss of one or even both of her parents. By cluttering the scene with as many human and animal figures as possible, she reassured herself that there would be substitutes for these potential losses. In line with this, I considered her symptoms of hyperactivity and attentional deficit to be concomitants of the fear that she felt in relation to her parents' illnesses. Furthermore, I considered her depression the predictable result of the spectre that hung over her household. Her depression served as a confirmation of my view that when someone is depressed, there is either something in the patient's reality that justifies a depressed reaction or he or she views the situation in such a way that depression is a predictable effect.

During her third month of treatment the following interchange took place while using *The Make-a-Picture Story* cards as a point of departure for mutual storytelling.

Therapist: Good afternoon, boys and girls, ladies and gentlemen. Today is Monday, the 28th of December, 1931—I mean 1981—and my guest and I are playing games. Now what we have here are these cards and our guest selects one card and then we have all these dolls here. We have these regular kinds of colored dolls like this, and we

have these black and white flat dolls like this—and you pick which-
ever ones you want—and you put them on whatever scene you want
and then you tell a story about it. Okay?

Patient: Okay. All right. (Patient creates a picture.)

Therapist: Let's see the card you have here. Now what is this card
of? What does that show?

Patient: The baby of the house.

Therapist: The baby of the house.

Patient: It's a picture with the mother, and the father, and the baby.

Therapist: Okay, the mother, father, and the baby. Go ahead.

Patient: Okay. I'll set this up.

Therapist: Set it up.

Patient: One day the mother and the father with their little baby
went into the mother's and father's bedroom. The baby was bouncing and bouncing and bouncing and bouncing on the bed. "It's time
for bed, Junior," said mother. Junior fell asleep right away.

Therapist: It's time for bed and then Junior fell asleep right away.
Okay, then what happened?

Patient: Then the mother and father climbed into bed. Junior was
their *only* child.

Therapist: Junior was their only child and they climbed into bed
with Junior.

Patient: And that night they had a real big dream.

Therapist: They had a dream. Yeah.

Patient: About them having a family to. . . .

Therapist: A dream that what?

Patient: About a family babysitting Junior.

Therapist: Oh, a family was babysitting Junior.

Patient: And they were out shopping for the night.

Therapist: The family was outside for the night? The babysitting
family?

Patient: No, the regular family. The mother and the father had
gone out for the night and this other family was babysitting little
Junior.

Therapist: Oh, in other words when the mother and father were
out this *whole* family was babysitting Junior. Is that right?

Patient: Hmm. (Patient adds family of five to the scene.)

Therapist: Okay, this *whole* family was babysitting Junior. Then
what happened? Where are they out? Now they're in bed there with
Junior?

Patient: Yeah, but they're dreaming.

Therapist: Oh, they're dreaming that they went out. They really
weren't out. They were just dreaming that they were out and they
were dreaming that this whole family was babysitting.

Patient: Yeah.

Therapist: Okay, then what happened?

Patient: Then when they woke up in the morning the baby started to . . .

Therapist: When they woke up in the morning, they what?

Patient: When they woke up in the morning the mother said to Junior, "We'll have a family babysit you today."

Therapist: The mother told Junior they're going to have the whole family babysit. Okay.

Patient: Junior soon got down behind mother. He didn't want mother to go to work. "I'm sorry, Junior, but I can't take care of you, but . . . (mumbles) . . . "

Therapist (interrupts): Wait a minute. Junior didn't want Mommy to leave for work and Mommy said what?

Patient: "I'm not going to work, Junior. I . . . (mumbles) . . . "

Therapist: I'm not going to what?

Patient: "I'm not going to work yet."

Therapist: "I'm not going to work yet?"

Patient: "Because you're going to have a new baby sister. Besides, you're already very little. I know that. You'll have to do with your new friend in the house."

Therapist: Wait a minute. You'll have to what with your new friend in the house?

Patient: "You'll have to do good with your *new* little kid in the house."

Therapist: "You'll have to do good with the new little kid in the house?" You mean the brother or the sister?

Patient: Yeah.

Therapist: Uh huh.

Patient: One day mother and father came home with twins!

Therapist: Wow! They came home with twins. Oh, twins. Instead of coming home with one, they came home with two. Then what happened?

Patient: Mother said, "Meet . . . " I mean mother said to Junior, "Meet Peter and your sister Ann."

Therapist: "Meet Peter and your sister Ann?"

Patient: Yeah.

Therapist: Oh, okay. So there was a Peter and Ann. Then what happened?

Patient: Peter's nickname is *clean*.

Therapist: Peter's nickname is what?

Patient: Is *clean*.

Therapist: Is *clean*?

Patient: Yes.

Therapist: Clean is his nickname and Ann's nickname is what?
Patient: Is *dirty.*
Therapist: Peter's nickname is *clean* and Ann's nickname is *dirty.*
Okay. Then what happens?
Patient: That night the mother and father slept in the bed with
Peter on the floor and the two twins at the foot of the bed.
Therapist: Okay. Okay, Peter on the floor and the two twins on
the bed.
Patient: And they woke up in the morning and they had no more
troubles with babysitting, because the whole family was babysitting!
(Patient now takes out the remaining dolls [about 15] and fills up all
the remaining spaces.)
Therapist: They had no more troubles because the whole family—
you mean, this wasn't a dream. They really were there?
Patient: Hh hmm.
Therapist: Is that the end of the story?
Patient: Yes.
Therapist: Okay. Now it's my chance to tell a story. Okay?
Patient: Oh, brother!
Therapist: Brother. You don't want me to tell a story?
Patient: Well, you can, but you can't use some of these characters.
Therapist: Okay. Which characters can I use and which charac-
ters can I not use?
Patient: Well, one thing. I just don't think you should use just those
four. (Patient sets aside four adult dolls, two males and two females.)
You can use any of the others.
Therapist: I can't use these four?
Patient: Yeah.
Therapist: I can't use these four over here, but I can use any of
the others?
Patient: Yes.
Therapist: Okay, I can use any of the others. Why can't I use these
four over here?
Patient: Because I'm going to need them for my next one and I
think I might want them. I know what they might do.
Therapist: Okay. I will not use them. I will use these others. Okay?
Patient: Okay.

My slip at the beginning of this interchange, in which I gave
the date as 1931, rather than 1981, like the overwhelming majority
of slips, is not without psychological significance. The year of my
birth is 1931. I suspect that I too was anxious about Ruth's parents
dying ("Send out not for whom the bell tolls, it tolls for thee.") and

probably unconsciously wished to regress back to a point where I could start all over again as a way of forestalling the inevitable. Had Ruth been old enough to understand the significance of this slip I would have certainly discussed it with her. It probably would have provided her some psychological benefit. Knowing that others have similar concerns can in itself be therapeutic. I suspect, as well, that other therapeutic benefits might have been derived from such a discussion.

This story is typical of those Ruth told in the early phases of her treatment. Rather than simply have a single babysitter she has a whole family babysitting. She starts off as an only child and when mother is expected to come home with one new baby, she comes home with two. By the end the babysitting family expanded to include just about every doll in sight, resulting in a total coverage of the card that she had chosen. Her final request that I not use the four adult dolls in my story was, I believe a reflection of her separation anxiety. She wanted to save them for herself, a symbolic reassurance that she would not be separated from them. I then told my story.

Therapist: Once upon a time there was a family and in this family was a Mommy and a Daddy. There was a baby and there was a girl. Okay? They lived together. Now this girl's father got sick one day, and he had to go to the hospital. But he came back! While he was away she was scared that he might not come back, but he came back and then her fears were over. But while he was there the mother said to the girl, "Are you scared that Daddy may not come back?"

And she said, "Yes, I am scared."

The mother said, "Well, it would be sad if he didn't come back. However, there are many other people in the world. There's this man over here. (Therapist picks up male doll.) There's an uncle. (Therapist displays another doll.) There's a grandpa. (Therapist picks up a third.) There's a grandma (and a fourth). There are lots of other people. In fact, while Daddy was in the hospital Grandpa came to the house to stay. Now when Daddy came back the Grandpa went home and lived with Grandma."

One day Mommy had to go to the hospital and the little girl got very sad, and she was worried that her mother might not come back. But the Daddy said, "Do you remember what your mother said when I was in the hospital?"

And the little girl said, "Yes."

And what had the Mommy said to the little girl when the Daddy was in the hospital?

Patient: I want to . . . (mumbles). . .

Therapist: What?

Patient: Let me think.

Therapist: Okay, you think.

Patient: That it would be sad if he didn't come back.

Therapist: That he would be dead?

Patient: It would be said if he didn't come back.

Therapist: It would be sad . . .

Patient (interrupting): Because there are lots of other people in the world.

Therapist: Right! If he didn't it would be very sad, but there are lots of other people in the world. Right. And then what happened was that the Mommy had to go to the hospital. And what did the Daddy say to the girl?

Patient: Probably the same thing.

Therapist: Which was?

Patient: It would be sad, but there are lots of other people in the world.

Therapist: Right. And he said, "There's Grandma." And Grandma came to the house and Grandma stayed at the house to help take care of the little girl and the baby while Mommy was in the hospital. Did the Mommy come back from the hospital? (All this is done with appropriate doll transfers.)

Patient: I don't know.

Therapist: Yes, she did. She came back and the little girl hugged her and kissed her, and her Daddy hugged her and kissed her, and the baby hugged her and kissed her, and everybody was glad she was back. And the Grandma said, "Okay, I don't have to stay here any more now, because your Mommy is back." And Grandma went home and stayed with Grandpa.

And then what happened was when the weekend came they had dinner guests. There was an uncle who came and there were friends. (Again appropriate dolls are introduced and removed.) There was a cousin—a teen-age cousin. Here is a teen-age cousin. And there was a boy. He was 12. He came. And there was another girl. And there was another uncle. And there was an aunt. And there were lots of friends and relatives that came. And so this made the girl feel very good, because she knew there were a lot of people in the world and that if ever anything were to happen to anybody in her family, like her mother or her father—if they were to get sick—she knew that there would be other people who could help take care of her.

And although she thought it would be very sad if something were to happen to one of her parents, she knew that there were a lot of other people. And do you know what the lesson of that story is?

Patient: No.

Therapist: What do we learn from that story?
Patient: Let me try and remember now. I don't know.
Therapist: We learn that if something happens to your mother or your father. . . .
Patient: Don't worry—that there are lots of others in the world.
Therapist: Right. Although it's very sad, there are lots of other people in the world. Okay? Now would you like to watch this television program?
Patient: Of course. . . .
Therapist: Okay, let's watch it.

Whereas in the patient's story the scene is cluttered with a multiplicity of figures simultaneously, in mine a more realistic approach to the parental substitute problem is provided. Specific individuals are defined and they are placed on the scene one or two at a time. At no time is the scene cluttered with a host of figures. I provided reassurance about the presence of substitutes, but introduced a healthier utilization of such surrogates, namely, one or two at a time rather than a horde. This is certainly more consistent with what would be her situation if her parents were indeed to die.

Ruth's therapy was conducted at what I considered to be a low level of efficiency. Had her parents not been sick, she probably would not have needed treatment. The most therapeutic experience that Ruth could have would be the total and complete cure of both of her parents. Because no one could honestly reassure Ruth that her parents would completely recover, it is not likely that her therapy could be completely successful.

At the time of this writing, she has completed three years of treatment. Fortunately, her mother is enjoying a prolonged period of remission from her multiple sclerosis and her father's condition still remains stable. There is no question that these are important factors in her improvement, although I would like to think that her therapeutic experiences have played some part. However, she still exhibits significant insecurity about her situation. In the middle of her second year of treatment she saw the movie *Annie* and became preoccupied with children who live in orphanages. This was primarily reflected in her therapeutic play. Clearly, she identified with the children whose parents had died and envisioned herself being placed elsewhere if this calamity were to befall her. Even though I had early in treatment advised the parents to discuss with Ruth who she would be living with if they were to both die, she still persisted in believing that she would somehow be cast out into an orphanage. Reassurances such as those provided in the aforementioned story played some role in reducing this fear.

CONCLUDING COMMENTS

I consider the mutual storytelling derivative games to be valuable therapeutic instruments. Although they are basically quite similar to one another with regard to the "rules," they are generally not considered so by most children (especially younger ones). The situation here is similar to that which is found in children's game in general. Many board games are basically identical with regard to the fundamental rules of play; the differences are the figures and equipment that are utilized when playing the seemingly different games. Accordingly, children are used to this sort of thing and generally do not object to these similarities in the derivative games. They are generally less valuable than pure mutual storytelling because the fantasy created with "Dr. Gardner's Make-Up-a-Story Television Program" is essentially completely free of external contaminations. These games should then be viewed as instruments of second choice. It is preferable for the therapist to be presented with a free self-created fantasy that is told into the atmosphere. Although the external facilitating stimuli here do provide some contamination, my experience has been that the pressure of the unconscious to project fantasies relevant to issues meaningful to the child at that particular time are far more powerful than the capacity of the external facilitating stimulus to provide significant contamination.

The mutual storytelling derivative games are generally useful for children from about the age of four (the earliest age at which I treat) to about eleven. At that age, children begin to appreciate that their stories are revealing of underlying psychodynamic processes over which they are likely to feel anxiety and/or guilt. Accordingly, most will then refuse to play the game with rationalizations such as: "This is a baby game" and "I'm not in the mood to play those kinds of games." This is one of the reasons why I devised *The Talking, Feeling, and Doing Game*, which I will be discussing in detail in the next chapter. Another reason for the game's development was that there were some children who were still not providing me with psychologically meaningful material, even though I presented them with one or more of the games described in this chapter. *The Talking, Feeling, and Doing Game* proved useful not only in eliciting material from these more resistant children but by extending, as well, the upper age limit for obtaining useful projective material that could readily be utilized in therapy. I found that I could engage most children up to the age of 14 or even 15 with *The Talking, Feeling, and Doing Game*, five or six years after the mutual storytelling technique and its derivative games were no longer therapeutically useful.

FOUR

The Storytelling
Card Game

The Storytelling Card Game* is the author's latest contribution to the mutual storytelling derivative games. Of the numerous games in this category that he has developed, he considers this to be the most predictably effective for eliciting self-created stories from children.

The Talking, Feeling, and Doing Game was originally devised to enable therapists to elicit psychodynamically meaningful material from children who were so resistant that they weren't even providing self-created stories. Most of the cards in this game are verbal projective in that they do indeed elicit unconscious material. However, many elicit material that is primarily in conscious awareness and very few elicit material as "deep" as that which is obtained from the self-created story. If one visualizes there to be a continuum from

---

*Manufactured by Creative Therapeutics, 155 County Road, P. O. Box R, Cresskill, New Jersey 07626.

material that is most readily accessible to conscious awareness at the one extreme to that which is most deeply repressed at the other, one could say that The Talking, Feeling, and Doing Game elicits information at the conscious end of the continuum and that the dream would provide information at the extreme unconscious end. Pure mutual storytelling, unaffected by the contaminants of play material, would be close to the dream end of the continuum. The mutual storytelling derivative games, affected as they are by external stimuli, represent a shift toward the conscious end of the continuum, but are still very much on the unconscious side. The Storytelling Card Game, then, can be viewed as an instrument that complements The Talking, Feeling, and Doing Game as a therapeutic modality.

EQUIPMENT

The equipment (Figure 4.1) consists of twenty-four picture cards of which twenty depict a scene that is free of either humans or animals

Figure 4.1

and four that are blank. All cards, including the blank ones, are numbered in the lower right corner. The cards portray common scenes: living room, classroom, kitchen, library, bathroom, backyard, meadow, etc. Fifteen human figurines are provided, depicting people from infancy to old age. The arrow spinner board is divided into sixteen sectors on which the arrow may come to rest. Ten sectors provide for winning or losing chips, either with the bank or the other player. The other six sectors instruct the player to select one of four specific picture cards from the stack of twenty-four and throw the die, for example "Select card 5, 6, 7, or 8 and throw the die." A die and tray of reward chips (the bank) are also provided.

BASIC FORMAT OF PLAY

The game begins with each player taking five "free" reward chips from the bank. These provide each with a "cushion" for any losses that may be incurred early in the game, before the player's personal treasury is enriched by chips acquired from storytelling. The spinner arrow is the central element in the game play. Each player in turn spins the arrow and follows the instructions indicated in the sector on which the arrow comes to rest. When the spinner comes to rest on one of the ten sectors involving chip gain or loss, the player wins or loses chips as indicated. Such activity is of little psychotherapeutic value, but it does enhance the child's excitement and involvement in the game. When the arrow comes to rest on one of the six sectors indicating card selection, the player selects one from the group of four cards indicated by the spinner and then throws the die. The number indicated by the die is the maximum number of figurines the player may choose from the array provided. Only one die is used in order to ensure that the number of figures chosen will be six or less, the usual number of people in a family. If two dice were to be used, it is likely that many of the throws would entail the child's using a larger number of figurines, beyond the number of people found in most families. And this might reduce the psychotherapeutic value of the stories so elicited. Once the figurines have been placed on the card a reward chip is given. If the player can tell a self-created story about the picture, two more reward chips are given. Finally, if the player can tell the lesson or moral of the story, an additional chip is earned. The story so elicited then serves as a point of departure for a wide variety of psychotherapeutic interchanges between the therapist and patient. The winner is the player who has acquired the most chips when the game is over.

TECHNIQUES OF PLAY

Although the players alternate turns, it is preferable that the patient spins first ("You're the guest, and guests go first"). This practice enables the therapist to obtain uncontaminated material from the child. If the therapist tells a story first, the material he or she provides may contaminate the child's subsequent responses.

The Creation of the Child's Picture

When the spinner arrow instructs the child to select one from four specific cards and to throw the die, the therapist does well to instruct the child to spread out all four cards, review them carefully, and then select one of them (Figure 4.2). This is preferable to the child's quickly selecting a card. Choosing one card in a relaxed fashion, with full opportunity to inspect all four, increases the likelihood that the card chosen will be relevant to the child's psychological processes. If the child selects the card simply on the basis of the number, before even seeing the four cards, the examiner should not respect the request; rather, the child should be required to inspect the cards carefully before making the selection.

Following the selection of the card the player throws the die. The number so obtained indicates the *maximum* number of figurines that the player may take from the array of fifteen provided. This allows the player some flexibility regarding the number of figurines chosen and is thereby less constrictive of the projections than would be the case if the player were required to take the exact number of figurines indicated by the die. Here too, the figurines should be spread out and the child encouraged to give thought to the selection. If the child chooses the figurines rapidly, it is less likely that the choices will reflect the most relevant psychological issues. The figurines are then placed on the picture selected and the player receives one reward chip (Figure 4.3). The child should be instructed to lay the figurines down on the picture card and not attempt to stand them up. They are not designed to be utilized in this manner, and attempting to do so will

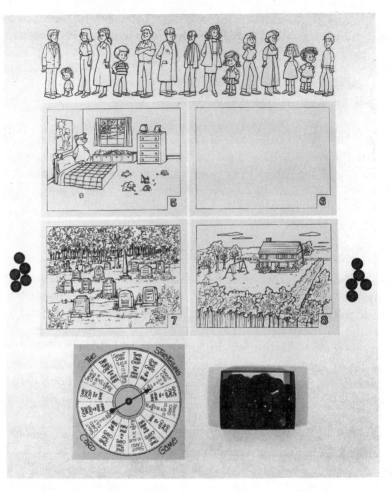

Figure 4.2

generally waste time. The player is also free to place the figures in any arrangement desired.

The Creation of the Child's Story

Next (and this is the most important part of the game), the player is required to tell a story about the picture so created. When first introducing the game, the therapist might say something to the child along these lines: "Now I want to see how good you are at making up a story about the picture you've just made. The rules of the game are

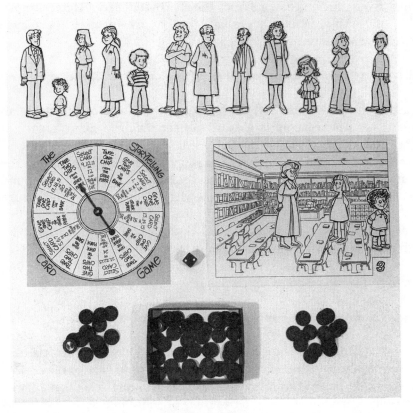

Figure 4.3

that the story must be completely made up from your own imagination. It can't be about anything that really happened to you or anyone you know. It can't be about anything you've read, seen on television, or videotape, or in the movies. It must be completely made up from your own imagination." If the game is being videotaped (an extremely valuable enhancement of the game's efficacy [submitted for publication]), then the therapist might add, "Naturally, the more interesting and exciting the story, the more fun it will be to watch on television afterwards." If the therapist suspects or concludes that the story so elicited is "lifted" from other sources, he or she does well to remind the patient that stories must be completely made up from the player's own imagination and they cannot be taken from other sources ("places"). Telling the child that the rules require that only stories that the child creates him- or herself will be rewarded with chips from the bank can enhance the child's "honesty." Upon completion of a self-created story about the picture formed, the player receives two more reward chips.

Eliciting the Lesson or the Moral of the Child's Story

Last, if the player can tell the lesson or the moral of the story, an additional reward chip is given. Younger children, who might not understand the meaning of the words *lesson* and *moral*, might be asked, "What do we learn from this story?" If the child claims that the story has no lesson or moral, the therapist does well to respond somewhat incredulously, "*Every* story has a lesson or moral. I'm sure you're smart enough to figure out what the lesson or moral of this story is." The lesson or moral assists the therapist in ascertaining which of the various themes that may be included in the story is likely to be the most important to focus on. Accordingly, a player can obtain up to four reward chips for each story.

The Therapist's Response to the Child's Story

After the patient has completed his or her story, the therapist may use the child's story as a point of departure for a wide variety of possible therapeutic interventions, e.g., a responding story in which adaptations are introduced that are healthier or more judicious than those utilized by the child (mutual storytelling technique). Other examples of therapeutic intervention would be discussion at the symbolic level ("Do you think that biting was the best way for the dog in your story to deal with that problem?"), general discussion ("Let's talk some more about the problem the boy had in your story, the problem of dealing with bullies"), or psychoanalytic inquiry ("Is there anything in your story that's like what is happening at home with you and your parents?"). It is important for the reader to appreciate that the responses presented herein are only suggestions and the game allows for great flexibility regarding the therapist's own individual style of responding to the child's stories.

The Therapist's Responding Story

If the therapist chooses to tell a responding story at that point (one based directly on the child's story), he or she may well request that the child "help" the therapist tell the story in order to incorporate the child's own resolutions and adaptations. If, however, the child's contributions reflect psychopathological patterns, the therapist should not include such in his or her story but present the healthier alternatives. The therapist might want to discuss these pathological contributions provided by the child or merely make a comment that he or she would prefer a different course for the story to take. The therapist then takes two reward chips for his or her story and may also reward the child with one or two chips for his or her contribution(s) (if "deserved"). The therapist's obtaining chips for providing a responding story encourages the child to respond similarly to the therapist's stories. When the therapist completes the story, he or she should ask the child to try to "figure out" the moral or the lesson, rather than immediately providing the moral or lesson him- or herself. In this way the child's involvement is elicited even further and the therapist can ascertain whether or not the child appreciates the story's fundamental message(s). If the child provides a reasonably good moral a reward chip is given; if not, the therapist then provides a lesson and takes the reward. Both can receive reward chips for the moral if each can provide a good lesson. (It is nowhere written that a story must have only *one* lesson or moral.)

In sum, the therapist is entitled to a maximum of three chips for a responding story (two for the story and one for the moral or lesson). Because the therapist has not created the picture, he or she is not entitled to the one chip provided the child for forming a picture with the card and figurines. The child, however, may earn extra chips by providing meaningful contributions to the therapist's story and moral. The therapist does well *not* to take chips for his or her contributions in discussions emerging from the child's story, but should judiciously award chips to the child for meaningful and therapeutically useful contributions to and remarks about the therapist's story.

The therapist may respond in any of the other aforementioned ways to the child's story or say nothing at that point and incorporate the information so gained into his or her subsequent responses during the course of the game. Whatever the nature of the therapist's response(s), an attempt should be made to play at a slow pace and discourage the child's providing quick responses in order to obtain chips. When played properly, both players are so engrossed in the stories and discussions that chips play a relatively minor role in the therapist-patient interchanges.

The Therapist's Initiated Story

When the therapist is the player directed by the spinner board to select one from four cards and then throw the die, he or she might display the four cards and ask the child to make the selection ("Can you please help me pick a card?"). In this way the card selected is more likely to touch upon issues relevant to the child. After the die is thrown, the therapist might enlist the child's assistance in selecting figurines and even allow the child to make the decision regarding which ones are chosen, how many (up to the maximum), and where they should be placed on the card. Such participation by the patient increases the likelihood that the picture created will be relevant to issues pertinent to the child. However, if the therapist has a particular theme in mind, he or she might choose the card and determine the figures to be selected. The therapist does well to utilize both methods of picture creation.

When the therapist tells a story, he or she should create stories that either are based on the child's previous stories (with the introduction of healthier themes) or incorporate other themes considered therapeutic. Just as is the case when the therapist tells a responding story, here too while telling his or her story, the therapist should try to involve the child, be receptive to the child's contributions to the telling of the story, and invite the child to try to figure out the lesson or moral of the story.

If, in spite of the therapist's courtesy that the "guest goes first," the spinner does not come to rest on a sector requiring storytelling until the therapist's turn (first, second, or third time around), the therapist will then be in the position of having no immediately preceding material on which to base a story. In such situations he or she might tell a story relevant to the child's clinical problems or topics focused on in the previous session (properly disguised by symbol and/or metaphor). If the therapist is concerned that such a story might be too contaminating of the child's subsequent responses (a reasonable consideration), then he or she might tell a more neutral story concerning issues relevant to practically all children, but not particularly relevant to the child's problems, for example, tolerating fears, enduring present frustrations for future rewards, self-expression, self-assertion, the value of practice, and so forth.

The Child's Response to the Therapist's Story

The therapist's story may serve as a point of departure for a variety of possible responses by the child, e.g., a responding story, discussion at the symbolic level, general discussion, and psychoanalytic inquiry. The therapist should encourage responses along these lines, but if the child chooses to go on and take his or her next turn, this should be respected. It is hoped that the therapist's stories and responses will become incorporated into the child's psychic structure and affect subsequent responses and stories. Even more important, it is hoped that the messages the therapist transmits will contribute to psychotherapeutic change—which, obviously, is the purpose of the game. Again, it is important to emphasize that the child should be discouraged from racing ahead simply to acquire more chips; rather, a slow pace is encouraged in order to get as much therapeutic mileage from each interchange.

Ending the Game

The play time is not fixed; rather, it is determined by the therapist's judgment regarding how rich the interchanges are and the time available during the session. When the play time is ended, the player with the most chips is declared the winner and receives a prize. Prizes are not provided as part of the game equipment. Traditional gumball machine trinkets will often serve well and can be readily purchased from supply houses and manufacturers of such materials.

INDICATIONS AND CONTRAINDICATIONS

The Storytelling Card Game is indicated for the wide variety of psychogenic problems for which children are brought to treatment. It is contraindicated for children who are psychotic and/or those who are significantly involved in fantasy. For such children the game might entrench their problems because it encourages further fantasizing. Such children do much better with more reality-oriented games such as The Talking, Feeling, and Doing Game.

The game is designed to be used in individual psychotherapy only. It would be injudicious for the therapist to use it in a group therapy situation because the first child's picture configuration and story are likely to contaminate the responses of the other children in the group. The best projections are made on a blank screen. Although there are some contamination of the screen by the picture card and figurines, at least the screen has been created to a significant degree by the individual who provides the projection. In contrast, if the game is used in a group therapy setting, the card screen (even when blank) is likely to be contaminated by the story provided by a previous child.

AGE RANGE

The game has proved most useful for children between the ages of 4 and 11. Children below 4 are not generally appreciative of the give and take of standard board-game play, do not wait their turns, and are not generally capable of providing the kinds of structured stories, that is, with logical sequences, that are the optimum kind to elicit for the purposes of therapy. Children of 4 and 5 may, however, provide story fragments that may still prove useful. Under these circumstances the therapist should try to surmise specific psychodynamic themes running through the child's story fragments. The upper age limit of 11 has been derived from empirical observations that youngsters beyond this age generally begin to appreciate that their self-created stories reveal personal information, and they may thereby become defensive and excuse themselves from play or refuse to participate with rationalizations involving their belief that the game is only for younger children.

MODIFICATIONS

It is important for the reader to appreciate that the instructions here should be considered as guidelines. Actually, the game allows for great flexibility and the therapist does well to consider his or her own modifications and innovations. Presented here are a few that the therapist may find useful.

The instructions allow the child to use fewer than the number indicated on the die to provide flexibility of figure choice. However, the examiner does well occasionally to permit the child to take a greater number of figurines than the die indicates—in order to enhance even further the potential variety of responses. Such expansion of the rules is especially justified if the request is not only reasonable but allows for the creation of a story that probably would be more meaningful than one created with a more limited number of figurines. Although allowing the child to take extra figurines should be judiciously permitted—because of the potential psychodynamic value of the stories thereby elicited—it would be an error to encourage the practice by using two dice. The "busy" stories created with many figures are less likely to focus on the specific intrapsychic and intrafamilial themes contributory to the psychopathological process. Accordingly, if the child routinely asks for extra figurines, then it is likely that pathological processes are operative—especially resistance to dealing with guilt-evoking and anxiety-eliciting material. Although the therapist would certainly want to understand the reasons for such pathological utilization of the figurines, he or she might still want to restrict the child to work within the maximum number provided by the die.

The game has been designed to elicit psychotherapeutically meaningful material from children who are resistant to discussing their difficulties directly. Accordingly, it is especially useful for resistant and uncooperative children. However, occasionally a child will be so threatened by storytelling that he or she will refuse to play the game. Such inhibited children may still be engaged in a modification in which they are not required to tell a story, but merely provide a statement about the picture created. Although such a statement will not generally provide as much psychodynamically meaningful material as a story, it can nevertheless provide the therapist with some useful information. This is especially the case if a particular theme pervades the various statements that the child provides. Generally, it is judicious to provide only one chip for a statement rather than two, in order to enhance the child's motivation to tell stories. Also, because the statement does not usually have a lesson or a moral, the child is further deprived of the more remunerative opportunities provided by a story and lesson.

Some children are so resistant and/or inhibited that they might not even be able or willing to provide a statement. The therapist does well not to simply "give up" on such children, but to try another modification. Specifically, the therapist might continue playing the game and provide stories him- or herself, without requiring of the child similar participation. Of course, the child will still be required to spin the spinner and is given the opportunity to acquire or lose chips when the spinner arrow comes to rest on one of the ten sectors indicating such transactions. Although the child may not avail him- or herself of the opportunity to acquire chips through storytelling, such a child might listen to the therapist's stories (always based on material relevant to the child) and derive some therapeutic benefit from such listening.

GENERAL DISCUSSION

The stories elicited in the context of The Storytelling Card Game are likely to be closer to issues relevant to the child's problems than those elicited from traditional picture cards utilized in many diagnostic projective instruments, for example, The Thematic Apperception Test (TAT) (Murray, 1936), The Children's Apperception Test (CAT) (Bellak and Bellak, 1949), and Roberts' Apperception Test for Children (Roberts, 1982). Generally, the scenes portrayed in these instruments, although sometimes vague, include a specific number of figures, each of whom is readily identifiable regarding sex and approximate age. Although there is a universe of possible responses to each of the scenes provided in these standard instruments, the pictures utilized in The Storytelling Card Game provide the opportunity for a greater universe of possible responses because the child has the option of deciding the sex, approximate age, and number of figurines (one to fifteen) to be included in the picture. Furthermore, the child determines the arrangement of the figures, and this, too, increases the variability of the responses when compared to traditional projective cards in which the relative positions of the figures affects the kinds of stories that will be elicited. Because the child creates the picture, rather than the creator of the drawings utilized in standard diagnostic projective instruments, the picture is more likely to tap the particular issues that are relevant to the child patient at that particular point. Last, The Storytelling Card Game provides four blank cards, reducing thereby the potential contamination of projections provided by traditional picture scenes. If all sixteen of the sectors were to involve storytelling, the game would be too high pressured because every spin would require a self-created story. This potential problem is obviated by utilizing only six of the sixteen sectors for storytelling and using the others for gaining or losing chips.

Besides the chips, other elements in the game enhance the likelihood that the child will provide self-created stories for the examiner. Spinning the spinner engenders excitement as the child hopes that the arrow will come to rest on a sector that will provide reward chips. The examiner does well to note that the ten sectors that are *not* involved in storytelling result in the gain or loss of *one or two* chips. In contrast, the six sectors that involve storytelling allow for the potential gain of *four* chips. Accordingly, the child is more likely to hope that the spinner will come to rest on one of the storytelling sectors. Throwing the die also enhances interest and excitement as the child generally hopes to obtain a high number in order to have the opportunity to utilize more figurines.

The game's mildly competitive element also enhances the child's involvement because of the prospect of winning the game and acquiring a prize at the end. Therapists are sometimes concerned about the potentially ego-debasing effects of competitive games in therapy, especially if the child loses frequently. The Storytelling Card Game is so structured that this potential risk is reduced significantly. Specifically, if each player were to take every opportunity to get as many chips as possible during every turn, then the winner would be determined by pure chance. The likelihood is that over the course of the game, the spinner will come to rest on both high- and low-yield sectors and this should ultimately even out. Furthermore, if the child avails him- or herself of the opportunity to earn extra chips by contributing to the therapist's stories and other responses, then the likelihood is that the child will win and that the potentially ego-debasing effects of losing will be obviated. However, as mentioned, when the game is played properly the therapist and child are so absorbed in the stories and other interchanges that little attention is paid to who has more chips and who ultimately wins.

CLINICAL EXAMPLE

Frank, a 6-year-old boy, was brought to treatment for help in dealing with his mother's illness. About six months prior to the first visit, his mother (age 43) was found to have cancer of the colon. Although there was a strong family history of this disorder, she had been negligent in getting frequent examinations. By the time the diagnosis was made, metastases to other parts of the body were found, especially in the bones of her spine. She was receiving chemotherapy as well as large doses of analgesics, and it was the opinion of all physicians that her prognosis was very poor. Frank had an older sister of 8 and both children exhibited behavior problems, especially tension, separation anxiety, and antisocial behavior. Furthermore, the children had not been told how seriously ill their mother was; rather, each time she was hospitalized they were sent to relatives and given various cover-up stories, excuses, and rationalizations.

During Frank's second session, the following interchanges took place while Frank and I were playing The Storytelling Card Game:

> *Therapist:* I'm going to select card 21, 22, 23, or 24 and throw the die. Okay? We've got these four: 21, 22, 23, and 24. Which one do you think I should talk about?

When the therapist is directed to select one from four cards, he or she does well to ask the child to determine which one of the four shall be used as a point of departure for the therapist's stories. This increases the likelihood that the story will relate to issues relevant to the child.

> *Patient:* I don't know. (Patient then points to card number 22, which depicts a stage.)
> *Therapist:* What is this one?
> *Patient:* Um, a stage.
> *Therapist:* A stage. And where is that stage?
> *Patient:* Uh, in a play.
> *Therapist:* Um, okay. Now what I do is, I throw the die. I got a four. I can take four people. I'm going to take three kids, and I'm going to take this teacher here. Let's get a teacher. Who looks like a teacher? Here's a lady who looks like a teacher. Okay.

The therapist might suggest that the child select the four figures because this will increase the likelihood that the story the therapist tells will relate to issues relevant to the child. However, at this point I decided to select the four figurines myself, four that would lend themselves well to utilization in the story that I had in mind, a story which I was certain would be relevant to the child. Accordingly I did not ask him to select the four figurines.

> Once there was a school and the school was going to have a play. There were three kids and they were going to be on the stage in the play. And one day the teacher got sick and they were very sad because they said, "Oh, my, my, my. The teacher's sick. What are we going to do? What are we going to do?"
>
> And they went to the principal of the school. And the principal said, "Well, when a teacher is sick we get a substitute." And so they got this substitute person and she was a substitute. Do you know what a substitute is?
>
> *Patient:* I don't know.
>
> *Therapist:* A substitute is the person who takes the place of somebody else. When a teacher is sick, they send in a substitute. And then the substitute came and she helped with the play. And then the original teacher came back. Then if the first teacher got sick again, they would bring in the substitute again.
>
> So the lesson of that story is: If your teacher is sick, usually they can get a substitute to take care of the kids. That's the lesson of that story. Do you remember the lesson? What's the lesson of that story?
>
> *Patient:* If your teacher's sick you could always use a substitute.
>
> *Therapist:* What is a substitute?
>
> *Patient:* Um, if your teacher gets sick, you get another, a whole new teacher.

The therapist does well to question the child about any words or concepts that might cause confusion. Otherwise, the therapist will not be certain that his or her messages are being received. Here it is clear that the patient understood the concept of the substitute.

> *Therapist:* Another teacher. Okay. Good. Okay, I get two chips for that story and I get one for the lesson. (Therapist takes three chips from the bank.)

I attempted here to introduce the important concept of the substitute because I considered it relevant to Frank's situation. It was likely that his mother would die. One way of dealing with this loss would be to involve himself with a substitute person, someone who could give him some of the affection, attention, guidance, etc. that his mother had been providing. I was planting a seed here, in advance, as a way of helping him with his forthcoming loss. I was introducing at this early point an option for adaptation to this loss, an option that might not have been in his scheme of things.

Therapist: Okay, now it's your chance. Let's put these four cards away. (Therapist replaces cards 21, 22, 23, and 24 in the stack.) Now you spin the spinner. Spin it again.

Patient: (spins the spinner)

Therapist (reading the spinner card): It says, "Take two chips from the other player." Okay, you get two chips from me. (Therapist gives patient two chips.)

Therapist: Now I go. And mine says, "Take one chip from the bank." (Therapist takes one chip from the bank.) Now you go.

Patient: (spins the spinner)

Therapist: And yours says, "Select card 21, 22, 23, or 24." Okay, now which one do you want to take of these four?

Patient (pointing to card 24): Um, I'll take that.

Therapist: What is that of?

Patient: A barn.

Therapist: A barn. Okay. Now you throw the die.

Patient (throws die): Two.

Therapist: Two. So you can take two people.

Patient: (selects two figurines and places them on the picture)

Therapist: Okay, what's the story?

Patient: This lady and this man, they just moved into a barn.

Therapist: A lady and man moved into a barn. Yeah.

Patient: And they liked it a lot.

Therapist: And they liked it a lot. Yeah.

Patient: Except for one thing, that the cows were bothering them because when they wanted to nap, they all kept going "Moooooooo."

Therapist (interrupting): Wait, a minute. Say that again about the cow. When they wanted to nap, the cow bothered them. Is that it?

Patient: Yeah.

Therapist: The cow bothered them when they took a nap. It said, "Moo."

Patient: Yeah.

Therapist: Then what happened?

Patient: Then they would keep on doing it when they were sleeping. But then the cows died.

Therapist: The cows died?

Patient: Yeah.

Therapist: And then what happened?

Patient: And then they won't bother them while they were trying to take a nap.

Therapist: And the cows didn't bother them and they got a nap.

Patient: Yeah.
Therapist: Is that the story?
Patient: Yup.
Therapist: Were they happy the cow died?
Patient: Uh, yeah.
Therapist: Why is that?
Patient: Because they couldn't sleep and they were like tired.
Therapist: Uh hmm. I see. Uh hmm. Okay. What's the lesson of that story?
Patient: The cows really bothered them when they were napping.
Therapist: Uh hmm. The cows what?
Patient: The cows bothered them when they were napping.
Therapist: Uh hmm. I see.
Patient: And the cows always died out so they don't worry.

Frank's mother was continually taking narcotics to ease the pain of her terrible disease. However, as is often the case, the analgesics she was taking were not completely successful in producing a pain-free state. At night, especially, when she was not distracted by the events of the day, her pain was often severe and she would cry out. The children could not but overhear her moans and sighs of grief. Of the various possible interpretations that this story had, the one that seemed to fit best was that it was a fantasy of cessation of exposure to his mother's moans that were interfering with his sleep, that is, if the mother were to die, he would get a good night's sleep!

The reader may consider this a somewhat surprising explanation, and it may be that the reader could come up with a better one. It was, however, the best one that I could think of—its morbidity notwithstanding. One can only wonder why Frank would entertain such a fantasy. He is basically wishing that his mother die soon in order that he may sleep uninterruptedly throughout the night. Is this not a cruel, and even sadistic fantasy for the child to have? I suspect that at his age Frank was incapable of fully appreciating the implications of his fantasy. Children of his age are traditionally egocentric and hedonistic. They have little ability to put themselves in the position of others. And he probably did not appreciate the finality of death. Accordingly, Frank had little capacity to appreciate the true implications of his fantasy.

I am reminded here of the 12-year-old girl whom I saw in treatment many years ago. Her mother was having visual difficulties and learned from the opthalmologist that she was suffering with retinitis pigmentosa, a disease of the eye that ultimately results in complete blindness. She imparted this terrible news to the family. The following day, during a joint session with the mother, I asked the girl what her reactions were to this terrible news. She replied, "Oh, goody. Now we'll be able to get a seeing-eye dog!"

It was with this understanding of Frank's story that I related mine:

> *Therapist:* Okay, now it's my time to tell a story. Once upon a time there was a man and his wife and they bought a barn. And there was a cow there and that cow was making a lot of noise. It was going "Mooooooooo. Mooooooooo. Mooooooooo." Did you ever hear a cow? Do they go like that? Can you make a cow sound?
>
> *Patient:* Mooooooooo. Mooooooooo.
>
> *Therapist:* Right. Mooooooooo, mooooooooo. That's how cows go. Right? Mooooooooooooooooo. Okay. It doesn't always sound like "Mooooooooooo" to me. Sometimes it sounds more like "Uhhhhhhhhhh. Uhhhhhhhhh." Like that.

The transcript cannot fully communicate the various cow sounds that the patient and I were making. I often do this when animals are depicted in a story. The imitations add a certain flavor and drama, which tends to enhance the attractiveness of the therapist's story. They also lend a note of levity to the therapy, which can often be a grim scene.

> *Therapist:* Anyway, the husband said, "Boy, that cow is making a lot of noise. I can't sleep." Now since cows can't understand, the husband couldn't go to the cow and tell her to stop making noise. If you go to a cow and say, "Excuse me, cow, would you please stop making that noise," do you think the cow will stop making the noise?
>
> *Patient:* No.
>
> *Therapist:* I don't think so either. And then the wife said, "Me, I wish that cow was dead."
>
> And the man said, "No, that doesn't have to happen. What we can do is we can take the cows and we can move them to another place—move those cows that are making the noise to another place, or *we* can move to another place. Instead of living here in this barn we can live in this house over here. We can send the cows over here so that they're so far away we won't hear the sounds.
>
> And then they thought that was a very good idea and then they weren't in any way bothered by the cows anymore. And they still had the cows, and they still got *milk* from the cows, and they still were able to have the

cows and have the *friendliness* of the cows. You know, the cows were around and they were friends. And the cows gave them milk, and they didn't have to hear the sounds. And that's the end of that story.

Obviously, my purpose here was to introduce another mode of adaptation to the mother's groaning. Specifically, I recommended the patient and/or the mother separate themselves more from each other so the patient would not hear her groans and be awakened at night. At the same time I emphasized that this mode of adaptation would still allow the patient to gain the gratifications of the cow's "milk" and "friendliness," that is, her love, affection, and attention.

> *Therapist:* Do you want to say anything about that story? Do you know what the lesson of that story is?

It is often preferable for the therapist to try to elicit a lesson or moral from the patient than to state it himself (herself). In this way the patient is given the opportunity to demonstrate whether or not the story's message(s) has been understood. It is only when the patient is not capable of providing such a lesson or moral that I will generally provide it.

> *Patient:* Um, they moved from the cow.
> *Therapist:* Uh hmm. They moved from the cows so that they didn't have to be bothered by the cows. Okay. You spin the spinner.
> *Patient:* (Patient spins the spinner.)
> *Therapist:* It says, "Select card 17, 18, 19, or 20 and throw the die." Okay, let's get 17, 18, 19, or 20. Okay, there are four pictures here. Okay, that's 17, 18, 19, and 20. Which of those four pictures do you want to take?
> *Patient:* (Patient points to picture number 20, a bathroom scene.)
> *Therapist:* Okay, this one. Okay, you throw the die now. Throw the die.
> *Patient:* (Patient throws the die.)
> *Therapist:* You got a four. That means you can take up to four people, and you put them in the picture and then tell a story. Which four do you want to take? Okay, now. Who are the people on the picture? Who are the people?
> *Patient:* This is, um (inaudible).
> *Therapist:* Is that the mother or the child or what?
> *Patient:* The mother.
> *Therapist:* It's the mother. Okay. And who's this?
> *Patient:* The little baby.
> *Therapist:* The baby. And who's this?

Patient: Um, child.

Therapist: Is it a boy or a girl?

Patient: A girl.

Therapist: It's a girl. About how old is she?

Patient: Hmm, six.

Therapist: Okay, and the baby? How old is the baby?

Patient: One.

Therapist: One, and who's this?

Patient: The father.

Therapist: Okay now, what's the story?

Patient: They were having trouble um. . . um. . . washing um the baby and their little girl came in and then she had no problem washing the baby.

Therapist (interrupting): Wait, they had trouble washing the baby? You mean the mommy and the daddy? And then the little girl came in and what did she do?

Patient: And she washed the baby and she had no trouble.

Therapist (repeating): Okay, the little girl washed the baby and she had no trouble?

Patient: Yup.

Therapist: Okay, she was able to do it.

Patient: Yes.

Therapist: The mommy and daddy were having trouble doing it, but the little girl helped. Is that it?

Patient: Yes.

Therapist: Now why were the mommy and daddy having trouble washing the baby?

Patient: Because they're too big and their back was hurting them when they bent down.

Therapist: Both the mommy and the daddy?

Patient (nods affirmatively).

Therapist (repeating): Their back was hurting when they bent down. So then the little girl helped. Is that it?

Patient: Hm hmm.

Therapist: Okay, is that the end of the story?

Patient: Yes.

Therapist: Okay, good. Okay, you get two chips for that. Okay. Do you know what the lesson of that story is? What do we learn from that story?

Patient: That the mommy and daddy had trouble washing the baby.

Therapist: Hh hmm. Okay, you get a chip for that.

As mentioned, the mother's metastases had spread to various parts of her body, including her lumbo-sacral spine. Not surprisingly, she could not bend over. I believed that the back trouble described in both parents related to the patient's fear that not only was his mother so incapacitated but that his father might become so as well. However, the older sister takes care of the child and washes it when the parents cannot. I believe that this story demonstrates the incorporation of my previous message into the child's psychic structure. Specifically, the child includes the concept of the substitute, an idea that I had introduced previously. This is one of the ways in which the therapist can ascertain whether his or her messages are being received by the patient. With this understanding of the patient's story I responded with my own:

Therapist: Now it's my time to tell a story about that picture. Once upon a time there was a family, and that family consisted of a baby, and a little girl, and a mommy, and a daddy. And one day they were washing the baby, the mommy and daddy, and the mommy said that she had some pain in her back. And she said to the daddy, "Will you please take over and wash this baby?"

The father said, "Sure." And then he took care of the baby.

And then one day the daddy had a little pain in his back and he said to the mommy, "Will you please wash the baby?"

And the mommy said, "Sure," because her back was better then.

And one day both of them had a little pain in their backs and then the little girl came and she washed the baby. And then what happened was that if anybody had any trouble, the other person took over and since there were four people in the family, there was always someone around to take over when there was some trouble.

Now, do you remember from my other story I used the word *substitute*? What does substitute mean?

Patient: When you . . . like when your teacher is sick. Then another teacher comes in.

Therapist: Right! That's what's called a substitute! The teacher is sick and can't teach that day. Another person can come around and that person can teach like in that other story I told. Now here these people are substitutes for one another. If someone has a pain in the back, the other person does the thing. Like if the mommy had a pain in the back, the daddy took over. Right? If the daddy had a pain in the back, the mommy took over. So there are always other people around to substitute. Right?

Patient: (nods affirmatively)

Therapist: Okay, listen, we have to stop this game now. Let's try to find out who the winner is. You count up your chips and I'll count up mine.

Patient and Therapist: (Both count chips.)
Patient: I got twenty-one.
Therapist: And I've got eleven. So who's the winner? Who has more?
Patient: (Patient raises his hand.)
Therapist: So you get the prize. Congratulations. (Therapist shakes patient's hand.) Good for you. Okay, now let's put this game away. This is the end of the program. We'll turn this off.

When a patient tells a story with a relatively healthy resolution of the presented problems (which was the case here), I generally emphasize or reiterate the healthy mode of adaptation in my responding story. And this is what I did here. My hope here was that I would engender in the patient the notion that there are people who can substitute for one another. Again, my hope was that this would be helpful to the patient in dealing with the forthcoming death of his mother.

Frank's situation is an excellent example of a situation for which the mutual storytelling technique may be useful. Clearly, dealing directly with his mother's forthcoming death would be extremely anxiety-provoking. The fact that he chose to present his conflicts over this issue at the symbolic and metaphoric level indicated that direct discussion of these issues would have been extremely anxiety provoking. Accordingly, I communicated my messages, advice, and coping mechanisms at the same level, thereby sparing him the anxieties that might have arisen had I attempted to bring into conscious awareness the meaning of his stories. In fact, had I decided to do so, I might have frightened him from further utilization of this technique. The Storytelling Card Game, which provides enjoyment, the fun of mild competition, and token reward chips, enhanced the likelihood that I would elicit this important material from Frank.

FINAL COMMENTS

Although designed to serve as a psychotherapeutic game, The Storytelling Card Game can also be used as a valuable diagnostic instrument. I am not referring to its use in providing diagnostic classifications, but to its value in providing examiners with information about underlying psychodynamics. The child is first provided with card 1, then asked to select one or more figurines from the array and place them on the picture. The examiner then asks the child to tell a story about the scene thereby created. This procedure is then repeated with cards 2, 3, and so forth. Generally, the examiner does well not to use all twenty-four cards in one sitting, but to spread the examination over two to three meetings. The Storytelling Card Game differs from traditional projective diagnostic instruments in that the children create their own pictures—thereby providing purer and more idiosyncratic projections.

The game may serve as an excellent companion to The Talking, Feeling, and Doing Game. The Storytelling Card Game taps primarily unconscious material. In contrast, The Talking, Feeling, and Doing Game is likely to elicit material more conscious in nature. Therefore, the two together provide the therapist with the opportunity to obtain material over the wide range from conscious to deep unconscious. Accordingly, the therapist does well to alternate the games, both within sessions and between sessions. Last, and most important, the use of these games should of course not preclude direct discussion with the child, work with parents and family, and other therapeutic modalities.

FIVE

Bibliotherapy

In the best books, great men talk to us, give us their most precious thoughts, and pour their souls into ours. God be thanked for books. They are the voices of the distant and the dead, and make us heirs of the spiritual life of past ages. Books are true levelers. They give to all, who will faithfully use them, the society, the spiritual presence of the best and greatest of our race.

William Ellery Channing

INTRODUCTION

I use the term *bibliotherapy* to refer to the use of books in the therapeutic process. I believe that this therapeutic modality has not been given the attention it deserves. My experience has been that this area is underrepresented in the psychotherapeutic literature, although one does occasionally come across articles on this subject. Psychoanalysts, especially classical psychoanalysts, generally frown upon therapists' recommending specific books to their patients, lest the "blank screen" be contaminated. I am in agreement that suggesting specific reading material to a patient may indeed bring about such compromise, but I also believe that this drawback may be more than compensated for by the advantages to the patient of such reading material.

I consider the educational element to be central to the psychotherapeutic process. And even in the most passive therapeutic approaches, the patient generally learns from the therapist about how better to cope with and adapt to life. There is deep wisdom in the aphorism "knowledge is power." Hans Strupp (1975), who has devoted himself extensively to delineating the elements in psychoanalytic psychotherapy that are of therapeutic value, considers a most important element to be what he calls "lessons in constructive living". The more knowledgeable one is about the world, the greater will be one's ability to cope with its inevitable problems, the greater will be one's capacity to adapt to it, and the less will be the likelihood that one will have to resort to pathological ways of dealing with life. Knowledge about the world may contribute not only to preventing the formation of psychological disturbances but to reducing them as well.

One of the most popular and ancient sources of such knowledge is books. Children often enjoy reading books and being read to from them. Books therefore provide a multisensory (visual and auditory) vehicle for the communication of therapeutic messages. They provide a mode of communication that might not be possible through simple discussion. Pictures and colors attract the child and enable the messages to be delivered "in an attractive package."

Books have been written to help prepare children for specific traumatic experiences, such as hospitalization (M. Pyne, 1962). There have been books written for adopted children (C. Livingston, 1978; F. Rondell and R. Michaels, 1951). Dozens (and probably hundreds) of books have been written for children on the subject of sex. Some of the most well known are by E.W. Johnson (1967), W.B. Pomeroy (1968, 1969), and P. Mayle (1973). Although these books can provide therapeutic benefit in a palatable format, it is important that therapists and parents select books that are appropriate to the child's intellectual and maturational levels. Goldings and Goldings (1972) have written an excellent article describing the various ways in which books can serve as a therapeutic modality.

My own contributions in this area generally fall into four categories: 1) expository, 2) reality-oriented, 3) fables, and 4) fairy tales. Although there are certainly other categories of children's literature, these are the four in which I have written. Furthermore, I have placed these categories in such an order that they represent a continuum from the most didactic to the most fantastic. This sequence may also be viewed as representing a continuum from the most to the least anxiety provoking, from those that may be the least interesting to children to those that are predictably the most attractive. Each type can be useful in therapy and all can be made attractive to children, especially if they deal with issues of psychological relevance to the child at the time he or she is reading the story.

THE EXPOSITORY BOOK

In expository books, the child is told directly the particular therapeutic information which the author wishes to convey. Of the four types of bibliotherapy discussed here, expository books are likely to be the ones to which children are least receptive because they do not contain any of the fanciful elaboration that is so predictably attractive to children. They may be more successful, however, if they deal with themes that are particularly relevant to problems that the reader is dealing with at the time the book is read. The child's interest, then, stems not so much from the desire for entertainment, but from the need for solutions to problems that are causing pain and stress.

It may be of interest to the reader to learn that the first book I ever wrote was in this category. In fact, it was not until 1964 that I first thought about writing a book. And the idea did not originate with me, rather it came from the father of a child in treatment. The child, then twelve, was known to be "brain injured" (the term used for what we presently call minimal brain dysfunction). During the three years prior to my consultation, he developed a series of superimposed symptoms that are generally considered psychotic: arm flapping, sitting on the floor, dropping blocks, and preoccupation with dinosaurs. In the initial screening interview the parents were particularly cautious about discussing the child's difficulties in his presence as they had been repeatedly warned by various authorities that they should never reveal to him that he was brain injured.

My evaluation confirmed the basic neurological impairments and revealed that the child was overwhelmed by anxiety. One of the primary sources of his anxiety was related to his ignorance of what was wrong with him. Accordingly, I advised the parents to tell the child what was wrong with him and to describe the nature of his problems and its causes. They flatly refused, quoting the various authorities who had warned them never to reveal to the child the nature of his illness. In the ensuing discussions I presented to the parents my various reasons for recommending that the information be revealed and managed to convey to them the judiciousness of such revelation. I explained to them how such withholding of information could cause distrust of the parents, how it was increasing the child's anxiety, and how it could make the child feel that his illness was worse than it really was. In one self-created story the child spoke of the dinosaurs as being stupid and as having small brains. I tried to impress upon the parents my belief that the dinosaur preoccupation was related to the child's view of himself as stupid, which was really not the case in that he was of average intelligence. I reassured the parents that I would schedule follow-up appointments and be available to help them and the child work through any possible untoward reactions he might have following the revelation.

Reluctantly, they went home and followed my advice. Within a few weeks there was a dramatic reduction (in fact, almost a disappearance) of the secondary psychogenic symptoms. The primary neurological manifestations, of course, still remained. The parents were most gratified over the results. In our closing session the father thanked me again for my help and suggested, "Doctor, you ought to write a book about brain injury for children. It really helped my boy and a book on this subject should certainly help others." Two years later, the New York Association for Brain-Injured Children published my *The Child's Book About Brain Injury* and my career as a writer was launched.

MBD: The Family Book About Minimal Brain Dysfunction

In 1973 this book was updated, expanded, and republished as *MBD: The Family Book About Minimal Brain Dysfunction* (1973a). The first half of the book is devoted to parents and provides them with advice that might prove useful to them in handling the special problems of the MBD child. The second half is written for MBD children and helps them understand the various manifestations of their disorder. Advice is provided in a concrete fashion to help them deal more effectively with their difficulties. The book is based on the principle that discussing the "undiscussable" makes the taboo subject less anxiety provoking. It is also based on the assumption that the more information one has about a disorder, the better the likelihood one will be able to deal with it as effectively as possible. In both the parents' and the children's sections, the importance of using the book as a point of departure for parent-child communication is emphasized. I have found the children's section especially useful in therapy. Reading the book along with the child can bring up a variety of issues that are useful to discuss in the therapeutic situation.

The Boys and Girls Book About Divorce

The Boys and Girls Book About Divorce (1970a, 1971b) has thus far been my most popular book. It is a source of deep gratification that it has undergone many printings, in both hard cover and paperback, and there have been a number of foreign translations as well. It may be of interest to the reader to learn that the book was originally rejected by sixteen major publishers. Finally, in 1970, it was published by Science House (now Jason Aronson, Inc.), a publisher of psychiatry and psychology books. But it was the Bantam paperback, which came out a year later, that enjoyed widespread popularity.

When writing the book, I faced the conflict of whether to write it in a novel or expository form. With regard to the novel, I wondered whether it might be more appealing because it would be closer to the type of story that is traditionally enjoyed by children. However, the primary drawback of using this format would be that I could not possibly create any story that would be specifically relevant to the experiences of more than a fraction of all children of divorce. For example, if the story was about a girl, it might be less likely that boys would identify with her. If a child's father left the home, the story would not be appealing to those children whose mothers had left. No matter how much I might try to relate common divorce experiences, the story could only be similar to what a small percentage of the target audience had actually experienced.

The expository form, I suspected, would have the advantage of enabling me to include a wider variety of experiences to which children of divorce were commonly exposed. There need be no limit on the number of possible situations I could cover. There was the risk, however, that the didacticism of such a presentation might be boring to the child. In considering the advantages and disadvantages of the alternatives, I decided to take my chances with the expository form. The success of the book suggests that my choice was a judicious one.

The book on divorce was written because I had observed that many parents were not being appropriately honest with their children regarding the major issues of the divorce. Such secretiveness was contributing, in a variety of ways, to the psychological problems with which these children often suffered. For example, a mother might complain that her son kept blaming himself for the divorce. Often a contributing factor (but by no means the only cause of such a preoccupation) was the fact that the child was not told anything about the reasons for the separation. In such situations, it was not surprising that the boy would tend to blame himself in his search for a possible explanation. The book encourages such children to ask important questions and it encourages parents to answer them. Another common problem that children of divorce suffer is that of anger inhibition. They may fear expressing anger toward the "abandoning" parent lest they see even less of that parent. And they may fear expressing anger toward the custodial parent, lest that parent "abandon" them as well—abandonment now being very much in the child's scheme of things. The book helps children deal with these, as well as a wide variety of other problems that are likely to arise in the lives of children of divorce.

After making the decision to write the book, I spent the next two years gathering data. I scribbled on scraps of paper any issue arising in my practice that I thought might be useful to include. Journal articles became a further source of information. And experiences of supervisees, colleagues, and friends provided further data. After two years of such data gathering, I organized my collection of scrap papers and notes. I found that they naturally fell into a number of discrete categories. Each pile of slips (representing a category) became a chapter in the book. And each pile was further subdivided with the result that these smaller piles became subsections of the chapters. It was from such pieces of paper that the book was written over a period of a few weeks.

During the next year the manuscript was lent to a series of children, for both parents and children's comments and reactions.

In this way, deletions were made and further material added. I was fortunate in meeting Alfred Lowenheim, a most talented artist, who did the illustrations. Of the many artists who submitted renditions, Al's were clearly the best. His capacity to draw a wide variety of children's facial expressions was unique. And more important was his ability to introduce a note of hope and optimism into the most morbid situations. Because the divorce issue is such a painful one, such qualities in the children's facial expressions were particularly important. Al's contributions to the book's success was formidable and my debt to him is great.

Down the years I have continued to receive letters from children. Invariably, they tell me how useful the book has been to them. In addition, many describe the difficulties they are having over their parents' divorce and will often ask me for advice. Every letter has been answered. Although attempts have always been made to provide advice, this obviously, at times, has had to be limited.

Particularly gratifying have been the foreign translations (Japanese, 1972e, 1980d; Spanish, 1972f; Dutch, 1972g, 1980c; Hebrew, 1977c; French, 1981d). The Japanese translation (1972e) contributed to my being invited in 1974 to present a lecture series in Tokyo, Kyoto, Kobe, and Hiroshima. The Dutch translation (1972g) played a role in my invitation to serve as a visiting professor at the University of Louvain in Brussels in 1980 and 1981. The popularity of the Japanese translation has always been somewhat puzzling to me in that cultural patterns would, I suspect, make it quite difficult for the average Japanese child to follow some of the recommendations made in the book. For example, it is hard for me to imagine a Japanese child telling his father that he is angry at him for being late at the time of his visits. Also, it is difficult for me to imagine a Japanese child taking my advice not to take seriously those who would ridicule him because of his parents' divorce. The Japanese are a shame-oriented people and are exquisitely sensitive to the feelings of others. In spite of these apparent problems that I suspect the book presents to the Japanese child, the book appears to have enjoyed considerable popularity there.

The book is written at a level understandable to the average six-to-seven year old when it is read to him or her. Most eight year olds can read the book with little or no help from parents. However, the book is also written for the parents, the third-to-fourth grade level notwithstanding. Most parents appreciate this and have found the book useful to read. Teenagers will often refuse initially to read it because they consider it beneath them with its obvious cartoon-like illustrations, large print, and elementary-grade reading level. Once they have overcome these initial hesitations, they have often found it very useful.

In a sense the book is a psychiatry primer, written for children. This is not, in principle, an inappropriate thing to do. There is no concept in all of psychiatry, in my opinion, that cannot be understood by the average 11 year old. Our terminology is often merely jargon that is designed to impress. It attempts to give a scientific ring to the commonplace. Accordingly, it often produces more confusion than elucidation, in that the psychiatric term becomes less well defined than the concept it was designed to describe.

As every writer of children's book knows well, it is the parents, not the children, who buy the book. They screen and censor and are not likely to buy a book that they would consider detrimental or offensive to their children. *The Boys and Girls Book About Divorce* certainly contains material that is considered such by many parents. A book that raises the question as to whether a parent loves a child is not one that some parents would consider proper reading material for their children, let alone something they would spend their money on. A book that encourages children to express their anger at their parents (albeit using words more polite than the ones that enter their minds) is also one that would make many parents hesitate.

Even in the introduction there are possible parental "turn-offs." Telling parents that they *should* tell the child that an absent parent does not love him or her (when such is really the case) is not considered the popular thing to do. And telling parents that they *should* criticize the absent parent to the child (in a balanced way in which assets are also presented), goes against traditional advice. Accordingly, I am sure that many parents put the book down as soon as they read my comments in the introduction. In spite of the presence of this somewhat unpopular material, the book has continued to grow in popularity—attesting to the fact that there are thousands who are willing to look at unpleasant truths and recognize that more euphemistic books, although less painful to read, are not as likely to be useful to children in such serious situations as divorce.

I think one of the book's appeals lies in the fact that I attempt to provide practical and concrete advice for every problem presented. The child is told what he or she can do to try to help him- or herself. Unrealistic solutions are discouraged and the possibility of both success and failure is presented.

In 1968, when the book was originally written, I called it *The Child's Book About Divorce*. An editor suggested that some children might consider the word *child* demeaning, and suggested *The Boys and Girls Book About Divorce* as a safer title. Recently (in the late 1970s), the use of the words *boys* and *girls* has come under attack. Making a distinction about sex, when such distinction is irrelevant, is considered "sexist." Such critics might consider the title *The Boys and Girls Book About Divorce* to be objectionable because it refers to the sex of the reader for no apparent purpose. Although I have not seen any children (yet) who have been offended by the title, I have to admit that the distinction is not particularly necessary for the purposes of the title or even the bulk of the contents of the book.

To rectify this "error" might bring me back to the original title, with the risk of using that. Of other options, each seems to have its drawbacks. *The Youngsters Book About Divorce* seems too stilted, *The Kids Book About Divorce*, too folksy and slangy. The word *kids* is also considered by some to be intrinsically demeaning because the word can connote young sheep. (Pedantic grade school teachers are particularly enthusiastic about this distinction.) Perhaps in the future my "error" will become ever more obvious and my title will invariably date the book. Although the title may, after more than 20 years, be on the verge of becoming dated, the book's contents, to the best of my knowledge, have not yet become so.

The Boys and Girls Book About One-Parent Families

On a number of occasions, I have received a telephone call from a distraught parent (usually a stranger) asking me for advice regarding a child's attending a parent's funeral. Usually my advice is requested to help resolve a family argument over whether or not the children should attend a parent's funeral. Often it is the grandparents who hold that the children's presence would be psychologically detrimental to them, while the surviving parent believes that it might be useful and/or desirable. Often the parent does not have the psychological strength or maturity to withstand and/or refute the grandparents' arguments and wants my support for his or her position. Feelings run strong on this issue and I cannot say that my advice that the children be invited (but not required) to attend is always heeded. Usually I provide some of the important reasons (Gardner, 1976b, 1976c,1977d,1979d), but these are not compelling to those who have been so deeply engrained with the notion that having children attend a funeral (like other exposures to death) cannot but be psychologically detrimental.

Because of such experiences with parents, I decided to write a book for children that could be useful to them in dealing with parental death. Thus my *The Boys and Girls Book About One-Parent Families* (1978, 1983c). Although optimally useful prior to the death of the parent, the book has not, to be the best of my knowledge, been commonly used during this period. It has been more frequently used at the time of death to help parents make such decisions as to what to tell the children, whether or not to take them to the funeral, and to help them work through their reactions. Like my *The Boys and Girls Book About Divorce* (1970a, 1971b), the book, although written for children, is written for the parents' guidance as well. The material not only provides the child with information that should prove of interest and use, but is also designed to serve as a point of departure for communication with the surviving parent and other adults. Such communication serves as a vehicle for the release of pent-up feelings—a release that is central to the mourning process. Such communication is also likely to provide the child with information that can be useful in facilitating the mourning process and information that could correct distortions that might contribute to the development of psychopathology. Furthermore the communication entrenches the child's relationship with the surviving parent—so vital a process at this unfortunate period in the child's life.

In addition, I provide information to children living in two other types of one-parent families, namely, divorced families and families in which a parent (usually a mother) has never been married. Although the unwed mother is far less the pariah today that she was in past years, children of such mothers still suffer some stigma as well as other difficulties specific to their situation. Overcoming old taboos and open communication are the best solutions to dealing with these problems. The material on divorce is a partial update of material previously presented in *The Boys and Girls Book About Divorce*. This book was also translated into Japanese (1981e).

The Boys and Girls Book About Stepfamilies

Considering my other books for children in the divorce situation, it was only natural that I write *The Boys and Girls Book About Step-families* (1981c). It too is a book in the expository vein. Again, it is most likely to be of interest to children in this situation or children anticipating entering into stepfamily life. It covers a wide variety of issues with which stepfamilies are commonly confronted: what to call a stepparent, the love between stepparents and stepchildren, loyalty conflicts, adjusting to new lifestyles, relationships between stepsiblings, and adoption by a stepparent. The issues raised are designed to serve as points of departure between the children and parents living under in what is often a difficult situation.

The Parents Book About Divorce

Each of my children's books is also written for parents. The parents are advised to read the book along with the child and to use the material therein as a point of departure for a wide variety of inter-changes. Furthermore, the parents have always been in mind as I write the children's books. I view them as reading these books as well. And many parents have confirmed my anticipations that they would find these books useful for themselves, even though they are written at the child's level. My *MBD: The Family Book About Minimal Brain Dysfunction* (1973a) has a section for the parents. *The Boys and Girls Book About Divorce*, however, has only an introductory chapter for them. Because I had so much more to say to parents, I decided to write a special book for them. Doubleday invited me to write *The Parents Book About Divorce* (1977b, 1979a), anticipating a book of about 200 pages. When I submitted my manuscript they were originally upset because they anticipated that my material would require a book of 350 to 400 pages and so they asked me to resubmit a smaller book with a substantial amount of material deleted. Considering practically *all* of it to be important and recognizing possible lack of objectivity regarding this conclu-sion, I requested that *they* review the manuscript and decide themselves what material they thought should be deleted, but requested that they discuss with me first any material they wished to omit. About a month later they informed me that they had carefully reviewed the book, with an eye toward omitting material, and could find nothing that would warrant omission. Although I recognized that some parents would be turned off by the book's length I consider it to contain only the minimal material necessary for parents to read in the divorce situation.

When I submitted the original manuscript to Doubleday I informed them that I was including an extremely important passage in the introduction and that I would omit this passage only with great reluctance. The passage:

> I believe that it (the book) provides an in-depth coverage of the most common problems that parents are confronted with when dealing with children's reactions to separation and divorce. It does not provide any simple answers. The problems dealt with here are complex. Those who would give simple answers to these complicated problems may initially attract a wide audience; however, their solutions are doomed to failure and those who rely on them are bound to become disappointed and disillusioned. This book, therefore, is for those who are suspicious of or fed up with simple solutions and are willing to expend the effort of dealing with these problems more realistically.

Clearly, this is not the kind of introduction that sells books in an age when people seem to be much more attracted to simple and quick solutions to complex problems. The fact that the book has gone through multiple printings over the last nine years is testimony to the fact that there are still many people who recognize that complex problems can only be dealt with with complex answers. This book has also gone into a French translation (1979e).

Understanding Children—A Parents Guide to Child Rearing

Mountains of books have been written on child rearing. There is not a year in which we don't see at least a few more added to the ever-growing heap. Generally, the most popular of these books are those that provide simple answers. Those who propose complex solutions are not likely to sell many books. The best way to write such a best seller is to take a few (at most) simple ideas and expand them into a book by repeating them over and over and then fattening the text with clinical examples (real or invented). By using large print, wide margins, and "filler" pages, the publishers can be relied upon to make the whole thing look like a book.

The next step is for the author to peddle the book on television. A few exposures is not likely to do much. A nationwide campaign is much more likely (but is in no way guaranteed) to be effective. The worst things that an author can say on such television programs are: "That's a very complex subject . . . ," "There's really no simple solution to that problem . . . ," or "I cannot really say why that particular child acted in the way that he did. . . . " Few today would buy a book written by someone who has no simple solutions. Few want to burden themselves with complex answers that may not even apply to one's own child. Success is much more likely if one provides a snappy answer to every question—no matter how complicated. In addition, if the responses are sprinkled with humor, and even slapstick, Mr. Funny is likely to sell even more books. Last, if the author has show-biz talent and can ham it up, he or she may become a TV celebrity—someone invited by the most popular talk shows. If the author feels that such appearances involve no compromise of professional dignity, if every remark made is used by the "M.C." as a taking off point for a joke, then he or she may be even more successful. And his book will make him a bundle.

My contribution to this "mountain of books" on child rearing is *Understanding Children—A Parents Guide to Child Rearing* (1973b). As might be expected from what I have said previously, the book has no simple answers or quick solutions. In fact, some of my explanations have turned off those readers who would have been much happier with shorter discussions. Where possible I have used in headings such traditional child-rearing clichés as: "My Joey would never do such a thing," "All I want is that my children should be happy," "We keep a united front," et cetera. Although this book is yet another addition to the sea of child-rearing volumes, I would like to believe that it is better than the majority of them. Although many parents have found it useful (it has gone through multiple editions), I have resigned myself to the fact that it will probably never enjoy widespread popularity because of its complexity. It too has undergone a Dutch translation (1975c).

REALITY-ORIENTED STORIES

As mentioned, the didacticism of the expository presentation has the drawback of increasing the risk that the child will lose interest. Children are more predictably attracted to stories that involve fanciful elaborations around their central messages. Accordingly, reality-oriented stories are generally less appealing (especially for younger children) than fables and fairy tales. Children, however, are likely to be attracted to reality-oriented stories if others, rather than the readers themselves, are the ones to whom the unpleasant things are happening or the ones who think and do the "bad" things. In addition, children are likely to be more involved if the story deals with issues that relate to the problems and conflicts with which they are directly dealing at the time. The "lessons in constructive living" are thereby assimilated in a way that is generally less confronting than the expository presentation, but more than in the fanciful categories described below.

We do well to appreciate that to view reality with perfect clarity all the time may be too painful for anyone. A certain amount of fantasy is pleasurable and may even be necessary to preserve our sanity. However, excessive involvement with fantasy may ill-equip us to deal with reality. Some balance, then, must be arrived at. This balance should be definitely weighted on the reality side of the scale, if one is to function most adequately in life.

At the time in the lives of our children when we are most concerned with teaching them about reality, we simultaneously expose them to a world of unreality—a world of fairy tale, fancy, and myth. Although the child certainly derives many benefits from fantasy, such exposure at the same time often engenders unreal expectations about living which may contribute to life-long feelings of dissatisfaction and frustration.

In the attempt to provide a contribution on the reality side of the balance, I wrote *Dr. Gardner's Stories About the Real World*, (1972a). These stories do not begin with *once upon a time* because they did not take place a long time ago in some mythical land, but are occurring now, everywhere around us. They are not stories about beautiful princesses, handsome knights, fairy godmothers, sorcerers, and wizards. They are not about perfect people and they do not offer perfect solutions. Rather, the problems which the children face in these stories are not quickly resolved and, in the process of solving them, the children suffer certain discomforts and inconveniences. The people with whom the children in these stories deal are genuinely human. They have their assets and their liabilities, their strengths and their weaknesses. They are often inconsistent and misguided. They lie, curse and exhibit the host of human frailties. But they are also benevolent, intelligent, fair and possess other human qualities which we all admire. This is the way people really are and children must come to appreciate this if they are to deal adequately with life.

These stories, then, are about actual things which have happened, and will continue to happen, to real children. Stories about reality, like stories about unreality, can capture the imaginations of our children and provide them with meaningful gratifications. Lastly, these stories do not end with *and they lived happily ever after*. No one lives ever after; we are all mortal. And no one is always happy. Life is a mixture, and unhappiness is an inevitable part of it.

Our hope, therefore, lies in achieving whatever satisfactions we may reasonably expect in the short time allotted to each of us. The likelihood of our gaining such gratifications depends, in part, upon how accurately we perceive the truths of life. Unreal fantasy, its gratifications notwithstanding, does not equip us to pursue our goals. These stories then enhance, rather than detract, from our children's chances for happy experiences in life—and this is their purpose.

When utilizing the mutual storytelling technique, my stories are designed to provide specific information that is directly relevant to issues that are important for the child patient at the very time we are involved with one another during the therapeutic session. The stories presented here are less specific. They deal with issues that are common, if not universal. However, their drawback is that they are not as likely to be as exquisitely relevant to the child at the time of presentation as those provided when engaging in mutual storytelling.

One could argue that reading children's stories such as these is like putting Penicillin in the drinking water. A small percentage of the population, those suffering at that particular time with certain types of infectious diseases, will profit from drinking such water. For the overwhelming majority of the rest, the Penicillin will have been wasted in that it will pass right out of the body and have little, if any, effect on the individual. And there will be a small percentage who will suffer some untoward reaction because of a special sensitivity to the drug. Or one could argue that reading such stories to children is like feeding a sick child every drug in the medicine cabinet, in the hope that one will get him or her better. I cannot disagree with such criticisms of bibliotherapy. However, my experience has been that the themes dealt with in my *Stories About the Real World* (1972a) are so common, again if not universal, that children have been drawn to them with a surprising and gratifying degree of consistency. I recognize my immodesty here, but that is what has happened with these stories. There are many children who have quoted them to other children and their parents. Others have put the book under their pillows at night. Others have carried it along for special guidance in tense situations. And others have asked parents to repeatedly read to them specific stories. There is no question that such utilization has been useful for these children. Not only does it help prevent the kind of distorted thinking that contributes to the formation of psychopathology and other forms of maladaption, but can contribute to the alleviation of such disorders as well.

The book contains six stories. *Oliver and the Ostrich* deals with the issues of avoidance and denial. ("There are some people who have a very strange idea. They believe that the ostrich hides his head in the sand when something dangerous is about to happen—such as when another animal is going to attack. This isn't true. The ostrich wouldn't do such a foolish thing.") *Say You're Sorry* focuses on the common utilization (by children as well as adults) of the "I'm sorry" manipulation to avoid facing up to or suffering the consequences of one's maltreatment of others. ("Eric did not want to be sent to his room and so he grumbled to Carol, 'O.K., I'm sorry.' But he really didn't mean it. He was lying. He just said he was sorry so he wouldn't be punished.") In *Peter and the Dog* I attempt to help children deal with frustration via the utilization of substitutive gratification. ("Peter loved his new pets and he played with them every day. He was no longer sad that he didn't have a dog.") *The Girl Who Wouldn't Try* encourages the use of conscious control, and toleration of anxiety as a method of desensitization to the inevitable fears that all must learn to accept in new situations if one is to gain the benefits to be derived from such involvement. In addition, it focuses on the "nothing ventured, nothing gained" theme. ("She knew it was going to be scary to try, but she also realized that you can feel pretty bad about yourself if you don't.") *Jerry and the Bullies* was originally entitled *Dirty Words*. The original publishers, however, decided that some of the expletives should be deleted and so the expurgated version is the one that was published. The story encourages healthy expression of anger, in a manner appropriate to the situation, in a way that is not simply cathartic but attempts to remove the noxious stimulus that is causing the anger to generate. ("It may surprise you but bad words can be very useful. They can help a person show his anger or disappointment in a way that really doesn't harm anyone.") Lastly, *The Hundred-Dollar Lie* deals with the injudiciousness of lying. It does not focus on the ethical or moral reasons for not lying as much as the practical and more mundane: the fear of disclosure, the lowered feeling of self-worth, the social rejection one suffers with the reputation of being a liar, etc. ("He was scared. He kept worrying about all the children finding out about his lie. He was afraid that they would all call him liar and that he wouldn't have any friends anymore.")

This book has also enjoyed foreign translations (Dutch, 1974e, and Italian, 1976d). In addition, the interest in this book was so great that I subsequently published a second volume, *Stories About the Real World, Volume II* (1983b). The stories in this second volume deal with such issues as the work ethic, the differentiating between things one can control from things one cannot control, cigarette smoking, toleration of the unpleasant, looking at naked children, and lying.

FABLES

Storytelling has proved to be one of the most powerful techniques that mankind has ever devised for molding human behavior. By telling stories about things that happened to *others*, unpleasant messages were found to be far more palatable than those pertaining to "present company." And the farther away and the more remote the "others" were, the less threatening the story was to the listeners. The important principle, however, could be retained. The lessons that were learned could still be transmitted as long as it was others, rather than present company, who had learned them. The essential precondition for such stories to be useful was that the leaders had to take the position: "Of course, no one here would do such things—or even think such things—but it is interesting to hear about others who have engaged in such nefarious practices and what they have learned from their experiences and misdeeds." And the farther away the story's characters lived, the more remote they appeared to be from the audience, the less threatened the listeners were. Last, making the men handsome, the women beautiful, and introducing adventure, humor, sex, violence, and dramatization, added to the attractiveness of the vehicle and insured greater receptivity to the messages, even those that were particularly anxiety provoking. The central philosophy of the method is well stated in a refrain from a song sung by Jack Point, the jester, in Gilbert and Sullivan's operetta *Yeoman of the Guard*:

> When they're offered to the world in merry guise
> Unpleasant truths are swallowed with a will—
> For he who'd make his fellow, fellow, fellow creatures wise
> Should always gild the philosophic pill!

The story can be attractive and nonthreatening. It allows for the imparting of important principles and guidelines without the listener experiencing personal guilt or fear of incrimination. The listeners are usually not even consciously aware that their interest is determined primarily by the fact that they harbor the same impulses (however unacceptable) as the story's protagonists, that they are grappling with the exact same conflicts as those who lived far away, long ago, in distant lands. The method is so powerful and useful that I would hazard the guess that it was crucial for the survival of the earliest civilizations and that those societies that did not utilize the method did not survive. Every society that I know of has its heritage of such stories. These were transmitted first by the spoken and then by the written word down the generations: the Bible, the Koran, various legends, myths, fairy tales, parables, and other traditional tales.

The fable is one such vehicle. Like the others it utilizes symbolization in order to disguise. Like the others, it uses allegory to transmit its messages. Allegory, by definition, involves the representation of an abstraction via a concrete or material form. It is a symbolic narrative. The fable is one of the purest forms of allegory. But the *sine qua non* of the fable is that its protagonists be animals. Without the animal, the story cannot justifiably be called a fable. An occasional human being may be found but, if there are too many, the story will no longer be a fable. But the animals in the fable are typically human, with all the human foibles: avarice, lust, jealousy, arrogance, false pride, and so on. Finally, the fable, if it is to be worthy of the name, has one or more morals or lessons. Too many lessons may reduce a fable's effectiveness. Burdening the mind of the listener with too many lessons is likely to reduce the impact of a single moral.

The use of the animal symbol for stories or other purposes dates back to the earliest civilizations. Animal drawings on cave walls probably antedated human figures. Anthropomorphization of animals is ubiquitous in primitive religions, animal worship being one manifestation of such anthropomorphization. (Anthropomorphization still persists in modified form in most modern and more sophisticated religions.) Children, who have much in common with primitives with regard to their thinking processes, are traditional lovers of animals. I am referring not only to the actual pleasure that children derive from animals in reality (from pets and visits to the zoo, for example), but to the use of animals as symbols in their fantasies. The animal appears to be the child's natural choice for allegorical symbolization.

Child therapists have known, since the second decade of this century, that children will tell them much about themselves if encouraged to relate self-created stories about animals. But if one tries to get the children to appreciate that they are really talking about themselves (i.e., "gain insight"), they are likely to become resistive and inattentive. This valuable source of information about their underlying psychodynamics may thereby be lost to the therapist. But discuss the animals as animals, and lengthy therapeutic conversations are possible. One seven-year-old child once said to me, upon being asked to make up a story about the animal figurines I provided him, "Remember, this story has nothing to do with me or anyone in my family. It's only about animals!" I agreed not to challenge him on this statement, and he was thereby allowed to provide me with a wealth of information about himself that was therapeutically useful. Had I tried to analyze his resistance to coming to terms with the fact that he was really talking about himself, I probably would not have been able to be of much help to him in the areas revealed by this story.

Without knowing that they have been doing it, children have been telling fables to therapists for years. Children are probably the best fabulists of us all. My experience as a fabulist comes through the mutual storytelling technique. It was through experience with the mutual storytelling technique, more than from any other source, that I came to create fables of my own.

Modern psychoanalytic theory provides us with a powerful tool for understanding the underlying meaning of children's stories, be they self-created fables or other symbolic narratives. It provides a depth of understanding far more profound than that which is generally appreciated by the listener. The same theoretical principles can be used in the creation of stories such as the fables I relate in my *Dr. Gardner's Fables for Our Times* (1981b).

In this book I present thirteen fables, each of which portrays the ways in which certain animals have dealt with a wide variety of "human" problems. *The Show-Off-Peacock* deals with exhibitionism. The problem of dependency is dealt with in *The Kangaroos and Their Pouch*. The problem of blind mimicry and submission to the opinions of others is dealt with in *The Parrot and the People*. In *The Squirrels and the Skunk* the squirrels learn that one should use concrete evidence rather than reputation before deciding about a person's (the skunk's) personality attributes. The problem of self-assessment as related to one's own opinion versus the opinions of others is dealt with in *The Pussycat and the Owl*. The *Wise-Guy Seal* learns that honest effort is more likely to produce results than dreamy procrastination. In *The Dogs and the Thieves* we learn about dogs whose barks are worse than their bites and the respect that is engendered in "dogs" who "speak softly and carry a big stick." In *The Ant and the Grasshopper* we learn about the efficacy of cooperative group effort in contrast to what an individual alone can do. *The Dolphin and the Shark* deals with the issue of sensitivity to other people's feelings. In *The Squirrel and the Nuts* we learn about the value of advanced planning. *The Ostrich and the Lion* deals with the denial mechanism. *The Beaver and the Owl* deals with the value of fortitude, knowing when to give up, and the respect one engenders in others when one is strong enough to admit mistakes. Last, in *The Fox and the Big Lie* we learn about the alienation one suffers from others by lying.

As I am sure the reader can appreciate these stories deal with central problems of life from which symptoms are often derived. As is most often the case when I utilize the mutual storytelling technique, each of these stories ends with a moral. And this, of course, is very much in the tradition of the fable. However, I have often found more than one moral to a story and have had no hesitation listing them. (It is nowhere written that a story must have only one moral.) In fact, in one story (*The Pussycat and the Owl*) I found no less than twelve (yes twelve!) lessons. The moral serves an important function. It "nails down" the story's main theme and increases the likelihood that the listener will "get the message."

FAIRY TALES

Introduction

The fairy tale has traditionally been one of the most attractive forms of children's literature. The fairy tale tradition is ancient and its appeal universal. Children's enjoyment of and widespread fascination with these stories is strong testimony to the fact that they provide important psychological gratifications. These tales have been passed down from generation to generation. However, over the years countless variations have been introduced. It is most likely that each modification satisfied the particular psychological needs and motivations of the individuals who introduced them. Many of these changes were probably not consciously made; rather, they were more likely the result of unconscious processes. It is reasonable to speculate that listeners repressed or suppressed from conscious awareness those aspects that were personally less significant and retained the more psychologically meaningful components. The story that was thereby "heard" was different from that which was then retold. The resultant version experienced similar modifications as each new generation of storytellers introduced its own alterations. The invention of the printing press in the fifteenth century brought about a certain stabilization to this process. However, no systematic publication of fairy tales was done on a large scale until the seventeenth century when Charles Perrault published his collection of such tales. In the early nineteenth century Jakob and Wilhelm Grimm, in Germany, and Hans Christian Andersen, in Denmark, published collections of known fairy tales as well as those of their own. These publications brought about even further standardization of the stories, but many versions of each story are still to be found.

Psychoanalytic theory provides us with a valuable instrument for understanding the underlying psychological meaning of many of these stories. There are certainly many schools of thought among psychoanalysts and their interpretation of fairy tales would certainly not be consistent. I believe, however, that most analysts would not take issue with most of the interpretations that I will propose below. Some of the stories have one or two basic themes that are consistently dealt with throughout. Other stories appear to be no more than a potpourri of many elements which do not lend themselves to any unified or consistent psychological interpretation. Psychoanalytic theory not only provides us with a tool for understanding the meaning of each individual fairy tale but, in addition, can provide us with insights as to why the fairy tale, in general, is so attractive to the child.

Reasons Why Fairy Tales Are Extremely Attractive to Children [of All Ages]

I believe that many factors contribute to the fairy tale's universal attraction to children. First, fairy tales allow the child to satisfy, in fantasy, wishes that would be impossible to gratify in reality. The child is small and weak in a world of adults, whom he or she views as giants. By identifying with the characters in the fairy tale the child can gain a sense of power that he or she does not actually possess. And with such power the child can acquire whatever one's heart desires may be—riches, wisdom, strength, etc. In *Jack and the Beanstalk, Jack*, on the brink of poverty and starvation, procures the giant's riches—enabling him thereby to support his mother in the style to which she had previously been accustomed prior to the death of his father. Similarly, *Hansel and Gretel* use the witch's jewels to provide their father and stepmother with enough financial stability to insure that the children will not once again be driven out of the house because of food privation. The *Ugly Duckling* becomes a beautiful swan. *Beast*, in *Beauty and the Beast*, becomes a handsome prince. Poor wretched *Cinderella* marries the rich handsome prince and lives happily ever after. *Thumbelina* and *Tom Thumb*, although minuscule, are able to enjoy the excitement of adult adventure, during which experiences they are magically protected from the inevitable dangers of the world of grownups. As enjoyable and appealing as these themes are, the methods by which the gratifications are achieved are usually magical, with little or no effort on the part of the story's protagonist. Although such fantasies provide solace and hope, they are clearly maladaptive ways for adjusting to the real world.

It is probable that those who are less deprived have less need for such tales. The pauper can enjoy a story in which a poor man becomes king; but a king is likely to have little interest because he already reigns. Similarly, adults have less need for fairy tales than children. Adults are more capable of providing themselves with what a child is unable to acquire. To children, the world is populated by giants. No matter how filled with love and material possessions their lives may be, they still envy the power and prerogatives of the adults around them. Therefore a child can be greatly inspired by a story in which the underdog magically triumphs over the powerful. The possible danger of such tales, however, is that they may encourage the child to hope for magic solutions to life's problems rather than to strive for the rewards that may be had by a more realistic approach.

Fairy tales simplify the world, making it easier to understand. This is especially attractive and comforting to children who, by virtue of their immaturity, inexperience, and naiveté cannot but find the world confusing and at times incomprehensible. In fairy tales everyone is stereotyped. There is no such thing as people with mixtures of assets and liabilities, with desirable and undesirable traits. People are clearly either good or bad. Things are either right or wrong. And one can tell from the outset the category into which the person or act will fall. In *Beauty and the Beast*, *Beauty* is pure beauty and *Beast* is ugliness incarnate. *Snow White's* queen mother is bad and is consistently so throughout. Stepmothers, like those of *Cinderella* and *Hansel and Gretel*, are perennially wicked. Such simplification of the world is appealing and is one factor in the fairy tale's attraction.

Unfortunately, simplifying a complex problem is not likely to be of help in solving it. And seeing people as simply all good or all bad ill equips us to deal adequately with real people who are inevitably a mixture of both. Believing that there are people who are all good cannot but be disillusioning as everyone will invariably reveal imperfections. And anticipating some people to be all bad will rob us of the gratifications of what might have been extremely satisfying relationships.

Fairy tales not only allow for the fantasized gratification of wishes for beauty, riches, power, etc., but allow for the release of hostile impulses as well. Children, like the rest of us, are frequently frustrated by the world around them. None of us can have more than an infinitesimal fraction of all the things we may want. So frustration is inevitable and frustration ultimately produces anger. However, survival of civilized society depends upon the repression and/or suppression of anger and its diversion into useful and/or innocuous channels. Long before written history, mankind must have appreciated that the proper control of anger was central to the viability of a civilized and productive society. With no restraints on the expression of anger there would be perpetual fear and chaos, a totally predatory and destructive world. But too much suppression of anger produced various kinds of personality problems that made such individuals ill-equipped to function adequately in society. Some middle path for anger expression had to be found.

One such method of innocuous release is provided by fairy tales. By identifying with characters who act out their anger the child can vicariously release hostility in ways that cause no actual harm to anyone. *Jack* kills the giant. *Hansel* and *Gretel's* stepmother abandons the children in the woods as her solution to the domestic food privation problem. The witch in turn would resort to starvation and cannibalistic devouring of the children for which, in retaliation, she is boiled to death in her own pot. *Snow White's* stepmother dances to her death on hot stones. Such innocuous release of anger notwithstanding, the fairy tale teaches violent solutions to interpersonal problems rather than more civilized methods. People in them rarely sit down and try to resolve their differences in humane and civilized ways. Killing off an adversary is suggested as the first, quickest, and cleanest way to solve a conflict.

In fairy tales the heroes and heroines traditionally live happily ever after. *Cinderella* marries the handsome prince and lives happily ever after. So do *Jack* and his mother and *Thumbelina* and her little prince, and *Hansel* and *Gretel*, and *Beauty* and *Beast* (the latter no longer as a beast, of course, but as a handsome prince), and so do countless others.

Life is a constant struggle for happiness, a state that somehow always seems to elude us. The best that most of us can hope for are intermittent states of happiness. Most recognize that life, at best, is a mixture of both happiness and unhappiness. One of the fairy tale's appeals, therefore, is that it provides fantasy gratification of the desire to live in a state of perpetual happiness and provides hope that such constant euphoria can indeed be obtained. As satisfying as such fantasies and hopes are, they have the drawback of lulling the individual into believing that such states of perpetual ecstasy can really be achieved. One of the reasons people marry is that they believe that it is a step not only to being happy, but to living happily ever after. And it is the *Cinderella* stories of our childhood and others like it that contribute to the inevitable disillusionment with marriage that results when one finds that it's just not producing the continued state of happiness that our childhood fairy tales promised.

A significant aspect of the fairy tale's appeal lies in the symbolic presentation of its messages. Long ago mankind must have realized that it was crucial to the survival of civilization to get as many members of society as possible to adhere to certain rules and regulations. It was also realized quite early that messages transmitting such rules, when presented directly, in undisguised fashion, were far less attractive than those conveyed in the form of exciting stories with appealing characters. Sermons can be dull and dry. Bible stories are more likely to attract the congregation's attention. Reading a list of rules of behavior is not likely to capture a large and enthusiastic audience. Legends, myths, and fables— which convey the same messages in symbolic form—are much more likely to be attended to and remembered. And fairy tales are in the latter tradition. Not only do they present their messages in an attractive package, but the characters utilized are from distant lands and lived long ago. Learning lessons from the experiences of such characters is far less anxiety provoking than hearing about the consequences of unacceptable acts performed by oneself or those close by. The audience can relax and listen with receptivity when hearing about the misdeeds of others because none of the listeners need reveal his or her own participation in similar behavior or need admit similar inclinations or desires. But the messages nevertheless sink in and the lessons are learned.

In the fairy tale such lessons are quite dramatically portrayed, again in simple and often stereotyped fashion. Good ultimately triumphs over evil. Hardworking and loyal *Cinderella* wins the hand of the handsome prince, while her self-indulgent and haughty stepsisters are left frustrated and enraged. *Hansel* and *Gretel* acquire the witch's jewels, implicitly as a reward for their continued loyalty to their father and stepmother. *Beauty*, although revolted by *Beast's* ugliness, agrees to marry him because of feelings of compassion, pity, and guilt. As the reward for her high principles and self-sacrificial decision, *Beast* is transformed back into the handsome prince he was before being bewitched. Via a series of harrowing experiences *Tom Thumb* learns how injudicious it is to run away from home.

What Should We Do with Fairy Tales?

What then should we do with these stories? On the one hand, they are an extremely effective method of communication and among the most powerful vehicles for attracting the attention of children and transmitting messages to them. On the other hand, fairy tales are filled with many elements that are sick and maladaptive. Because of these detrimental factors there are some who would dispose of them altogether. I believe that we should try to retain those elements of the fairy tale that have proved useful and discard that which appears to be harmful. One can create stories in which the rich visual imagery and dramatic qualities of the fairy tale are retained and healthy messages substituted for the unhealthy.

As discussed throughout this book, I am a strong believer in the therapeutic value of a storytelling mode of communication—especially when dramatization, allegory, and metaphor (elements invariably found in the fairy tale) are utilized. Messages so communicated are much more palatable and much more likely to be appreciated and retained than those directly stated. Sterile facts are not as likely to be remembered as those which are provided in an attractive package. And fanciful elaboration, so typical of the fairy tale, provides such packaging. The fairy tale is a proven vehicle for evoking the kind of visual imagery that enhances the impact of a communication. For example, one can use judiciously the magic element of the fairy tale. Children enjoy magic as a source of drama and excitement. And if the magic is *not* used to solve a character's central problem, it can add to the reader's pleasure and not foster unreal expectations. The same is true for the element of triumph. We all need to win once in a while, but winning in the real world involves effort, trial, and error. If our children are exposed to stories that demonstrate these processes, they can be helped to mature. The hostility in fairy tales can also be useful. However, it must be channeled into healthy directions. By confining themselves to self-defense and not indulging in sadistic gratification, the heroes can serve as models for the civilized release of anger.

Modern psychoanalytic theory has provided us with valuable tools to accomplish these goals. Psychodynamic insights have enabled us to understand more deeply than ever before the nature of the unhealthy elements in the fairy tale. And such knowledge has enabled us, as well, to create stories with more salutary themes.

Fairy Tales for Today's Children

In my *Fairy Tales for Today's Children* (1974a) I have taken four popular fairy-tale themes, dispensed with or revised elements that I consider pathological, and replaced them with what I consider to be healthier resolutions of the problems confronting the protagonists. My favorite is *Cinderelma*.

The terms *Cinderella* and *they lived happily ever after* have become almost synonymous. The story is one of many that children are exposed to at the most impressionistic time of their lives. Stories such as these contribute to the notion that marriage per se can provide not only happiness, but eternal happiness (or at least happiness until the end of one's days). The theme is multiplied many times over during a child's formative years and even later. Believing it cannot but produce frustration in one's real relationships with members of the opposite sex. It is a contributing factor to disillusionment in marriage and divorce. It is a contributing factor to general dissatisfaction in life, as one is led to believe that there are indeed individuals who live continual euphoric existences. Although all know of beautiful movie stars with multiple marriages and others who kill themselves (either quickly or slowly), the myth does not seem to be dispelled by these confrontations with reality.

In my story, *Cinderelma*, the heroine, is not rescued by a prince. Nor is she magically transformed by a fairy godmother. Her attempts to seek easy, quick, and magic solutions to her problems prove futile. But ultimately, via her own efforts (coupled with a little bit of luck and some craft), she is able to led a productive and gratifying life—not forever, but "until the end of her days."

In *The Princess and the Three Tasks*, I have borrowed elements from stories written in the chivalric tradition in which the suitor must prove his worth and affection by exposing himself to significant travail and suffering on behalf of the loved one. My hope here is to communicate in the allegorical mode just how irrational this common masochistic mechanism is for the suitor and insensitive and egocentric for the lady so courted.

In *Hans and Greta*, I use the universally absorbing theme of parent-child hostility and conflict, but have modified it. The children's problems are not solved by killing the witch and by the stepmother's convenient death. These are clearly unrealistic and unsuitable solutions. We can not so readily murder those who maltreat us; nor do they so conveniently die. (In fact, they often appear to have a greater longevity than those who treat us kindly.) In my story the children's hostilities are confined to self-defense. In addition, the stepmother is depicted somewhat less stereotypically. She is occasionally fun to be with. Also, the children do not come to the family's rescue by bringing home the witch's treasure. Children are rarely able to solve a family's problems and it is unfair to suggest that this is possible.

In *The Ugly Duck*, I do not accept the attractive solution that those who are scapegoated because of inborn differences may wake up someday with their liabilities turned into assets. The little duck in my story doesn't discover he's really a swan. But, with the help of the wise old owl, he manages to work out a reasonable solution to the social alienation he suffers.

Modern Fairy Tales

My second book of modified fairy tales, *Modern Fairy Tales* (1977a), provides four more stories in which I have removed what I consider detrimental in traditional fairy-tale themes and substituted what I consider to be more salutary. My favorite in this collection is *Mack and the Beanstalk*.

Jack and the Beanstalk is one of the "purer" fairy tales. It does not appear to contain the multiplicity of psychoanalytic themes so often seen in the fairy tale which, as mentioned, is often a potpourri of many elements contributed by a long succession of individuals down the generations. I believe that its purity, in part, is related to the fact that it is such a powerful oedipal statement. The story is basically one in which *Jack* accomplishes all his oedipal desires. The giant in the sky represents *Jack's* father. From the psychological point of view, he has already been ejected from the household and can be considered to be dead in that he resides in the sky, that is, in heaven where dead people supposedly go. Although *Jack* has, thereby, gratified his oedipal wishes, he does not have the wherewithal to support his mother in the style to which she had been accustomed prior to the death (or perhaps more correctly, murder) of his father. In order to provide himself with the funds that would enable *Jack* to support his mother in the style to which she had been accustomed, Jack makes three trips up to heaven in order to acquire from his father possessions that would be of use to Jack in gratifying his oedipal desires. Jack's father appears to have accomplished the enviable feat of "having died and taken it (his money) with him." Interestingly, the little old lady who resides in the giant's castle exhibits amazing disloyalty to the giant. She, of course, is an alter ego of Jack's mother and serves to help him in the acquisition of the giant's possessions. The trading of the cow for the beans and the growing of the beanstalk are merely mechanisms that serve to provide Jack with a route (the beanstalk) to his father in heaven.

First, the giant's treasure of gold coins is stolen. This provides Jack with the wherewithal to support his mother in grand style. However, monetary sources have a way of being depleted and before long Jack is once again in want of funds. And so he returns to heaven, this time to steal the giant's goose that lays the golden eggs. Like the legendary money tree, funds are now provided by a living form and so the supply is richer and seemingly endless. In addition, an egg-laying goose is an excellent representation of the mature female, that is, Jack's mother. The eggs, as the product of the mother's procreative endeavors, readily symbolizes Jack himself. The fact that the eggs are golden serves to gratify Jack's wish that he be precious and desirable.

One would think that Jack would now be satisfied. The golden eggs supply him with an endless source of funding for his oedipal gratifications. But Jack is not an easily satisfiable young man. He once again returns to the giant's home, this time to steal his most treasured possession, the golden harp. This curvaceous, sweet-music producing instrument, on which one plays with one's hands, lends itself well to symbolizing the sexual female—in Jack's case, again his mother. The sexual element here is more overtly symbolized. Now that Jack has everything that he has wished to obtain from his father, he kills him by chopping down the beanstalk. This act may also serve as a symbolic castration of his father in retaliation for possible unconscious fears that his father will castrate him for his oedipal wishes.

As mentioned, *Jack and the Beanstalk* is one of the purer fairy tales from the psychoanalytic point of view. However, its attraction, in part, lies in the unrealistic and usually unattainable oedipal gratification that Jack enjoys. Jack's counterpart in my version of the story, *Mack and the Beanstalk*, has no such luck. Other than Sophocles' Oedipus in the original Greek tragedy, and possibly a few others whom I do not personally know, most boys do not have the opportunity to gratify their unrealistic and impractical oedipal fantasies. My story provides what I consider to be a more realistic solution for Jack's oedipal desires, while retaining much of the richness of the original tale. I believe that my story, if read to boys at the three-to-five-year age level, can be useful in helping them resolve in a more realistic way any oedipal conflicts they may have. I have not conducted any formal studies to ascertain whether it has indeed been useful in this regard. I have, however, learned of a few boys (through their parents) who have been very moved by this story, have repeatedly asked that it be reread to them, and who have demonstrated their appreciation of the sharing element in their relationship with their fathers.

Draco the Dragon is not derived from any particular fairy tale; rather it utilizes the common fairy tale theme of the fire-breathing dragon for the purpose of dealing with the common problem of hostility expression. The theme of hostility in fairy tales is ubiquitous. The most gory and sadistic kinds of torture and murder are depicted. There are many who would "clean them up" by omitting the hostility. I believe that this is not only naive but also a disservice to children. Anger is part of our psychological repertoire. It enhances our efficiency in protecting ourselves. Without it mankind would probably not have survived. One of the greatest problems we have in the world today is that of learning how to use our anger most effectively and advantageously. Like electricity and atomic power, although potentially lethal, it can also be an immensely useful servant. My story attempts to portray some of the valuable uses of anger through the experience of *Draco*, the fire-breathing dragon.

In *The Adventures of Sir Galalad of King Arthur's Court*, I have taken some well-known themes from Arthurian legend and modified them in ways that I consider salutary. The issues of magic acquisition of power and blind fealty are especially focused upon. However, there are some more subtle messages as well that should be appreciated by most adults.

There is probably no one who ever lived who has not at one time or another wished that he or she had been born someone else, or wished that he or she could change places with someone considered more fortunate. *The Prince and the Pauper* tells of the outcome of one such transformation. My story of *The Prince and the Poor Boy* also deals with this wish. The theme of searching for a better home elsewhere is an ancient one and appears in stories as far removed from one another as L. Frank Baum's *The Wizard of Oz* and Voltaire's *Candide*. My rendition throws in for good measure a few elements from *Aladdin's Lamp*, *Dick Whittington and His Cat*, and *The Elves and the Shoemaker*—all modified, of course, along the lines of the principles mentioned above.

Dorothy and the Lizard of Oz

The Wizard of Oz, written by L. Frank Baum and first published in 1900, is probably the most popular fairy tale of the twentieth century. The book enjoyed widespread popularity even before its MGM movie version appeared in 1939. The movie rendition significantly enhanced its popularity, and its exposure on television each year has become a tradition that has ensured its transmission to further generations of children. The story certainly satisfies the major criteria for being considered a fairy tale. There are the magic solutions that instantaneously solve the most complex problems. Rich fantasy and dramatization, so characteristic of the fairy tale, enhance the story's attractiveness. There is the satisfaction of wishes that cannot be gratified in reality. There is the stereotyped world in which all people and things are immediately recognized as either good or bad, right or wrong. And all consistently remain in the assigned role throughout the story. And, of course, like all good fairy tales, it ends with everyone presumably living happily ever after. Unless something comes along to replace or surpass it in the next fourteen years, future generations will probably come to consider *The Wizard of Oz* to be the twentieth century's major contribution to the fairy tale genre.

When a story enjoys such widespread popularity, it usually provides important psychological gratifications. Modern psychoanalytic theory provides us with a tool for understanding these to a degree not previously possible. Let us see what such an inquiry can teach us about *The Wizard of Oz*. Let us start with *Dorothy's* three friends, as their stories are easier to analyze than *Dorothy's*. The *Strawman* does not have a brain, that is, he feels that he is stupid. In the original book the *Wizard* gives the *Strawman* a brain of bran and nails, "a bran new brain" with nails to make him "sharp." In the movie version, the *Strawman* is given a diploma. This is not only designed to give the *Strawman* and everyone else the impression that he is now smart (*Dorothy*, the *Tin Woodman*, and the *Cowardly Lion* are certainly convinced), but somehow gives the *Strawman* actual knowledge as well. (Immediately after receiving the diploma he suddenly spouts the Pythagorean theorem as applied to an isosceles triangle.) There is no one, no matter how well educated and/or brilliant (the two do not necessarily go together) who does not feel, at times, intellectually inadequate. At best, even the most gifted and dedicated scholar can only grasp and feel competent with an infinitesimal fraction of all there is to know. And the child cannot but feel even more inadequate with regard to the knowledge of and capacity to deal with the vast world. By identification with the *Strawman*, one gratifies the wish for feelings of intellectual competence. And better yet, little effort is required. Whereas others have to attend universities for four or more years before being granted their diplomas, the *Strawman* earns his university degree in less than a minute. In the short time it takes the *Wizard* to bestow the diploma upon the *Strawman*, he becomes "smart"—an appealing shortcut, especially to the child who faces what may appear to be an endless educational process.

Now to the *Tin Woodman*. His problem is that he doesn't have a heart, only an empty tin chest. His problem is ostensibly solved when the *Wizard* gives him a heart. In the original Baum version, the heart is made of stuffed silk. In the MGM version, it is a red, ticking clock-heart. Wearing this around his neck and listening to the ticking sounds convinces the *Woodman* and others around him that he now can love. Again, little effort is required to enjoy the benefits of being capable of loving. Presumably, one of these benefits is that one will be loved in return. Although not elaborated upon in the story, the main drawback to being unable to love is that one is not likely to engender loving feelings in others. However, some reference is made to this by the MGM *Wizard* who, when giving the *Tin Woodman* the clock-heart, states, " . . . a heart is not judged by how much you love, but by how much you are loved by others." It is not, then, that altruistic needs are being thwarted here but self-serving gratifications. The *Tin Woodman's* grief here is not only that he is being deprived of the good feelings that come when one loves another, but of the pleasures derived from being loved as well. Giving love is the most predictable way to get love. When one doesn't give love, one is not likely to get it. The heart, then, is to provide the *Tin Woodman* with both—the capacity to give love and the hope of receiving it. However, no work, no effort is expended in order to get his heart. None of the traditional factors that we consider indispensable to the loving relationship seems to be necessary. No giving, no sacrifice, no sympathy, empathy, toleration, admiration, respect, sexual attraction, or sharing of experiences are warranted. This capacity to love and be loved is suddenly acquired, merely by wearing a little ticking clock.

Everyone wants to be loved and everyone wants the pleasure of loving. The infant's need to be loved is vital. Without the love of parents and/or other significant figures in his environment the infant will be deprived of the necessities vital to life, and he or she may even die. All of us, no matter how independent of others we may come to be, still crave for the love, affection, and attention of others. And all of us, once we have known the feeling of giving love, seek to enjoy that emotion again, no matter how elusive and transient it may be. Part of the appeal of *The Wizard of Oz* is that it enables us, via identification with the *Tin Woodman*, to gratify vicariously our need to be loving people, capable of both giving and receiving love.

Now to the *Cowardly Lion*. All of us are afraid at times. The younger we are the more fears we are likely to have. The infant finds himself helpless in a world of giants, some of whom he depends upon for his very existence. And no matter how old we get, no matter how competent we may become, we still live in fear of many things. If we are to achieve many of our goals in life and if we are to fight off those who may threaten us, we need the stamina to tolerate these inevitable fears, to suffer them rather than to avoid them. This is what we call courage. Such willingness to suffer these uncomfortable fearful feelings is crucial if we are to fight off those who would endanger us or if we are to acquire what is frightening or dangerous.

Intimately associated with courage is potency. It is difficult to imagine courage without power. We do not speak of courage alone, but courage to do something: courage to fight, courage to stand up, courage to strive. The *Cowardly Lion*, then, is not simply looking for courage, he is also looking for the power that comes with courage. Courage is the prerequisite for the more important gratification of power. The *Wizard* provides these in the medal for bravery that he gives the *Lion*. The *Lion* does earn his medal (a "triple cross") in that it is awarded for "bravery against wicked witches." However, this one act and its reward produce a total conversion from cowardice to bravery. The cowardice problem is instantly cured, and the cure, presumably, is lifelong.

In infancy we are fearful and weak. As we grow older, we

become less fearful and less impotent. But no matter how old and competent we become, we all at times become fearful. All of us, at times, wish for greater courage to sustain us during our fearful periods. And all of us look for the power to help us overcome the fearful situation. Such courage and power only come with time, experience, and endurance. The *Wizard of Oz* provides courage (and presumably power) in as much time as it takes him to pin the medal on the *Cowardly Lion's* chest. Not only is the *Lion* convinced that he is brave, but his friends are convinced as well.

The attraction of the *Strawman*, the *Tin Woodman*, and the *Cowardly Lion* is that they provide children (and, to a lesser extent, adults) with vicarious gratification of needs that are central to their well-being, if not their very existence. By identification with these figures, children gain intellectual competence in compensation for feelings of ignorance of how to deal with the world. They are provided with the capacity to love and thereby are provided with the most powerful and predictable tool for gaining the love of others. And they gain courage, the prerequisite of power, in compensation for the sense of impotence that is intrinsic to childhood. There are few needs that are more important to children. No surprise then that the *Strawman*, the *Tin Woodman*, and the *Cowardly Lion* are so universally loved.

And now for *Dorothy*. Her main problem is that Miss Gulch, the mean woman from the town near her aunt and uncle's farm, has an order from the sheriff empowering her to take *Dorothy's* dog *Toto*. It seems that *Toto* got into Miss Gulch's garden. She threatened him in such a frightening way that he bit her, thereby providing her with the justification for taking him away from *Dorothy*. We presume he will be put in such a place or state (the story is not clear about his exact disposition) that there will be no further danger that he will ever bite anyone again. Unfortunately, her aunt and uncle (law-abiding citizens that they are) do not support *Dorothy* in her attempts to thwart Miss Gulch, and they tell *Dorothy* to hand the dog over to her. The story deals with this problem by the mechanism of escape. In the land of Oz *Dorothy* and *Toto* are supposedly safe from Miss Gulch, the sheriff, and anyone else who would want to take *Toto* away from her.

The Oz solution, however, is not without its drawbacks. Not only is *Dorothy* exposed to a whole new host of problems (a realistic element in an otherwise unrealistic tale), but she sorely misses her aunt and uncle (their disloyalty to her in the Gulch incident notwithstanding). The *Wizard* does get *Dorothy* back to Kansas, thereby removing her from the dangers she is exposed to in Oz and gratifying her desire to return once again to her loved ones. Also, she learns an important lesson in Oz (again in the MGM version): " . . . if I ever go looking for my heart's desire again, I won't look any further than my own backyard. Because if it isn't there, I never really lost it to begin with." This, of course, is an ancient wisdom. However, although *Dorothy* does finally return to Kansas, the problem with Miss Gulch is not dealt with at the end of the story. *Dorothy* fled Kansas, and then flees Oz. The problem that originally caused her flight from Kansas is not solved. This flaw in the tale notwithstanding, *Dorothy* is still a beloved figure for children and adults as well. I believe that the atttraction comes from another factor in the story, one that is far larger than the lesson that *Dorothy* learns. In fact, I believe that most children (or adults) cannot say what the lesson is that *Dorothy* learned, so small a role does it play in the movie. I would go further and say that most younger children (under seven or eight) do not even know what *Dorothy* is talking about when she relates the lesson she has learned.

Dorothy's main attraction is that she visits the "land over the rainbow." She gratifies our desire to go to a land where "bluebirds fly," the land where "the dreams that we dare to dream really do come true," the land where "troubles melt like lemon drops, away above the chimney tops." In short, *Dorothy* gratifies our desire to go to paradise. Although Oz is not continual pleasure for *Dorothy*, by the end of the story she manages to clear the place of its only flaws: the two wicked witches. The story implies that after she has left, the Munchkins and other denizens of the land will now lead the life of eternal peace and bliss that Oz was designed to provide.

Life is, at best, a continual struggle, and the desire for a paradise is universal. Dreaming of a land over the rainbow can provide us with just the kind of narcosis that can make life more bearable and at times more pleasurable. To recognize that this is only an unrealistic dream can enable us to enjoy the gratifications of such fantasies without being too swept up by them. To believe that one can really find such bliss in life, on an ongoing basis, may produce grave disappointment and disillusionment. Judy Garland, the actress who played *Dorothy*, was ever associated with the song "Over the Rainbow." Throughout her career, audiences repeatedly asked her to sing the song. A performance was rarely considered complete without it. Her name became inextricably bound to the song and its myth of a paradise land over the rainbow. It is public knowledge that Judy Garland's life was anything but happy. To the best of my knowledge she found little gratification in her marriages and for many years fought, but never overcame, a drinking problem. In her later years people did not attend her performances primarily to hear a beautiful voice (so much had it deteriorated), but many came out of pity, to help her make a comeback. She probably appreciated this, but such awareness must have been extremely distressing and debasing. One could speculate that she, like so many others in Hollywood, got swept up in their screen fantasies. They, like their audiences, come to believe that paradise can be found on earth and they will never be satisfied until they find it. People whose lives are a constant quest for such "happiness" are doomed to deep frustration. The main attraction of *The Wizard of Oz*, then, is that it fosters the hope for such a paradise on earth. It gratifies vicariously our desire to live in such a world. Its main drawback, of course, is that it contributes to the disillusionment that inevitably must come to those who believe in and pursue such fantasies.

In *Dorothy and the Lizard of Oz* (1980b), I have tried to retain what is healthy in the Baum and MGM versions and to omit what I consider to be unhealthy and contributory to inappropriate and maladaptive ways of looking at and dealing with life. Although I have taken away some of the attractiveness of the original, my hope is that I have provided even more attractive substitutes. And if they are not as attractive, they will at least ultimately be more gratifying because they are based on reality and real possibilities for living in the real world.

CONCLUDING COMMENTS

It is my hope that the reader will agree with me that child therapists do not utilize frequently enough bibliotherapeutic techniques. This is unfortunate because both attempts to do just those things that we are trying to do in psychotherapy, namely, to change the way people think about the world and the methods they use to deal with it. I believe that these offerings have not only proved useful for children whom I have seen in therapy, but for others as well. Writing books such as these has given me the feeling that I have been able to use what I have learned from my patients to bring about therapeutic change in a large audience of other people whom I have never personally met. Unlike the surgeon who can see within minutes the products of his labors, we in psychiatry must patiently hope that a small fraction of our efforts will prove useful. Writing books such as these has enhanced my ability to gain, as a psychiatrist, this important gratification.

References

Bellak, L., and Bellak, S. S. (1949). *Children's Apperception Test*. Larchmont, NY: C. P. S.

Conn, J. H. (1939). The child reveals himself through play. *Mental Hygiene* 23:1–21.

_____ (1941a). the timid, dependent child. *Journal of Pediatrics* 19:1–2.

_____ (1941b). The treatment of fearful children. *American Journal of Orthopsychiatry* 11:744–751.

_____ (1948). The play-interview as an investigative and therapeutic procedure. *The Nervous Child* 7:257–286.

_____ (1954). Play interview therapy of castration fears. *American Journal of Orthopsychiatry* 25:747–754.

Freud, S. (1909). A phobia in a five-year-old boy. In *Collected Papers*, vol. 3, pp. 149–209. New York: Basic Books, 1959.

_____ (1924). The passing of the Oedipus complex. In *Collected Papers*, vol. 2, pp. 269–276. New York: Basic Books, 1959.

Gardner, R. A. (1968). The mutual storytelling technique: use in alleviating childhood oedipal problems. *Contemporary Psychoanalysis* 4:161–177.

_____ (1969). Mutual storytelling as a technique in child psychotherapy and psychoanalysis. In *Science and Psychoanalysis*, ed. J. Masserman, Vol. 14, pp. 123–135. New York: Grune & Stratton.

—— (1970a). *The Boys and Girls Book About Divorce*. New York: Jason Aronson.

—— (1970b). Die Technik des wechselseitigen Geschichtenerzahlens bei der Behandlung eines Kindes mit psychogenem Husten. In *Fortschritte der Weiterentwicklung der Psychoanalyse*, ed. C. J. Hogrefe, vol. 4, pp. 159–173. Göttingen, Germany: Verlag für Psychologie.

—— (1970c). The mutual storytelling technique: use in the treatment of a child with post-traumatic neurosis. *American Journal of Psychotherapy* 24:419–439.

—— (1971a). *Therapeutic Communication with Children: The Mutual Storytelling Technique*. Northvale, NJ: Jason Aronson.

—— (1971b). *The Boys and Girls Book About Divorce* (Paperback edition). New York: Bantam.

—— (1971c). Mutual storytelling: a technique in child psychotherapy. *Acta Paedopsychiatrica* 38:253–262.

—— (1972a). *Dr. Gardner's Stories About the Real World*. Vol. I. Cresskill, NJ: Creative Therapeutics.

—— (1972b). Little Hans—the most famous boy in the child psychotherapy literature. *International Journal of Child Psychotherapy* 1:27–32.

—— (1972c). "Once upon a time there was a doorknob and everybody used to make him all dirty with fingerprints . . . " *Psychology Today* 5:67–92.

—— (1972d). The mutual storytelling technique in the treatment of anger inhibition problems. *International Journal of Child Psychotherapy* 1:34–64.

—— (1972e). *The Boys and Girls Book About Divorce* (Japanese edition). Tokyo, Japan: Mikasa-Shobo.

—— (1972f). *The Boys and Girls Book About Divorce* (Spanish edition). Buenos Aires, Argentina: Editorial Galerna.

—— (1972g). *The Boys and Girls Book About Divorce* (Dutch edition). Wageningen, Holland: L. J. Veen's Vitgeversmaatschappij N. V.

—— (1973a). *MBD: The Family Book About Minimal Brain Dysfunction*. New York: Jason Aronson.

—— (1973b). *Understanding Children—A Parents Guide to Child Rearing*. Cresskill, NJ: Creative Therapeutics.

—— (1973c). *The Mutual Storytelling Technique* (12 one-hour audio cassette tapes). Cresskill, NJ: Creative Therapeutics.

—— (1974a). *Dr. Gardner's Fairy Tales for Today's Children*. Cresskill, NJ: Creative Therapeutics.

—— (1974b). La technique de la narration mutuelle d'historettes. *Médecine et Hygiène* (Geneva) 32:1180–1181.

_____ (1974c). Dramatized storytelling in child psychotherapy. *Acta Paedopsychiatrica* 41:110–116.

_____ (1974d). The mutual storytelling technique in the treatment of psychogenic problems secondary to minimal brain dysfunction. *Journal of Learning Disabilities* 7:135–143.

_____ (1974e). *Dr. Gardner's Stories About the Real World* (Dutch edition). The Hague, Holland: Vitgeverij Bert Bakker BZ.

_____ (1975a). *Psychotherapeutic Approaches to the Resistant Child* (2 one-hour audio cassette tapes). Cresskill, NJ: Creative Therapeutics.

_____ (1975b). Techniques for involving the child with MBD in meaningful psychotherapy. *Journal of Learning Disabilities* 8:16–26.

_____ (1975c). *Understanding Children—A Parents Guide to Child Rearing* (Dutch edition). Bilthoven, Holland: Vitgeverij Amboboken B. V.

_____ (1976a). *Psychotherapy with Children of Divorce*. New York: Jason Aronson.

_____ (1976b). Helping children deal with parental death (two 1½-hour cassette tapes). Cresskill, NJ: Creative Therapeutics.

_____ (1976c). Easing the damage of divorce and death. *Blue Print for Health*, Vol. 26, no. 1, pp. 49–56. Chicago: Blue Cross Association.

_____ (1976d). *Dr. Gardner's Stories About the Real World* (Italian edition). Rome, Italy: Editore Armando Armando.

_____ (1977a). *Dr. Gardner's Modern Fairy Tales*. Cresskill, NJ: Creative Therapeutics.

_____ (1977b). *The Parents Book About Divorce*. New York: Doubleday.

_____ (1977c). *The Boys and Girls Book About Divorce* (Hebrew edition). Tel Aviv, Israel: Sadan Publishing House.

_____ (1977d). Children's guilt reactions to parental death: psychodynamics and therapeutic management. *Hiroshima Journal of Psychology* 4:45–57.

_____ (1978). *The Boys and Girls Book About One-Parent Families*. New York: G. P. Putnam's Sons.

_____ (1979a). *The Parents Book About Divorce* (Paperback edition). New York: Bantam.

_____ (1979b). Helping children cooperate in therapy. In *Basic Handbook of Child Psychiatry*, ed. J. Noshpitz, vol. 3, pp. 414–433. New York: Basic Books.

_____ (1979c). Psychogenic difficulties secondary to MBD. In *Basic Handbook of Child Psychiatry*, ed. J. Noshpitz, vol. 3, pp. 614–628. New York: Basic Books.

_____ (1979d). Death of a parent. In *Basic Handbook of Child Psychiatry*, ed. J. Noshpitz, vol. 4, pp. 270–283. New York: Basic Books.

_____ (1979e). *The Parents Book About Divorce* (French Edition). Paris, France: Ramsay "image."

_____ (1980a). The mutual storytelling technique. In *The Psychotherapy Handbook*, ed. R. Herink, pp. 408–411. New York: New American Library.

_____ (1980b). *Dorothy and the Lizard of Oz*. Cresskill, NJ: Creative Therapeutics.

_____ (1980c). *The Boys and Girls Book About Divorce* (Dutch edition). Deventer, The Netherlands: Van Loghum Slaterus B. V.

_____ (1980d). *The Boys and Girls Book About Divorce* (Japanese edition). Tokyo: Shakai Shisa Sha Ltd.

_____ (1981a). The mutual storytelling technique and dramatization of the therapeutic communication. In *Drama in Therapy*, ed. G. Schattner and R. Courtney, pp. 211–235. New York: Drama Book Specialists.

_____ (1981b). *Dr. Gardner's Fables for Our Times*. Cresskill, NJ: Creative Therapeutics.

_____ (1981c). *The Boys and Girls Book About Stepfamilies*. Cresskill, NJ: Creative Therapeutics.

_____ (1981d). *The Boys and Girls Book About Divorce* (French edition). Montreal, Canada: Presses Sélect Ltée.

_____ (1981e). *The Boys and Girls Book About One-Parent Families* (Japanese edition). Tokyo, Japan: Kitaoji Shobo.

_____ (1983a). Treating oedipal problems with the mutual storytelling technique. In *Handbook of Play Therapy*, ed. C. E. Schaefer and K. J. O'Connor, pp. 355–368. New York: Wiley.

_____ (1983b). *Dr. Gardner's Stories About the Real World*. Vol. 2. Cresskill, NJ: Creative Therapeutics.

_____ (1983c). *The Boys and Girls Book About One-Parent Families*. New York: Bantam.

_____ (1988). *The Storytelling Card Game*. Cresskill, NJ: Creative Therapeutics.

Goldings, R., and Goldings, H. (1972). Books in the playroom: a dimension of child psychiatric technique. *Journal of the American Academy of Child Psychiatry* 12:52–65.

Hug-Hellmuth, H. von (1913). *Aus dem Seelenleben des Kindes*. Leipzig: Deuticke.

_____ (1921). On the technique of child analysis. *International Journal of Psycho-Analysis* 2:287–305.

Johnson, E. W. (1967). *Love and Sex in Plain Language*. Philadelphia: Lippincott.

Livingston, C. (1978). *"Why Was I Adopted?"* Secaucus, NJ: Lyle Stuart.

Mayle, P. (1973). *Where Did I Come From?* Secaucus, NJ: Lyle Stuart.

Murray, H. (1936). *The Thematic Apperception Test.* New York: The Psychological Corporation.

Pomeroy, W. B. (1968). *Boys and Sex.* New York: Delacorte.

_____ (1969). *Girls and Sex.* New York: Delacorte.

Pyne, M. (1962). *The Hospital.* Boston: Houghton Mifflin.

Rondell, F., and Michaels, R. (1951). *The Family That Grew.* New York: Crown.

Roberts, G. E. (1982). *Roberts Apperception Test for Children.* Los Angeles, CA: Western Psychological Services.

Schneidman, E. J. (1947). *The Make-A-Picture Story Test.* New York: The Psychological Corporation.

Solomon, J. C. (1938). Active play therapy. *American Journal of Orthopsychiatry* 8:479–498.

_____ (1940). Active play therapy: further experiences. *American Journal of Orthopsychiatry* 10:763–781.

_____ (1951). Therapeutic use of play. In *An Introduction to Projective Techniques,* ed. H. H. Anderson and G. L. Anderson, pp. 639–661. Englewood Cliffs, NJ: Prentice-Hall.

_____ (1955). Play technique and the integrative process. *American Journal of Orthopsychiatry* 25:591–600.

Strupp, H. H. (1975). Psychoanalysis, "focal psychotherapy," and the nature of the therapeutic influence. *Archives of General Psychiatry* 32:127–135.

Index

Abuse, sex, 51
Adventures of Sir Galalad of King Arthur's Court, 259
Age, for mutual storytelling and derivative games, 5–6, 204
Alphabet Soup Game, 174–186
Ambivalence, introduction through mutual storytelling of, 25
Anger
  displaced, 162
  fairy tales and release of, 252–253
Anger inhibition problem
  during divorce, 235
  mutual storytelling technique in case of, 27–34
  story about healthy expression of anger, 246
Animal symbols in fables, 247–250
Antisocial behavior
  due to feelings about competent sibling, 67–96
Anxiety. See also Separation anxiety disorder
  from ignorance, 232–233
Apathy, mutual storytelling technique in case of, 12–14, 27–34

Atmosphere of story, analyzing, 10–11
Audio tape recorder, use of, 6–7

Bag of Things Game, The, 140–147
Bag of Toys Game, The, 129–140
Bag of Words Game, The, 147–155
Baum, L. F., 260
Beauty and the Beast, 251, 252
Bellak, L., 194
Bellak, S. S., 194
Bibliotherapy, 230–266
  expository books, 232–242
    Boys and Girls Book About Divorce, The, 234–238
    Boys and Girls Book About One-Parent Families, The, 238–239
    Boys and Girls Book About Stepfamilies, The, 240
    MBD: The Family Book About Minimal Brain Dysfunction, 233–234
    Parents Book About Divorce, The, 240–241

Bibliotherapy (continued)
  expository books (continued)
    Understanding Children—A
      Parents Guide to Child Rearing,
      241–242
    fables, 246–250
    fairy tales, 250–265
      Fairy Tales for Today's Children,
        256–257
      reasons for attraction to, 251–255
      use of, 255–256
      Dorothy and the Lizard of Oz,
        260–265
    reality oriented stories, 243–246
Birth of sibling, 67, 77–80
Blank screen approach, 230
Board Games. See Mutual storytelling
  derivative games
Board of Objects Game, The,
  120–129
Boys and Girls Book About Divorce,
  The (Gardner), 234–238
Boys and Girls Book About
  One-Parent Families, The
  (Gardner), 238–239
Boys and Girls Book About
  Stepfamilies, The (Gardner),
  240

Castration threats, 50, 52, 53, 55. See
  also Oedipal problems
CAT, 194
Channing, W. E., 230
Child rearing
  Understanding Children: A Parents
    Guide to Child Rearing,
    241–242
  Children's Apperception Test
    (CAT), 194
  Child's Book About Brain Injury,
    The (Gardner), 233
Cinderella, 252–254
Cinderelma, 256
Clinical examples
  of Alphabet Soup Game, 176–186
  of Bag of Toys Game, 130–140

  of Bag of Words Game, 150–155
  of Board of Objects Game,
    124–129
  of dramatized storytelling, 65–115
  of Feel and Tell game, 169–174
  of Make-a-Picture Story Cards,
    195–204
  of mutual storytelling technique,
    12–61
  of Pick-a-Face Game, 188–192
  of Scrabble for Juniors, 158–167
Communication, after parental death,
  239
Competition
  healthy vs. unhealthy, 119
  in mutual storytelling derivative
    games, 118–119
Compulsion, touching, 176–186
Conflicts, intrapsychic, 75–77
Conn, J., 3
Conscious awareness of unconscious
  material, 2
Cooperation, fable about, 249

Death, of parent, 238–239
Defense mechanisms. See Denial
  mechanisms
Denial mechanisms, 79–80, 85
  fable about, 249
  Pick-a-Face Game, use in case of,
    188–192
  stories dealing with, 245
Dependency, 249. See also
  Overprotectiveness of mother
Deprivation, cases of, 85, 167
Desensitization, 118, 172–174, 245
Divorce. See also Marriage
  Boys and Girls Book About Divorce,
    The, 234–238
  Boys and Girls Book About
    One-Parent Families, The,
    238–239
  Parents Book About Divorce, The,
    240–241
Doll play, 68–96
Dorothy and the Lizard of Oz, 265

Dr. Gardner's Fables for Our Times
(Gardner), 249
*Dr. Gardner's Stories About the Real
World* (Gardner), 243–246
Dramatized storytelling, 62–115
clinical examples, 65–115
antisocial behavior due to sibling
rivalry, 67–96
in neurologically based learning
disability cases, 65–67, 96–115
parental involvement, 64

Educational experience, therapy as,
231
Egocentricism, 67
Expository books, 234–242
*Boys and Girls Book About Divorce,
The*, 234–238
*Boys and Girls Book About
One-Parent Families, The*,
238–239
*Boys and Girls Book About
Stepfamilies, The*, 240
*MBD: The Family Book About
Minimal Brain Dysfunction*,
233–234
Parents Book About Divorce, The,
240–241
*Understanding Children—A Parents
Guide to Child Rearing*,
241–242

Fables, 246–250
Fairy tales, 250–265
Fairy Tales for Today's Children,
256–257
Modern Fairy Tales, 257–260
reasons for attraction to, 251–255
use of, 255–256
Dorothy and the Lizard of Oz,
260–265
Father. *See* Parent(s)
Feel and Tell, 167–174
Formal operations stage, 2
Freud, A., 2
Freud, S., 48–49

Funeral, child's attendance of
parent's, 238–239. *See also*
Death of parent

Games, board. *See* Mutual storytelling
derivative games
Gardner, R. A., 60, 70, 147, 239
Garland, J., 264–265
Gaudi, A., 1
Gilbert, W. S., 116
GMBDS. *See* Group of Minimal Brain
Dysfunction Syndromes
(GMBDS)
Goldings, H., 231
Goldings, R., 231
Grab-bag games, 129–155
Bag of Things Game, 140–147
Bag of Toys Game, 129–140
Bag of Words Game, 147–155
Grimm, J., and Grimm, W., 250
Group of Minimal Brain Dysfunction
Syndromes (GMBDS)
*MBD: The Family Book About
Minimal Brain Dysfunction*,
233–234
Gunplay, influence of, 128

Hans and Greta, 256–257
Hansel and Gretel, 251, 252, 253
Hostility
in fairy tales, 259
playing tricks as expression of, 100
Hug-Hellmuth, H. von, 1, 2

Interpretation. *See* Mutual storytelling
derivative games; Mutual
storytelling technique

Jack and the Beanstalk, 251, 253,
257–258
Johnson, E. W., 231

Klein, M., 2
Kritzberg, N. I., 120, 155

Learning. See also Educational
experience; Neurologically
based learning disability;
School
from fairy tales, 254–255
Little Hans case, 48
Love in *The Wizard of Oz*, 237–238
Lowenheim, A., 236
Lying, 20, 246, 249

Mack and the Beanstalk, 257,
258–259
Magic
cure fantasies, 17–25, 96–115, 133,
135–136
in fairy tales, attraction to, 252,
255
Make-a-Picture Story Cards (MAPS),
192–204
diagnostic utilization, 192–194
therapeutic utilization, 195–204
"Malevolent transformation," 44
MAPS. See *Make-a-Picture Story
Cards* (MAPS)
Marriage
Cinderelma story, 256
Mayle, P., 231
MBD. See Group of Minimal Brain
Dysfunction Syndromes
(GMBDS)
*MBD: The Family Book about Minimal
Brain Dysfunction* (Gardner),
233–234
Metaphor, value of. See Dramatized
storytelling; Mutual storytelling
technique; Mutual storytelling
derivative games
Michaels, R., 207
Minimal brain dysfunction. See Group
of Minimal Brain Dysfunction
Syndromes (GMBDS);
Neurologically based learning
disability
Modern Fairy Tales (Gardner),
257–260
Morals in fables, 249–250

Mother. See also Parent(s)
overprotectiveness of, 169–174
sexual seductivity of, 50, 51,
150–155, 176, 186
unwed, 239
Murray, H., 194
Mutual storytelling derivative games,
116–205
Alphabet Soup Game, 174–186
Board of Objects Game, 120–129
competition in, 118–119
Feel and Tell, 167–174
Grab-bag games, 129–155
Bag of Things Game, 140–147
Bag of Toys Game, 130–140
Bag of Words Game, 147–155
Make-a-Picture Story Cards,
192–204
Pick-a-Face Game, 186–192
Scrabble for Juniors, 155–167
Mutual storytelling technique, 1–61
basic technique, 5–7
clinical examples, 12–61
fundamentals of story analysis,
10–12
historical background, 1–5
self-created stories, specific
technique for eliciting, 7–10

Negative reinforcement, 117–118
Neurologically based learning
disability
cases of
Bag of Things Game, use in,
145–147
dramatized storytelling used in,
65–67, 96–115
in sibling, 136

Oedipal interest, 48–49
family factors and development of,
186
Oedipal problems
author's approach to alleviation of,
51–52

cases of
  Alphabet Soup Game, use in,
    176–186
  Bag of Words Game, use in,
    150–155
  mutual storytelling technique in,
    53–60
  tics developed due to, 176
  touching compulsion due to,
    176–186
  fairy tales on, 257–259
  family factors and development of,
    186
Oedipus complex
  author's view of, 49–51
  Freud's theory of, 48–49
One-parent families, 238–239
Options, expanding patient's
    repertoire of, 33–34
Overloading of messages, 129, 136
Overprotectiveness of mother,
    169–174

Parental involvement in child's
    treatment
  in dramatized storytelling, 64
  Little Hans case, 48
Parent–child relationship
  alleviation of oedipal problems and,
    52
  fairy tales about, 251–252, 256–259
Parent(s). *See also* Marriage; Mother
  accepting reality about, 139–140,
    167
  illness of, 197–204
Parents Book About Divorce, The
    (Gardner), 240–241
Participation, parental. *See* Parental
    involvement in child's
    treatment
Passive role for therapist, problems
    with. *See* Blank screen
    approach
Peer relationships
  Scrabble for Juniors, use in case of
    difficult, 158–161

Perrault, C., 250
Phobic child
  Little Hans case, 48
Pick-a-Face Game, 186–192
Play. *See also* Dramatized storytelling
  doll, 68–96
Pomeroy, W. B., 231
Positive reinforcement, 117–118
Prince and the Poor Boy, The,
    259–260
Princess and the Three Tasks, The,
    256
Projection. *See* Mutual storytelling
    derivative games; Mutual
    storytelling technique
Psychoanalysis. *See* Freud, S.
Psychotherapeutic process, central
    elements in
  as educational experience, 231
Pyne, M., 231

Reality about parents, child's
    acceptance of, 139–140, 167
Realilty-oriented stories, 243–246
Repetition in dramatized storytelling,
    106, 110

Schneidman, E. J., 192
School
  behavior, 162–167
Scrabble for Juniors, 155–167
Self-assertion, *Bag of Things Game*
    focusing on, 141–147
Self-created stories. *See also* Mutual
    storytelling derivative games;
    Mutual storytelling technique
  specific technique for eliciting,
    7–10
Separation anxiety disorder
  Feel and Tell game, use of, 169–174
  mutual storytelling technique, use
    of, 34–41
  over potential loss of parents,
    197–204
Sex abuse, 51

Sexual seductivity of mother, 50, 51, 150–155, 186
Shakespeare, W., 62
Sharing
  concept in alleviation of oedipal problems, 52, 57–60, 155, 181
  of parental attention with siblings, 78–79, 80, 96
Siblings
  antisocial behavior disorder over, 67–96
  birth of, 67, 77–80
  separation anxiety over loss of, 34–41
  sharing of parental attention with, 78–79, 80, 96
Snow White, 252, 253
Solomon, J. C., 3
Stepparents, 240
Stereotypes in fairy tales, child's attraction to, 252
Stories About the Real World (Gardner), 85
Story analysis, fundamentals of, 10–12
Storytelling. See Bibliotherapy; Dramatized storytelling; Mutual storytelling technique
Strupp, H., 231
Substitutive gratifications, providing, 14, 38–39, 52, 155, 201–202, 245
Sullivan, H. S., 44
Superego
  development
    intrapsychic conflict and, 75–77
    in neurologically based learning disability case, 65–67
    reiterative process for, 74
  deficiencies, case of, 26–27

Symbols. See also Mutual storytelling derivative games; Mutual storytelling technique
  in fables, 247–250
  story analysis and significance of, 10
Symptoms, oedipal, 50–51

Tactile projective game, 167–174
Talking, Feeling, and Doing Game, The, dramatized storytelling and, 70–73
TAT, 194
Teenagers, use as authority in stories, 21, 144
Thematic Apperception Test (TAT), 194
Tics, 589
Transformation, "malevolent," 44

Ugly Duck, The, 257
Ugly Duckling, The, 251–252
Unconscious material and processes bringing into conscious awareness, 2
Understanding Children: A Parents Guide to Child Rearing (Gardner), 241–242
Universal symbols, notion of, 71

Video tape and cassette recorders, use of, 6–7, 64–65

"War games," influence of childhood, 128
Wizard of Oz, The (Baum), 260–265
Work ethic, developing, 147